"A wonderful blend of normative and empirical analysis, which asks important questions about whether the judicial review we experience meets democratic standards, as opposed to the more common concern of whether an idealized form of judicial review might meet democratic standards."
—**Mark A. Graber,** *Regents Professor, University of Maryland Carey School of Law*

"Creatively blending political theory and institutional analysis, Watkins and Lemieux show why tired arguments over the dangers of judicial activism overlook the courts' crucial function of protecting democracy from political failures. Their repositioning of courts as unique but fundamentally political institutions challenges both conventional legal and political science understandings of judicial behavior. The book reconfigures American politics by bringing the courts into the picture as necessary partners in ensuring democratic legitimacy and preventing domination."
—**Julie Novkov,** *Professor of Political Science and Women's, Gender and Sexuality Studies, University at Albany*

"This pioneering book challenges conventional thinking about judicial review and moves the field in an exciting new direction. It dismantles minimalist and 'instructions for judges' approaches rooted in the wrong-headed countermajoritarian paradigm and redirects our attention to how well courts, as compared to other veto points, contribute to the anti-domination aim of democracy. The authors' approach—simultaneously theoretical, practical, and comparative—yields properly modest conclusions about the virtues and vices of judicial review."
—**Terri Peretti,** *Professor of Political Science, Santa Clara University*

# JUDICIAL REVIEW AND CONTEMPORARY DEMOCRATIC THEORY

For decades, the question of judicial review's status in a democratic political system has been adjudicated through the framework of what Alexander Bickel labeled "the countermajoritarian difficulty." That is, the idea that judicial review is particularly problematic for democracy because it opposes the will of the majority.

*Judicial Review and Contemporary Democratic Theory* begins with an assessment of the empirical and theoretical flaws of this framework, and an account of the ways in which this framework has hindered meaningful investigation into judicial review's value within a democratic political system. To replace the countermajoritarian difficulty framework, Scott E. Lemieux and David J. Watkins draw on recent work in democratic theory emphasizing democracy's opposition to domination and analyses of constitutional court cases in the United States, Canada, and elsewhere to examine judicial review in its institutional and political context.

Developing democratic criteria for veto points in a democratic system and comparing them to each other against these criteria, Lemieux and Watkins yield fresh insights into judicial review's democratic value. This book is essential reading for students of law and courts, judicial politics, legal theory, and constitutional law.

**Scott E. Lemieux** is a Lecturer in Political Science at the University of Washington. His research interests include the relationship between the courts and other political branches, the impact of (and backlash against) judicial rulings, and the democratic legitimacy of judicial review. He has written or co-written articles in journals including *Perspectives on Politics, Polity, Studies In Law, Politics and Society, New Political Science*, the *Maryland Law Review*, the *Journal of Supreme Court History*, and the *American Journal of Comparative Law*. He is also a co-founder of the blog *Lawyers, Guns & Money* and contributes regularly to publications including *The New Republic, The Week*, the *Guardian*, the *Los Angeles Times*, and the *American Prospect*.

**David J. Watkins** is Associate Professor of Political Science at the University of Dayton, where he teaches historical and contemporary political theory courses, as well as courses on democracy and democratization. His research focuses on contemporary political theory, with particular attention to neorepublican thought. Recently, his work has appeared in journals such as *Perspectives on Politics, Political Theory*, and *Polity*.

# Law, Courts and Politics
Edited by Robert M. Howard
*Georgia State University*

In *Democracy in America*, Alexis de Tocqueville famously noted that "scarcely any political question arises in the United States that is not resolved, sooner or later, into a judicial question." The importance of courts in settling political questions in areas ranging from health care to immigration shows the continuing astuteness of de Tocqueville's observation. To understand how courts resolve these important questions, empirical analyses of law, courts and judges, and the politics and policy influence of law and courts have never been more salient or more essential.

*Law, Courts and Politics* was developed to analyze these critically important questions. This series presents empirically driven manuscripts in the broad field of judicial politics and public law by scholars in law and social science. It uses the most up to date scholarship and seeks an audience of students, academics, upper division undergraduate and graduate courses in law, political science and sociology as well as anyone interested in learning more about law, courts and politics.

For a full list of titles in this series, please visit www.routledge.com

6. **Judicial Politics in Mexico**
   The Supreme Court and the Transition to Democracy
   *Edited by Andrea Castagnola and Saúl López Noriega*

7. **Judicial Elections in the 21st Century**
   *Edited by Chris W. Bonneau and Melinda Gann Hall*

8. **Regulating Judicial Elections**
   Assessing State Codes of Judicial Conduct
   *C. Scott Peters*

9. **Varieties of Legal Order**
   The Politics of Adversarial and Bureaucratic Legalism
   *Edited by Jeb Barnes and Thomas F. Burke*

10. **Judicial Review and Contemporary Democratic Theory**
    Power, Domination, and the Courts
    *Scott E. Lemieux and David J. Watkins*

# JUDICIAL REVIEW AND CONTEMPORARY DEMOCRATIC THEORY

Power, Domination, and the Courts

Scott E. Lemieux and David J. Watkins

NEW YORK AND LONDON

First published 2018
by Routledge
711 Third Avenue, New York, NY 10017

and by Routledge
2 Park Square, Milton Park, Abingdon, Oxon, OX14 4RN

*Routledge is an imprint of the Taylor & Francis Group, an informa business*

© 2018 Taylor & Francis

The right of Scott E. Lemieux and David J. Watkins to be identified as authors of this work has been asserted by them in accordance with sections 77 and 78 of the Copyright, Designs and Patents Act 1988.

All rights reserved. No part of this book may be reprinted or reproduced or utilised in any form or by any electronic, mechanical, or other means, now known or hereafter invented, including photocopying and recording, or in any information storage or retrieval system, without permission in writing from the publishers.

*Trademark notice*: Product or corporate names may be trademarks or registered trademarks, and are used only for identification and explanation without intent to infringe.

*Library of Congress Cataloging-in-Publication Data*
Names: Lemieux, Scott, author. | Watkins, David J., author.
Title: Judicial review and contemporary democratic theory : power,
     domination and the courts / Scott E. Lemieux and David J. Watkins.
Description: New York : Routledge, 2017. | Series: Law, courts and
     politics ; 10 | Includes bibliographical references and index.
Identifiers: LCCN 2017030534 (print) | LCCN 2017035334 (ebook) |
     ISBN 9781315105765 (Master) | ISBN 9781351602136 (WebPDF) |
     ISBN 9781351602129 ( ePub) | ISBN 9781351602112 (Mobipocket/
     Kindle) | ISBN 9781138095199 (hardback : alk. paper)
Subjects: LCSH: Judicial review. | Democracy.
Classification: LCC K3175 (ebook) | LCC K3175 .L46 2017 (print) |
     DDC 347/.012—dc23
LC record available at https://lccn.loc.gov/2017030534

ISBN: 978-1-138-09519-9 (hbk)
ISBN: 978-1-138-09521-2 (pbk)
ISBN: 978-1-315-10576-5 (ebk)

Typeset in Bembo
by Apex CoVantage, LLC

# CONTENTS

| | |
|---|---|
| *Acknowledgments* | ix |
| Introduction | 1 |
| **PART I** | **7** |
| 1 Beyond the Countermajoritarian Difficulty | 9 |
| 2 How Not to Argue about Judicial Review and Democracy | 45 |
| 3 The Revolution Will Be *Sub Silentio*: The Roberts Court and Judicial Minimalism | 63 |
| **PART II** | **101** |
| 4 Democracy-Against-Domination and Contemporary Democratic Theory | 103 |
| 5 Compared to What? Judicial Review as Just Another Veto Point | 130 |
| 6 Judicial Review in a Comparative Context | 160 |

**viii** Contents

7 Conclusion: Toward a Realist, Institutional Democratic
Theory 173

*Index* *181*

# ACKNOWLEDGMENTS

This project benefitted from the input of a substantial number of first-rate scholars, to whom we're immensely grateful. A far from exhaustive list would include Eva Bellin, Jeff Dudas, Lenny Feldman, Michael Forman, Russell Arben Fox, Jackie Gehrig, Michael Goodhart, Mark Graber, Jeffrey Isaac, Angela Ledford, Jacob Levy, George Lovell, Ryane McAulliffe-Straus, Chris Manfredi, Jamie Mayerfeld, Michael McCann, Julie Novkov, Erik Olsen, Terri Peretti, Mitch Pickerill, Andy Polsky, Mark Rigstad, Melissa Schwartzberg, and Ken Sherrill. An earlier version of this manuscript was presented at both the Association for Political Theory (APT) First Book Manuscript Workshop in 2015 and a section of it at the McGill Legal Theory Workshop and benefitted immensely from both. The APT workshop was particularly valuable thanks to the incisive readings and valuable advice provided by the workshop participants: Simone Chambers, Sonu Bedi, Lucas Swaine, Lisa Conant, and Vanessa Baird. We would also like to thank the discussants, fellow panelists, and audience members at multiple different conferences as well as multiple anonymous reviewers for their valuable feedback. This collaboration began when we were both PhD students in the Political Science Department at the University of Washington, where we were fortunate to find a supportive environment among the faculty and our fellow students, and the boundary between political theory and (the rest of) political science was porous and routinely crossed by people who make their home on both sides; it's difficult to imagine this collaboration taking productive form without that initial environment.

Scott E. Lemieux would also like to thank his wife, Emily; parents, Elaine and Harold; and sister, Michelle, without whom this project would be inconceivable.

x   Acknowledgments

David J. Watkins would like to thank his colleagues in the Political Science Department at the University of Dayton, who provided a collegial and supportive environment for this project that has been highly beneficial. In particular, two department chairs, Jason Pierce and Grant Neeley, provided support, encouragement, and valuable advice. The democratic theory articulated in this book has roots in my doctoral dissertation; my committee was the aforementioned Jamie Mayerfeld as well as Karen Litfin and the late Nancy Hartsock. Most of all, thanks to Amy for everything.

An earlier version of chapter one was published as "Beyond the Counter-majoritarian Difficulty: Lessons from Contemporary Democratic Theory" in *Polity* 41:1 (2009), 30–62, and an abbreviated version of chapter five was published as "Compared to What? Judicial Review and Other Veto Points in Contemporary Democratic Theory" in *Perspectives on Politics* 13:2 (2015), 312–326. We thank the journals and Palgrave MacMillan and Cambridge Publishers for permission to use the material here.

# INTRODUCTION

In his inaugural address as the sixth holder of the Chichele Chair of Social and Political Theory at Oxford University, Jeremy Waldron outlined a vision for contemporary political theory, premised on a conceptual map containing three main varieties of political theory. First, there are political theorists who attend to normative concepts: justice first and foremost among them, followed by liberty, community, equality, human rights, and others: "the aims and ideals that direct our politics."[1] Second, political theorists can and occasionally do turn their attention to the virtues: the character and qualities we hope to find—or wish to instill—in good citizens. The purpose of Waldron's conceptual exercise is to make the case that we should turn more of our focus to a third kind of political theory, one that is present in the canon, but all too often downplayed or ignored at the expense of the other two: political theory about institutions and structures—what Waldron calls a *political* political theory. This book falls primarily, but not exclusively, in Waldron's third category. The turn to *political* political theory need not entail a rejection of "moralism" in political theory, as some self-described political realists claim, or even a retreat to presumably less demanding moral values such as order and security we find in, for example, the work of Bernard Williams and other proponents of the "realist" turn in contemporary political thought.[2] Waldron argues the nature and character of our political institutions have profound moral resonance—in particular, the dignitarian value of laws that best instantiate equal political participation rights.[3] Values—sometimes including idealistic values—can remain important even as we examine them in the context of their fraught, contingent, and probabilistic relationship with political institutions and structures through which they will work.

The particular institutional structure we'll examine here is constitutional courts (in general) and the power of constitutional judicial review (in particular). As

**2** Introduction

judicial review's role in democratic political systems has expanded in the late 20th and 21st centuries, so too has scholarly attention to the phenomenon. This attention has come from both empirical and normative approaches, although the line separating them is frequently breached by those primarily operating on both sides of it. A central preoccupation for this literature has been judicial review's status in democratic political systems: What does it mean for democracy? Does judicial review save us from too much democracy, or does it cut off, replace, or thwart democratic politics with elite control of important political decisions? Or is it properly understood as a democratic feature of a democratic political system? The focus on the first question came courtesy of the dominance of Alexander Bickel's framework in legal scholarship about judicial review, particularly his notion of the countermajoritarian difficulty. Both defenses and critiques of judicial review generally take its countermajoritarian (and therefore undemocratic) nature as a given. The shortcomings of this framework, which are substantial, will be given considerable attention in the first chapter. In recent years, several legal scholars, including Barry Friedman, Mark Graber, and Terri Perreti, have begun to challenge the countermajoritarian difficulty thesis in empirical grounds, demonstrating a far more complicated relationship between constitutional courts and other political actors. This book seeks to advance this effort to move beyond the countermajoritarian difficulty in the realm of democratic theory. Contemporary democratic institutions and practices are complicated, and cannot be easily sorted into the categories of "majoritarian" and "countermajoritarian"; further democratic assessment and criteria are needed. This book seeks to correct that imbalance, analyzing judicial review in its institutional context. Once we see past the flawed framework of the countermajoritarian difficulty, we can ask if it makes sense to treat judicial review as a democratic institution. But how would we make such a determination? What sorts of empirical and normative questions would help us answer a question like that?

The first chapter gives a full account of the impetus of the project and previews our arguments, reviewing the problems with the countermajoritarian difficulty's empirical assumptions, and beginning to think through their implications for democratic theory. A persuasive account of judicial review's democratic shortcomings, we argue, is not based on its countermajoritarian status, but its capacity to allow political actors to evade democratic responsibility. The second and third chapters continue to explore and address the shortcomings with existing approaches to judicial review and democracy. The second chapter focuses specifically on a strategy for justifying judicial review that we argue has limited value for political theory, which we call the "instruct judges" approach. A number of democratic theorists have argued judicial review's democratic value comes from judges conducting themselves in accordance with certain constitutional and/or democratic virtues—upholding the right values, limiting their interference in legislation to particular issue areas, using particular kinds of arguments, and so on. Whatever substantive differences we may have with this approach, the core of our critique here is methodological; such approaches avoid the realm of *political* political theory, in the Waldronian sense, in favor of a combination of conceptual and virtue-based approaches. Our project is to identify institutional designs more likely to be amenable to democratic politics, even in circumstances when various actors (including judges) fail to perform their office in the manner we'd hoped they would. Following Brian Carey's formulation, we need an institutional democratic theory for the range of people that exist, including the excessively partisan, the irrational and vengeful, and "jerks"—all of whom might be judges.[4] The third chapter takes a closer look at a specific judicial doctrine— that is, a set of "instructions for judges"—designed to render judicial review more amenable to democratic politics: judicial minimalism, particularly the version embraced by Cass Sunstein. Our sustained exploration of "minimalism" as practiced in recent Supreme Court jurisprudence demonstrates not just the empty nature of minimalism as a doctrine, but also the uselessness of a doctrine-based approach to assessing judicial review's democratic status.

Throughout, we develop and deploy a theory of democracy we refer to as "democracy-against-domination." We'll briefly introduce this approach in chapter one, give a more thorough account of it in chapter four, and deploy it to develop a set of evaluative criteria for veto points in democratic politics in chapter five. Chapter four gives an in-depth account of this approach to democracy and situates it in present debates and controversies in contemporary democratic theory. We demonstrate how democracy-against-domination can help us make sense of the debate between deliberative and agonistic accounts of democracy by situating both those approaches in democratic contexts. It is also an approach to democracy that's particularly useful for our substantive focus. A significant part of its appeal, for us, is that it is a democratic theory attuned to both the dangers of excessive state power (*imperium*) and abusive private power (*dominium*). The challenge of institutionalizing democracy-against-domination, then, involves identifying strategies likely, or at least capable, in promoting both goals simultaneously; that is, designing a state with the capacity to prevent private domination while avoiding becoming a *dominus*. No veto point can clear the high bar of guaranteeing success here—domination isn't the kind of problem that can be solved with an institutional fix, and any democratic institutional arrangement will sometimes fail—but some will offer greater upsides and fewer downsides than others. Chapter six turns to precisely that issue. Having established, in chapter five, that we have some *prima facie* reasons to think judicial review is a relatively attractive veto point from a democracy-against-domination standpoint, we place judicial review in a directly comparative context, comparing the case for its democratic value to federalism, bicameralism, and other veto points. We then conclude with some reflections on how the approach developed here lives up to the challenge of crafting an institutional, "realist" democratic theory.

The 13th Amendment to the United States Constitution reflects the relevance of this approach to democratic theory to constitutionalism, the practical

**4** Introduction

limitations of applying it, and the necessity of institutional analysis to do so. The text of the 13th Amendment, unlike most of the rights protected by the Constitution, applies to private as well as state actors: "Neither slavery nor involuntary servitude, except as a punishment for crime whereof the party shall have been duly convicted, shall exist within the United States, or any place subject to their jurisdiction." The 13th Amendment is generally understood today as a provision with the narrow goal of eliminating chattel slavery. As Balkin and Levinson observe, however, many contemporaneous Republican framers and supporters of the amendment believed that it enacted a broader non-domination principle.[5] This broader understanding can be traced back to the founding, when many believed that "the true marker of slavery was that slaves were always potentially subject to domination and to the arbitrary will of another person."[6] Because the text of the 13th Amendment reaches private as well as state actors, reading the amendment according to this understanding would have radical implications.

However, as Balkin and Levinson conclude, it was precisely those radical implications that caused the amendment to be read more narrowly. For strategic reasons, abolitionists—who had to hold together a coalition in which many members had conservative economic views—emphasized narrow reading of the amendment, applying it only to chattel slavery. The 14th Amendment—which by its text constrained only the state and not private actors—became the locus of expanded judicial protections of rights in the 20th century.[7] The history of the 13th Amendment indicates that there is a longstanding link between constitutionalism and theories of democracy and/or republicanism that emphasize non-domination. It also shows that such constitutional principles are not logically confined only to restraints on state action. Finally, it shows that textual principles of non-domination will only be effectuated if they retain substantial political support going forward.

## Notes

1 Jeremy Waldron, "*Political* Political Theory: An Inaugural Lecture," *Journal of Political Philosophy* 21:1 (2013): 1–23; see also his *Political Political Theory: Essays on Institutions* (Cambridge, MA: Harvard University Press, 2016).
2 Bernard Williams, *In the Beginning Was the Deed: Realism and Moralism in Political Argument* (Princeton, NJ: Princeton University Press, 2005); Raymond Guess, *Philosophy and Real Politics* (Princeton, NJ: Princeton University Press, 2008); Mark Philp, "Realism without Illusions," *Political Theory* 40:5 (2012): 629–649; and Edward Hall, "How to Do Realistic Political Theory (And Why You Might Want To)," *European Journal of Political Theory* 16:3 (2017): 283–303. For a sympathetic overview of the Guess and Williams-inspired 'realist' turn in contemporary political theory, see Enzo Rossi and Matt Sleat, "Realism in Normative Political Theory," *Philosophy Compass* 9:10 (2014): 689–701. Our approach in this book shares a great deal with the realist turn in political theory, but probably foregrounds the normative ideal of freedom as non-domination too much to entirely satisfy most realists. Waldron's conception of a "political political theory," on our reading, also decenters moral ideals in favor of institutions, but does so

in a way that retains a greater range of possible positions regarding the status and role played by moral ideals in politics and political theory.

3  Waldron, "*Political* Political Theory," 12–14.

4  Brian Carey, "Justice for Jerks: Human Nature, Selfishness, and Non-Compliance," *Social Theory and Practice* 42:4 (2016): 748–766.

5  Jack Balkin and Sanford Levinson, "The Dangerous Thirteenth Amendment," *Columbia Law Review* 112:7 (2012): 1459–1500; see also Rebecca Zeitlow, "Free at Last! Anti-Subordination and the Thirteenth Amendment," *Boston University Law Review* 90 (2010): 254–312.

6  Balkin and Levinson, "The Dangerous Thirteenth Amendment," 1484.

7  Mark A. Graber, "The Thirteenth and Fourteenth Amendments," *Columbia Law Review* 112:7 (2012): 1501–1549.

# PART I

PART 1

# 1

# BEYOND THE COUNTERMAJORITARIAN DIFFICULTY

## 1.1 Introduction: The Difficulty with the Countermajoritarian Assumption

The landmark decisions of the Warren Court provoked a crisis within American legal theory. Liberal legal scholars generally found the substantive outcomes of landmark Warren Court decisions desirable in policy terms, but had more difficulty in defending them as acceptable exercises of judicial power according to traditional theories of how judicial power should be exercised.[1] What they perceived as poor legal reasoning was particularly troubling to them because they even saw *principled* legal reasoning as presenting serious problems for American democracy. Alexander Bickel, whose work was enormously influential within these debates, famously stated the problem this way: "The root difficulty is that judicial review is a countermajoritarian force in our system . . . when the Supreme Court declares unconstitutional a legislative act or the action of an elected executive, it thwarts the will of representatives of the actual people of the here and now; it exercises control, not in behalf of the prevailing majority, but against it. That, without mystic overtones, is what actually happens."[2] While democracy was admittedly more complex than town-hall plebiscitarianism, "none of these complexities can alter the essential reality that judicial review is a deviant institution in the American democracy."[3] Bickel's articulation of the "countermajoritarian difficulty" was not a new development in legal theory,[4] but distilled and formalized a set of longstanding worries among legal scholars in a way that was enormously influential, and became a major part of the way in which constitutional theorists evaluated the Warren Court.[5] Theorists assessing the legitimacy of judicial review have frequently started from the assumption that judicial review is "countermajoritarian," and therefore presumptively at odds

**10** Part I

with democracy. The question, then, is whether or not judicial review could nonetheless be democratically legitimate, at least if practiced or constituted in a particular way.

We argue that a useful analysis of the democratic status of judicial review must abandon the "countermajoritarian difficulty" as an underlying premise. The assumption that judicial review is "countermajoritarian" and, therefore, a "deviant" institution is critically flawed in two critical respects. First, Bickel's framework is often not an accurate empirical description of the nature of judicial power, and its corollary assumption that the political branches represent popular majorities has similar empirical problems. Second, even if the description of courts as inherently "countermajoritarian" was accurate, this does not necessarily present the normative difficulties claimed by Bickel and his adherents. All liberal democratic systems have significant "countermajoritarian" elements (including within the political branches themselves), and few would argue that all of these mechanisms are necessarily "deviant." Yet few legal scholars write anguished papers about the deviant nature of the Senate, congressional committees, or the Federal Reserve.[6] For judicial review's democratic status to be meaningfully assessed, a more nuanced, comparative perspective is required.

Although the difficulty asserted by Bickel is often used as a starting point to attack judicial review (or at least some particular manifestation of judicial review), this argument can be turned on its head. The most common way of solving the "countermajoritarian difficulty" is to turn this alleged vice into a virtue: the countermajoritarian nature of the courts is a good thing. Courts are uniquely well-situated to protect the rights of individuals or disadvantaged groups against an excessively powerful majority. Judicial review, on this more positive account, is not a "deviant" institution but one that upholds fundamental democratic values. And, of course, Bickel himself concluded that judicial review could be legitimated because the courts could serve as a forum of principle and reason that would inject higher constitutional values into the interest aggregation and horse-trading of legislative politics.

Whether framed in positive or negative terms, however, theoretical assessments of judicial review that start from the premise that the courts are countermajoritarian all make the same mistake of treating institutions as engaged in zero-sum struggles for power. It is assumed that when courts exercise judicial review, they are contravening the will of the political branches and, therefore, by extension, the will of the majority. While sometimes useful, this underlying assumption also distorts many aspects of the practice of judicial review. We argue, based on a growing literature in political science, that the courts are often the accomplices of political actors, rather than being at loggerheads with them. Judicial review tends more often than not to represent the values of the governing coalition. We maintain that any theoretical assessment of judicial review must take this into account.

To question the usefulness of the "countermajoritarian difficulty" as a way of conceptualizing the legitimacy of judicial power is not, however, to say that judicial review (and other forms of judicial policy-making) is normatively unproblematic. A relational model of interbranch dynamics raises significant concerns about judicial policy-making: the inapplicability of the countermajoritarian difficulty cuts both ways. If courts are unlikely to successfully usurp legislative prerogatives on a consistent basis, they are also likely to be unreliable protectors of the rights of oppressed minorities. Using a more sophisticated analysis of interbranch relations also reveals additional potential problems with judicial review from a democratic standpoint, such as the evasion of legislative responsibility and the potentially distorting effects of "dialogues" between legislatures and courts.

Ultimately, then, the democratic legitimacy of courts depends entirely on the democratic theory being advocated. As we will argue in detail in the next section, conflating "democracy" with "majoritarianism" and "majoritarianism" with the political branches of government is not a productive starting point. But while it is necessary to go beyond a simplistic majoritarianism that virtually nobody would defend outside of the context of analyzing judicial review, each alternative democratic theory raises particular questions about it. To use the broad categories of democratic theory described by Ian Shapiro, judicial review has different potential strengths and weaknesses depending on whether one conceives of democracy in terms of republican self-governance, deliberative democracy, or democracy as a means of minimizing domination.[7]

This chapter will use recent developments in democratic theory to clarify some important questions about the democratic legitimacy of judicial review. First, we will explain in more detail why the "countermajoritarian difficulty" does not ask the right questions about judicial review. Second, we will explain how contemporary democratic theory can inform evaluations of the relationship between judicial review and democracy through its attention to the specific relationships between the normative point of democracy and its institutional manifestation in democratic theory. We will focus on democracy as a means of minimizing domination, as we find this approach provides both the most normatively useful and most realistic framework for assessing the democratic legitimacy of judicial review. Rather than attempting to assess how judicial review might function in a theoretical polity of equal citizens carefully deliberating about issues of public policy, for example, it is important to evaluate judicial review within actually existing institutional contexts. The fact that the "countermajoritarian difficulty" does not provide a good basis for critiquing judicial review, however, does not guarantee its democratic value: we must also question whether or not judicial review can actually be expected to reduce domination. From a democracy-against-domination perspective, we argue—with certain caveats—that judicial review can play a positive role, and should not be considered *inherently* undemocratic.

**12** Part I

This chapter will introduce and preview many of the arguments developed further in the rest of this book. The next two sections will lay out the empirical and theoretical flaws in the "countermajoritarian difficulty" framework for assessing judicial review, respectively. Rejecting it on theoretical grounds requires rethinking the relationship between majoritarianism and democracy. From there, the remainder of this chapter is occupied with four tasks. Once we recognize that democracy and majoritarianism cannot be easily conflated, we must look to democratic theory for alternatives. In section 1.4, we reject one alternative to majoritarianism, deliberative democracy, and focus on a more attractive alternative amenable to our realist institutional approach. We examine some recent work in democratic theory that emphasizes the opposing domination as democracy's central point to demonstrate this approach's strengths and weaknesses. Although the theorists we discuss consider the implications of their democratic theories for judicial review, they fail to consider much of what is known about judicial review in practice. We then return to a discussion of some empirical literature on judicial review in a comparative context to better consider how, and to what extent, judicial review might be valuable from the perspective of democracy-against-domination. Section 1.6 briefly notes that from an anti-domination perspective, the oft-neglected distinction between different kinds of judicial review—specifically, the difference between review of legislative and executive/administrative actors—should not be ignored. We close with an examination of how this discussion might shed a different and more productive light on the democratic status of judicial review than the "countermajoritarian difficulty" framework, and conclude with a preliminary account of some of the implications of this approach to democracy for judicial review.

## 1.2  Why the "Countermajoritarian Difficulty" Framework Is Inadequate as a Standard of Democratic Legitimacy

We contend that normative assessments of judicial review should examine the institution in practice; as a result, it is useful to briefly outline the normative and empirical problems with Bickel's framework. His formulation of the problem, unfortunately, is "so weakly grounded empirically" that it obstructs, rather than illuminates, consideration about the democratic legitimacy of judicial review.[8] In particular, it is important to avoid the rigged contests that are common when evaluating judicial review: critics of judicial review comparing legislatures passing legislation resulting from the constructive deliberation of knowledgeable citizens versus an entirely unaccountable (and disproportionately old and affluent) small group of lawyers, or supporters of judicial review comparing crude interest aggregators with no interest in constitutional values in the political branches with judicial "forums of principle." The central empirical

## Beyond Countermajoritarian Difficulty

problem with the "countermajoritarian" framework is twofold: it overstates the countermajoritarian nature of courts as well as the majoritarian nature of legislatures.

### *Majoritarian Courts*

Several political scientists have shown that courts tend to be closely tethered to the dominant political factions at any given time.[9] In the 20th century, this became a commonplace and ordinary part of the case for the court's legitimacy.[10] Even the decisions that are often the primary subject of controversies about "countermajoritarian" courts are better described as reflecting majority preferences, or at least the preferences of some powerful members of governing majorities. Powe's excellent study demonstrates that the Warren Court, despite often being used as a symbol of countermajoritarian judicial activism, was in fact very much in line with and supported by the governing coalition of the time.[11] Decisions like *Brown v. Board* and *Griswold v. Connecticut* are more plausibly described as a governing majority imposing uniformity on outliers than as countermajoritarian activism. As Mark Graber observes, "a generation of law professors analyzed Warren Court decisions as if Barry Goldwater had won the 1964 national election."[12] Similarly divisive decisions, including *Dred Scott, Roe v. Wade*, and *Bush v. Gore*, also—at least arguably—represented majoritarian preferences.

Another important factor limiting the "countermajoritarian" nature of courts in practice is the fact that courts necessarily rely on other institutional actors to implement their directives. Lisa Conant's study of compliance with the European Court of Justice, for example, found that courts are unable to make a substantial impact when they attempt to engage in policy-making that faces strong opposition within member states. Governments can use a wide array of passive and active strategies to resist implementation in ways that leave the courts little recourse.[13] For this reason, the assumption that courts readily impose their will on other political actors is misleading.

Bickel's claim that judicial review has a "tendency over time to weaken the democratic process"[14] is also subject to question. Most importantly, judicial review "can sometimes facilitate participation."[15] Several important studies in the law and society tradition have demonstrated that the courts both require democratic mobilization to initiate litigation and rely on democratic mobilization to implement their directives; in this way, the courts can be seen as strengthening democratic self-governance.[16] In a related finding, Tom Ginsburg's study of Asian constitutional courts demonstrates that judicial review is often a bargain among political factions that ensures representation of minorities and facilitates legitimate democratic successions: "in this sense, judicial review *reflects* democratization and is not antidemocratic, as asserted by theorists who focus on the countermajoritarian difficulty."[17] That courts are generally undemocratic in the sense of

**14** Part I

consistently producing policy outcomes that contradict majoritarian preferences simply cannot be held as an unquestioned assumption.

It is important not to exaggerate the extent to which courts mirror the preferences of governing coalitions. Recent scholarship, while accepting the basic insight that courts rarely swim far out of the political mainstream, has also found that conflicts among governing elites may give courts more relative autonomy than the landmark work of Robert Dahl suggested.[18] As Thomas Keck notes, while the appointment process tends to produce judges broadly sympathetic to the policy goals of the governing regime, institutional differences and disagreements about governing priorities mean that judges and legislators will sometimes differ even if they can be reasonably considered members of the same governing coalition, and some judges may be holdovers from a previous governing coalition.[19] In moving beyond the countermajoritarian difficulty, it is also important not to assume that judges and legislators will precisely mirror each other's preferences. As we will argue, considering potential differences between courts and legislatures is crucial in evaluating the legitimacy of courts, even if the nature of these differences is not what conventional frameworks assume.

### Non-Majoritarian Legislatures

In addition to the fact that courts are not, in practice, consistently countermajoritarian, political institutions are not necessarily majoritarian in either theory or practice. This is particularly evident in the American case. Checks and balances, a Senate that greatly overrepresents small states and has many countermajoritarian rules, the gatekeeping role of legislative committees, and various other mechanisms act as crucial checks on majority rule. As the recent work of Jacob Hacker and Paul Pierson demonstrates, legislatures can diverge from popular opinion on a range of issues for a considerable period of time.[20]

Institutions other than courts can also seriously consider constitutional questions. Legislatures engage in serious constitutional discourse, and moreover, do not always interpret constitutional texts in ways that maximize their authority.[21] Powerful legal norms and rights discourse do not exist purely within the judicial sphere, but also affect political actors (in and outside of formal political institutions). For example, even in the absence of a judicially enforced First Amendment, Congress and the executive branch during the Civil War consciously tried to avoid the worst excesses of the Alien and Sedition Acts.[22] It should not simply be assumed that only courts have the institutional ability to enforce constitutional norms.

### The False Assumption of Conflict

In the United States, much of the power of the federal courts is not the result of fixed constitutional powers, but rather the result of legislation that expands the jurisdiction of the courts.[23] While Bickel's framework generally assumes a zero-sum struggle for power among the branches, in practice, legislatures sometimes use the courts to defer and delegate policy choices in divisive social disputes.[24] Lovell's study of labor legislation in the United States provides further empirical ammunition for this theoretical insight.[25] While scholars had generally assumed that the American judiciary inhibited the strength of the American labor movement through conservative judicial activism against legislatures that were sympathetic to the interests of labor,[26] Lovell points out that this picture of the courts is highly problematic. Congress, in fact, passed intentionally vague legislation with the full knowledge that courts were overwhelmingly likely to resolve ambiguities against the interests of organized labor. The strategic benefits are evident: members of Congress could appease their labor constituencies while assuring businesses that the policy impact of reform legislation would be minimal, resolve legislative logjams, and evade responsibility for potentially unpopular policy outcomes. Similarly, Graber found that on issues such as slavery, antitrust, and abortion that threaten to destabilize governing coalitions, political actors will defer important policy choices to the courts.[27]

This tendency of legislatures to defer and delegate policy choices to the courts raises its own questions of democratic legitimacy, as this kind of blame-shifting has the obvious potential to undermine the accountability of the political branches. There is also the possibility of judicial distortion of legislative policy that, although its democratic implications will vary from case-to-case, must be taken into account.[28] Janet Hiebert, for example, found that while the Canadian government was generally able to pursue desired ends in the wake of judicial nullifications of particular legislation, having to pursue these ends in new ways still had important consequences whose desirability is not self-evident.[29] This literature is also important because it reminds us that judicial review can act as an "overhang" that may affect the construction of legislation even in cases where the courts do not nullify legislation.[30] But assessing these potential effects demands that we move beyond the simplistic assumption that courts are "countermajoritarian" and that judicial review necessarily "usurps" a clear legislative preference.

A curious aspect of Bickel's framework is that it causes scholars to work from underlying premises that they would almost certainly be unwilling to defend independently. Obviously, nobody—including Bickel—would mount a robust defense of the claim that American political institutions are designed to be "majoritarian." Although this sometimes drops out of his later analysis, Bickel, when laying out his theory, emphasizes the importance of electoral accountability in democratic institutions rather than simple majoritarianism *per se.*[31] This is true not only with respect to empirical questions, but to normative ones, as well. Again, very few theorists believe that democracy consists of *nothing but* majority rule, although majority rule is certainly of crucial importance. Most democratic theories make some accommodation for the protection of the rights of minorities and the necessity for fair procedures, and representative government also

**16**  Part I

places filters between legislative outcomes and majority will. The legitimacy of judicial review simply cannot be effectively analyzed without specifying how these complex tradeoffs are made.

## 1.3 Democratic Theory, Judicial Review, and the Countermajoritarian Difficulty Framework

Under the framework of the "countermajoritarian difficulty," judicial review is either normatively problematic due to its anti-democratic status or normatively valuable precisely because of its anti-democratic status. Even if we were to accept the empirical validity of the "countermajoritarian difficulty" thesis, it ought not to be assumed to necessarily be a "problem for democracy" because majoritarianism is not the same as democracy. The conflation of democracy with majoritarianism is, while common, deeply problematic from the perspective of any number of influential schools of democratic theory.[32]

The temptation to view judicial review as *inherently* countermajoritarian and legislative action as majoritarian (or at least much more so) may be driven in part by flawed assumptions about democracy that are overly procedural on one hand, and insufficiently attentive to procedural detail on the other. They are overly procedural to the extent that they assume that elections—the most concrete, tangible moment of political participation—constitute the *sine qua non* of democracy, and legislative action is one step removed from these elections than the courts. Lovell refers to this as the "electoral constraint" assumption, which entails the belief that "[t]he presence (or absence) of electoral constraints on the principal decision makers in a branch of government normally determines whether outcomes produced by that branch are democratic."[33] The "electoral constraint" assumption is excessively procedural in that it assumes that this central democratic procedure—citizen voting—is, in essence, indistinguishable from democracy's *normative* point. On the other hand, this assumption is insufficiently attentive to the actual procedural details that govern the legislative process, which contain (varying considerably in different times and places, of course) a great deal of countermajoritarian elements. The "countermajoritarian difficulty" thesis contains an unjustified and problematic assumption about the nature of the relationship between democracy's procedural manifestations and its normative point.

Yet democratic theorizing that adopts the framework of "the countermajoritarian difficulty" is quite common. Bickel and other prominent liberal jurisprudential and democratic theorists, as well as public choice theorists like William Riker, have embraced judicial review as a potentially useful and necessary antidote to democracy's potential flaws, errors, and excesses.[34] Conversely, a number of theorists of different stripes take judicial review to be problematic on precisely democratic grounds, as it unduly replaces the judgments and decisions made through the democratic process with those of an unelected group of judges who cannot be held accountable for their decisions.[35] Our task in this section is not to pick a side on this issue, but to question the assumptions that ground the debate. On what grounds is judicial review automatically conceptually outside of democracy? Even if democracy were simply equated with majoritarianism, as we have shown, rejecting judicial review as anti-democratic would be potentially problematic. The countermajoritarian difficulty framework continues to haunt democratic theory's consideration of the question of judicial review for many of both its advocates and opponents.

## 1.4 Alternatives to Majoritarianism in Democratic Theory

If we are not going to follow the theorists who assume that democracy is equal to majoritarian decision procedures, we must identify and defend an alternative conception of democracy's normative point. Democratic theory construction requires attention to two distinct democratic components. There is first the question of democratic procedures—which institutional arrangements, voting procedures, and so on, are required, acceptable, and unacceptable in a democratic polity. The second component is the normative point of democracy—the fundamental purpose and values of these procedures. Democracy is a concept infused with both normative meaning and empirical assumptions and claims. It is both difficult and unwise for democratic theorists to attempt to avoid serious consideration of either dimension of democracy in favor of the other.[36]

### *Deliberative Democracy*

As a normative starting point for democratic theory that moves beyond the conflation of democracy with majoritarianism, we propose deliberative democracy. This approach offers a more useful way to consider the democratic *bona fides* of judicial review than the "countermajoritarian difficulty" framework. Deliberative democratic theory shifts attention away from "mere" aggregation of votes and interest-based theories of political participation and toward a focus on a specifically democratic form of discourse and decision-making. Deliberative democratic theorists are most concerned not with the quantity of votes, but the quality of the reasoning that motivates them.

The deliberative democratic approach offers new ways to look at judicial review. Admittedly, some deliberative democrats have been quite skeptical of judicial review on the grounds that judicial reasoning by constitutional courts is an inherently elitist and undemocratic process.[37] Yet, the focus on discourse and reasoning provides a lens through which to evaluate the reasons behind particular acts of judicial review.[38] Jurgen Habermas, the noted proponent of deliberative democracy, sees a place for judicial review in an ideal deliberative democracy. He maintains that new laws must fit within the existing legal and constitutional framework. First and foremost, judicial review in a deliberative

**18** Part I

democracy is a means to ensure "fit" and "coherence" in the law.[39] For Habermas, this necessity outweighs any concerns he might have about the democratic value of judicial review. Aside from this observation, however, Habermas devotes surprisingly little attention to the details of his case for judicial review in a democratic society.

The recent work of Christopher Zurn addresses this gap in Habermas's account.[40] Although Zurn recognizes the empirical and conceptual problems with the "countermajoritarian difficulty" critique of judicial review, he focuses on the similar (and often conflated) "paternalist objection" to judicial review raised by Learned Hand.[41] This sees judicial review not so much as a violation of majority rule than as interference with self-government. For deliberative democratic theorists, such judicial paternalism violates core democratic norms because democracy is fundamentally about fostering the discursive habits and institutional arrangements necessary for facilitating the process of making democratic decisions together as a democratic community. Much of Zurn's book is given over to the task of demonstrating that existing deliberative democratic justifications for judicial review have failed to fully and successfully respond to this objection.

Nevertheless, Zurn concludes that judicial review (while not necessary) can be justified and valuable as a part of democracy under the right circumstances, as it has the potential to provide an independent "referee" in the constitutional deliberations of citizens,[42] and its very presence might serve to keep the deliberative attention of lawmakers and the public on the substantive and procedural requirements of the Constitution.[43] In particular, by using techniques such as the overbreadth doctrine, courts can encourage further deliberation by ruling out particular legislative *means* rather than substantive legislative *ends*.[44] Rightly puzzled by Habermas's evident lack of interest in developing a deliberative democratic theory of the institutional design of normatively justified judicial review,[45] he concludes with an extensive discussion of institutional reforms that could improve the democratic value of and justification for judicial review. Zurn has done democratic theorists an important service by turning the question of judicial review's democratic value away from simple majoritarian assumptions about the meaning of democracy.

That said, deliberative democratic theory is not the only new direction in recent democratic theory. In this chapter and the next, we introduce another normative starting point for democratic theory in our consideration of judicial review: democracy-against-domination. A primary strength of the democracy-against-domination approach is that it has normative purchase in a variety of political contexts. Deliberative democratic theorists have often lamented that deliberative democracy has limited value in circumstances in which there is an insufficient amount of "background equality," a category that for many deliberative democrats goes well beyond simply equal voting rights.[46] For deliberative democratic norms and institutions to properly function and have their desired effects, a good deal of domination must already have been eliminated. We wish to explore the implications of democracy-against-domination in part because it has the potential to speak directly to a wide array of contexts deliberative democracy does not. We do not reject the normative appeal of deliberative democracy—indeed, in chapter four, we'll argue that deliberative democracy can be best understood as a part of democracy-against-domination. Our project here is to develop an account of democracy that has a broader application across non-ideal contexts.

## 1.5 Democracy-Against-Domination and the Question of Judicial Review

The notion that democracy is best understood as a defense mechanism against or a means to attack practices and institutions of domination is a powerful one.[47] While it has a long history in democratic thought, this understanding of democracy's normative point has seen increased attention in recent years in part because it has been central to the recent work of prominent theorists, such as Philip Pettit and Ian Shapiro, among others. This conception of democracy's appeal and capacity to provide a better conceptual map of contemporary democratic theory will be explored and advanced at length in part two, when we develop our own alternative framework in earnest, particularly in chapter four. Here, however, we give a brief introduction to some parts of this approach to democratic theory particularly relevant to our task of rethinking the countermajoritarian difficulty, and offer something more helpful than the antidemocratic critique or valorization of the practice of judicial review.

### Shapiro, Pluralism, and Process Theory

Central to Shapiro's recent work on democratic theory is the understanding of democracy as "a means to manage power relations so as to minimize domination."[48] This colors Shapiro's view of hierarchies generally, especially their institutional manifestations. Hierarchies are not inherently dominative (organization hierarchies such as teachers over students and officers over subordinates are potentially just), but they are inherently "suspect." It is all too easy for just hierarchies to atrophy into domination if "left unchecked," so hierarchies should be "structured so as to minimize the likelihood they will atrophy into domination."[49] It is from this starting point that Shapiro considers and rejects judicial review as a necessary or valuable constraint on the excesses of democracy as it has often been understood.

However, Shapiro does see an alternate democratic justification for judicial review. Specifically, he considers the appropriate role of judicial review to be the development of a "middle-ground" sort of jurisprudential intervention into legislative decision-making. By this, he means that judicial review is ideally

**20**  Part I

reserved for cases when, "[t]he problem is real, but the proffered solutions over-reach, suggesting the desirability of finding a middle ground. 'More than process, less than substance' might be an appropriate slogan."[50] The goal of "middle-ground jurisprudence" is not to correct legislative error, but to send directions to the legislature to make another effort to solve the particular problem in a way that contributes to less, rather than more, domination.[51] Shapiro's framework for evaluating the democratic content and legitimacy of judicial review offers an improvement on Bickel's. Shapiro's "middle ground" jurisprudence also shares a number of similarities with the "representation review" theory put forward by John Hart Ely in *Democracy and Distrust*.[52] Ely's theory attempted to solve the countermajoritarian difficulty (and defend the legacy of the Warren Court) by arguing that judicial review was legitimate if it corrected failures of representation in democratic institutions. Ely's theory, while illuminating, has a number of significant problems. First, it fails to provide a convincing account of how judges should apply constitutional provisions—such as the Fourth and Eighth Amendments—that clearly place substantive restrictions on government ends rather than simply structuring decision-making procedures. Second, and more importantly, Ely's theory is just as subject to judicial manipulation as the constitutional theories he decries, relying on "substantive judgments, many of which are extremely controversial."[53] In particular, judgments about what constitutes a functional exclusion from the political process and what constitutes a "discrete and insular" minority require value judgments just as originalist, aspirationalist, and natural law constitutional theories do.[54] The second problem is especially relevant to our discussion here because it suggests that neat divisions between "substantive" and "representation reinforcing" constitutional doctrines cannot be effectively established in practice.

Shapiro's awareness of these problems suggests why he is staking out a middle ground between a process-based theory such as Ely's and a substantive theory, although the contours of his theory evidently remain quite vague. In addition, it is more useful as a tool to evaluate specific judicial actions than as a means of structuring judicial review because (even if we could reliably tell the difference between substantive and procedural judicial interventions) it would be exceptionally difficult to prevent judges given the power to enforce more procedural requirements from enforcing substantive limits based on the broad principles that are found in most constitutional texts.[55] Nevertheless, Shapiro's approach to democratic theory provides some insight into a democratic evaluation of judicial review.

Shapiro makes an important innovation in democratic theory by abandoning the Rousseauian notion of some sort of general will as the expected and proper outcome of democratic politics, a lingering assumption of both aggregative and deliberative democratic theorists. Furthermore, he is (properly, in our view) skeptical of the notion that legislative institutions can be reliable sites of robust democratic deliberation. Freed from these demanding and empirically suspect assumptions about its value, majority rule remains an important part of democracy, but not in the central way often assumed. Shapiro decenters the institutional practice of majority rule in favor of what he considers a more limited substantive point behind democracy's value. When the task of minimizing domination is seen as central to democracy, it becomes clear that the value of majoritarianism to democracy is contingent on what majority rule can contribute to that goal.

Ostensibly, majoritarian political institutions, such as popularly elected legislatures, offer mechanisms through which potential statist domination of the people can be avoided, but they open up other potential avenues for domination. From Shapiro's perspective, and the democracy-against-domination approach more broadly, it is difficult to offer a general account of constitutional judicial review as a mechanism to limit and prevent the practice of domination, however. Whether such an outcome is a likely result of judicial review is contingent on the content of the constitution and the common methods of interpretation, the prestige and power of the court, and the particular forms of domination prominent in the society in question. Still, if the constitutional rules include provisions of substantive equality, and must address potential democratic failure due to the presence of (in the famous formulation of Chief Justice Stone) "discrete and insular minorities,"[56] constitutional judicial review might provide an important mechanism to reduce domination.[57]

Shapiro argues that democratic theorists frequently make the mistake of paying insufficient attention to the ways in which power works in society. Specifically, he directs us to examine the ways in which social power allows for the domination of minorities in ways that are consistent with a general commitment to rights in a society. People are quite capable of holding many inconsistent views simultaneously,[58] and the social and discursive processes that undergird domination in a political community that values liberal norms make this clear. Judicial review critic Jeremy Waldron provides a possible response to this line of reasoning:

> A practice of judicial review cannot do anything for the rights of the minority if there is no support at all in the society for minority rights. The affirmative case that is often made for judicial review in these circumstances assumes that there is some respect for the relevant minority's rights outside the minority's own membership, but that it is largely confined to political elites.[59]

This is an important and valuable point, and one that warns against placing too much democratic hope at the feet of constitutional courts.

However, if we hold the view that democracy's normative purpose is the amelioration of domination, we do not need judicial review to serve as a "silver bullet" solution to the problem of domination to sustain its democratic *bona fides*. The ongoing domination of unpopular minorities by majorities ought to

**22** Part I

be understood as a problem without a single simple institutional solution. Indeed, the democracy-against-domination approach counsels against placing too much hope in any specific institutional arrangement, no matter how well-designed.[60] If ending or lessening domination is the normative point of democracy, the imperative shifts from finding precisely the right procedural way to alleviate the domination of these minorities to providing multiple possible procedural avenues to alleviate this domination, as their unfortunate status means no single procedure is particularly likely to resolve these problems. The task of democratic theory cannot be reduced to simply developing a precise account of institutional arrangements to identify precisely how it is to be done (and we might be well-served by acknowledging complex social, political, and economic problems such as these don't have a simple institutional answer). Even if judicial review provides only one possible and plausible avenue for reducing this persistent form of domination among many, it is an important point in favor of its democratic legitimacy.

## *Imperium* and *Dominium*: Pettit and Democracy-Against-Domination

This idea—that if democracy's central normative point is opposition to domination, then multiple procedural avenues to contest domination are democratically legitimate—is also a guiding principle in the democratic theory of Philip Pettit. Pettit is not primarily a democratic theorist; his central concern is rehabilitating a conception of republican political theory based on a distinctly republican conception of freedom—that is, freedom as non-domination, as opposed to the dominant Hobbesian and liberal notion of freedom as non-interference.[61] Democracy is valuable to Pettit only to the extent that it serves the value of freedom as non-domination. The intermediate normative point of democracy, suggested by this understanding of freedom, is to "bring government under the control of the governed"[62] to lessen the chances of domination occurring. Domination comes from one of two sources: *imperium* (domination by the state itself) and *dominium* (domination through private actors and elements of civil society). A democratic government must find a way to combat *dominium* while limiting itself in ways that will prevent slippage into *imperium*.[63] This understanding of the point and the appointed tasks of democratic government leads Pettit to suggest a two-tiered form of democratic politics.[64] On the first level, politics is deliberative, public, and legislative. There is little space for judicial review at this stage as the idea is to be as deliberative as possible,[65] and the ultimate decision (at this stage) should be made by electoral means.

In Pettit's view, this is simply the beginning of democratic governance in a republican polity. In addition to an electoral (authorial) stage, democracy must also have a contestatory dimension. The electoral/deliberative/authorial stage of democratic governance is analogous to a "first draft" on the path to the realization of the common good through law. The contestatory stage serves the function of the editor: "The first dimension will guard against false negatives by allowing every possible common-interest policy into consideration. The second dimension will guard against false positives by subjecting the policies adopted and their mode of implementation to a rigorous testing and filtering procedure."[66] The construction of a policy based on the common good (which is delimited and shaped by his republican conception of freedom as non-domination) is likely to require multiple stages and potentially multiple "drafts" to better eliminate practices and outcomes that increase rather than decrease domination. For Pettit, broad access to contestation is also based on a commitment to political equality. The contestatory dimension of democracy should not be understood as identical to judicial review—one could easily envision this imperative applied to the institutional structure of some parts of the administrative bureaucracy as well—but constitutional judicial review might play an important role. For Pettit, the specific contours of democracy's institutional complexity ought to be guided by a commitment to limiting and, if possible, eliminating domination. Democracy's multiple layers can do that—the authorial/electoral stage of democracy serves to prevent domination collectively (and to generate ideas for preventing domination of individuals), but the second, contestatory stage of democracy serves as an opportunity to prevent domination at the individual level.

At this point, we can identify three key ideas that emerge from these theorists. First, a significant strain of democratic thought claims that the central focus of democracy is to avoid domination, not simply to sustain majority rule (although, of course, majority rule is generally a major component of preventing domination by the state). Judicial review's usefulness, then, is dependent on whether or not it reduces the possibility of domination of individuals or groups, and whether or not this can be done without reducing the ability of the legislature to limit domination of the public by powerful elites.

Second, theorists such as Shapiro emphasize the potential value of judicial review as a means of preventing failures of representation within political institutions. Judicial review may be democratically legitimate—and the opposition of courts to "democratic" legislatures seen as potentially false—to the extent that it can keep democratic channels open and facilitate further effective political participation.[67]

Finally, these theories suggest that the value of judicial review is likely to be contingent. For democracy-against-domination theorists like Shapiro and Pettit, judicial review is not *necessary* to a liberal democratic state, but may play a useful role in certain circumstances. A consideration of Pettit's twin threats to freedom as non-domination—*dominium* and *imperium*—helps to contextualize this point. On the one hand, governments must be armed with enough power and capacity to act so as to facilitate their ability to strike against *dominium* when and where it arises in society. On the other hand, the institutions and powers of the state should be organized to lessen the likelihood of the state to slip into *imperium*.

**24** Part I

However, which kind of institutional arrangements and checks on power will reduce the possibility of *imperium* without unduly constraining the ability and likelihood of state power being effectively used to limit *dominium* is not a question that can be answered in a general and abstract way. The particular contours of social power within a political community, for example, will likely play a major role in our understanding of how this question might be answered, and how judicial review might play a valuable role. Yet, this explanation remains unsatisfying; as described here, it is a just-so story about judicial review's value. We aim to move beyond such an approach.

For the democracy-against-domination approach to be useful, we must say something more concrete and specific about judicial review. The democracy-against-domination approach is suspicious of all forms of hierarchy and power, as the fear that they might atrophy into domination remains strong. In this vein, both legislative democracy with constitutional judicial review and legislative supremacy clearly have the potential to allow and enact domination. There never can be an ideal institutional solution to the problem of domination; no configuration of institutional powers is guaranteed to save us from it. So we must turn to the issue of the likelihood of judicial review to ameliorate domination with greater frequency and intensity than it facilitates it.

## *Democracy-Against-Domination and Recent Empirical Studies of Courts*

Empirical scholars of judicial review in a comparative context disagree about the democratic valence of judicial review. One skeptic is Ran Hirschl, who has recently conducted an examination of the transition to more codified constitutional texts and the consequences of judicial review in Israel, South Africa, New Zealand, and Canada.[68] Hirschl finds that threatened political elites, eager to preserve their current status beyond future majoritarian elections, press for the constitutionalization of rights (as they understand them) to preserve their policy preferences: "judicial empowerment through the constitutionalization of rights and the establishment of judicial review may provide an efficient institutional means by which political elites can insulate their increasingly challenged policy preferences against popular pressure, especially when majoritarian decision-making procedures are not operating to their advantage."[69] Hirschl's careful case studies regarding the politics of the creation of judicial review suggest that this may indeed be an accurate description of how judicial review came into being. Hirschl also demonstrates that political elites eager to create judicial review have some shared ideological proclivities—namely, a neoliberal conception of rights, which offers strong protections for property rights while placing significant constitutional barriers in the place of the amelioration of economic inequality. The social and political forces behind this transformation are alternatively described by Hirschl as being the "secular bourgeoisie" (in Israel) and "the urban intelligentsia, legal profession, and managerial classes."[70]

The constitutional entrenchment of the elites' rights, Hirschl shows, becomes the constitutional entrenchment of the elites' preferred vision of rights. For example, he demonstrates convincingly that in Israel, the process of constitutionalization of rights and the creation of judicial review was pressed by a cross-party coalition of secular bourgeois Ashkenazi Jews. This group had dominated the Israeli political elite from independence well into the 1970's, but had seen its power declining and expected it to continue do so. Prosperous secular Jews sought to constitutionalize their preferred conception of human rights before they lost their political majority (which the shifting demographics of Israeli society made very likely). Tellingly, given this class's general neoliberal political preferences, two basic laws designed to protect subsistence rights and workers' rights were controversially excluded from the final version of the Basic Law before it was submitted for legislative approval.[71] Similar dynamics were identified to varying degrees in all four of Hirschl's cases; a neoliberal, negative conception of human rights was constitutionalized that favored the political ideology and interests of a group of declining political elites while excluding important social and economic rights (or, in the case of South Africa, restricting their impact).

Although Hirschl's narrative provides some *prima facie* reasons why adherents to the democracy-against-domination approach might not enthusiastically embrace judicial review, the generalizability of his account is put into question by the recent work of Kim Lane Scheppele. She has also examined recent examples of newly empowered constitutional courts and comes to the conclusion that "courtocracy" (as she calls it) can be, under the right circumstances, a compelling form of democracy.[72] This is most aptly demonstrated, according to Scheppele, in the context of the powerful Constitutional Court of Hungary in the 1990's. This court had powers that extended well beyond the typical powers of judicial review—for example, it had the power to review "non-action" by the legislature and declare it unconstitutional, effectively ordering the legislature to pass a law on a particular subject. Contrary to the pattern Hirschl identified with respect to social and economic rights, the constitutional court often pressed the legislature to protect them as required by the Hungarian constitution. The Hungarian court during the 1990's is also one of the most dramatic cases of a constitutional court with substantially more public support than elected political officials.[73] Party turnover was high in government, and the political parties had a tendency to fill their legislative agenda with largely symbolic gestures of little significance. In what many citizens considered much worse than a mere preoccupation with trivia, the legislature also succumbed to international pressure to overturn popular programs, producing a constitutional challenge that led to the so-called "Bokros package" cases, an incident that has significant implications for our discussion.

**26** Part I

The 1994–1995 Bokros package laws, named for the Finance Minister who championed them (after his predecessor resigned in protest over this plan), substantially cut or eliminated child supports, sick leave benefits, pregnancy benefits, and a host of other social insurance programs. This legislation was passed by parliament's unenthusiastic socialist majority due largely to considerable pressure from the International Monetary Fund (IMF), which had threatened to close its Budapest office and pull out of the country if social spending was not dramatically reduced. The post-communist Hungarian constitution contained a number of strong social and economic rights, although the programs cut in the Bokros package legislation were not specifically constitutionally mandated. The Court, too, faced pressure from IMF and World Bank officials to uphold the legislative rollbacks, but, unlike the legislature, refused to give in.[74] Although in the end the court did not reject reducing program spending and coverage, the legislature was told it needed to do so in a gradual manner that would allow those relying on these programs to adjust to the changes. The judges argued from the constitutional principle of legal security that the law could not change so rapidly and unexpectedly when dealing with entitlements that are deeply connected to the provision of constitutional rights.[75] Even though the court-ordered revisions did not meet the IMF's budget-cutting threshold, the IMF, not eager to be seen as undermining a constitutional court in good standing, did not follow through on its threat to withdraw from Hungary.[76] In this case and others throughout the 1990's, the court was exercising considerable policy discretion and doing so in a fashion that deserves to be called democratic by generally respecting the basic rights of citizens and plausibly reducing domination (through decisions that were also generally widely supported by the public).[77]

To be sure, Hirschl's pessimism and Scheppele's optimism regarding the democratic value of judicial review is likely driven in no small part by the cases they chose to study. One guiding assumption of this study is that judicial review, like many institutional arrangements and powers, will not be inherently or reliably democratic or undemocratic. Nonetheless, these cases help point us beyond merely noting judicial review's contingent value. These accounts, in addition to the earlier discussion of research on interbranch relations, can help guide us toward some general conclusions about the relationship between judicial review and democracy-against-domination as a democratic theory. We will turn to those in section 1.7.

## 1.6  A Note on Judicial Review and Non-Legislative Actors

Some arguments against judicial review are directed at the practice in general, and do not distinguish between legislative and executive acts. At least two prominent critics of judicial review, however, have left open the possibility that

Beyond Countermajoritarian Difficulty  **27**

judicial review that is not justified in the case of legislative enactments might be justified for actions of the executive branch. Jeremy Waldron's most comprehensive case against judicial review is explicitly limited to the "judicial review of legislation, not judicial review of executive action or administrative decision-making."[78] While Waldron does not rule out the possibility that his conditional opposition to judicial review would extend to the actions of executive branch officials or unelected state actors, at a minimum, he identifies the judicial review of executive actions as a distinct question that might entail a greater legitimate role for judicial review. This is a logical outgrowth of Waldron's commitment to the inherent value of legislative procedures and deliberation, as well as the capacity of legislators to engage in rigorous constitutional and right-based discourses, which are critical to his fundamental skepticism about the practice of judicial review.[79]

Mark Tushnet, another prominent critic of judicial review, similarly focuses on statutes passed by elected officials and brackets questions about the justifiability of the judicial review of executive actions. In *Taking the Constitution Away From the Courts*, he concludes his multi-pronged critique of judicial review by posing a hypothetical in which the Supreme Court announced that "[w]e will no longer invalidate statutes, state or federal, on the ground that they violate the Constitution."[80] The exclusion of the actions of executive branch officials or unelected state actors in this hypothetical Supreme Court withdrawal from the field of the judicial review of statutes is surely intentional, although he does not discuss his reasons for doing so explicitly. In a subsequent essay, Tushnet proposed a constitutional amendment (modeled on similar language in the Dutch constitution) that would codify the principle that "[t]he constitutionality of acts of Congress shall not be reviewed by any court in the United States."[81] Both thought experiments suggest that his critique of judicial review is focused on laws duly passed by elected legislators and does not necessarily apply to the actions or regulations of officials in the executive branch. Like Waldron, he implies that legislation is different and more troubling than other applications of judicial review.

From a democracy-against-domination standpoint—although not from the standpoint of, say, deliberative democracy—the issues involved with judicial review of elected chief executives are similar, although not identical, to those involved with the judicial review of legislative enactments. The more interesting question concerns unelected officials. The case for substantive judicial scrutiny of the actions of police officers—unelected officials who wield literally life-or-death powers—would appear, all things being equal, to be even stronger in this respect.[82] Waldron's point about executive branch officials being expected to act on the basis of *ex ante* legal authorization potentially justifying a higher level of judicial scrutiny seems particularly relevant to officials who carry firearms, can conduct privacy-invading searches, make decisions to arrest suspects, and levy fines. Police officers inevitably have to act with a substantial measure of discretion, and a

**28** Part I

good case can be made that this provides a particularly good reason for the courts to scrutinize policy actions for violations of constitutional rights.

This class of public officials is important for reasons of quantity as well as quality. A very useful empirical study conducted by Seth Kreimer found that the vast majority of lower-court incidences of judicial review involved scrutinizing the acts of police officers and bureaucrats as opposed to statutes passed by elected officials.[83] This most common form of judicial review does not even in theory pose the "countermajoritarian difficulty" that the judicial review of legislative enactments does. Responding to the frequently used assumption that judicial review necessarily involves "countermajoritarian" actions against elected officials, Kreimer makes the following observation:

> The problem, of course, is that the "electorally accountable officials" against whom the courts most frequently enforce constitutional norms include police, prison guards, and prosecutors whose accountability hardly equates with a popular mandate. Indeed, a primary characteristic of these street-level bureaucrats is the difficulty in prospectively constraining their discretion.
>
> Both of these concerns—the single-mindedness of the focus on bureaucratic missions and the relative unreliability of street-level bureaucrats as constitutional decisionmakers—are particularly salient in the areas of corrections and law enforcement which account for such large portions of the trial courts' constitutional review. In each setting, a bureaucratically monochromatic view of the world is exacerbated in total institutions where officials confront potentially hostile "clients" (with associated cognitive dissonance), where danger imposes the need for mutual loyalty among an insular corps of officials, and where individual "clients" are disenfranchised or powerless.[84]

No matter how sanguine one's view of the legislative process, the "countermajoritarian difficulty" framework is severely limited by the fact that the typical act of judicial review involves public officials who are not directly electorally accountable and are indirectly accountable only in a highly attenuated sense. From an anti-domination perspective, once we recognize the potential street-level bureaucrats have to wield functionally arbitrary power over individuals, additional mechanisms of accountability such as the possibility of constitutional review seem potentially appealing on democratic grounds.

Most of our analysis will focus on the judicial review of legislative acts, which is the tougher case for judicial review. But it should be kept in mind that the case for judicial review for unelected officials with broad discretion is almost certainly stronger. And, certainly, while there may be a sound case against judicial review in this context, the "countermajoritarian difficulty" cannot be an adequate basis for it.

## 1.7 Democracy-Against-Domination and Judicial Review: Some Preliminary Conclusions

We close this chapter with some preliminary conclusions, which will be further explored and refined in coming chapters.

### Democracy-Against-Domination Does not Require Judicial Review, but it Requires Some Effective Contestatory Institutions

In Scheppele's terminology, democracy takes place not just during elections, but between them.[85] The mere threat of losing the next election is often insufficient to prevent *imperium* on the part of the legislative or executive branches of government. In the case of Hungary, no ruling coalition has survived a re-election bid in the post-communist era, and on numerous occasions, the decisions (and inaction) of parliament have threatened the rights of Hungarian citizens. We confront the government as a people in national elections, but we also confront the state as individuals and private groups. A democratic institutional order must contain multiple methods of self-defense against both *imperium* and *dominium*. Judicial review certainly is not the only institutional arrangement that can provide this function, but it can be part of one. It might serve this function particularly well if the court can be petitioned by individual citizens, as is the case in both Russia and Hungary.

### The Circumstances under Which Judicial Review Is Adopted Matters

This is a central insight from Hirschl's work. Democracy-against-domination theorists ought to be concerned when the creation of a system of judicial review appears to be in large part an exercise in hegemonic preservation. This, Hirschl argues, is most likely to be the case when the creation of judicial review takes place under circumstances of "normal politics" and not as part of a larger political transition. As Hirschl notes, regimes transitioning from authoritarian to democratic institutional arrangements present a different set of challenges, and the hegemonic preservation hypothesis may not apply. Scheppele further makes the case that the post-communist transition in 1989 was particularly well-suited for thick constitutionalism with judicial review: publics in Eastern Europe and much of the post-communist world had had their fill of constitutions filled with promises of rights and no mechanisms to enforce them. Furthermore, the legislative process in such countries could not be expected to run smoothly from the very beginning: civil society was not robust enough to produce the kind of interest groups that generate potential citizen influence between elections (the Bokros package laws, for example, were enormously unpopular, but little pressure

**30** Part I

was mounted to encourage legislators to vote against them). We conclude that democracy-against-domination may direct us to oppose the institutionalization of judicial review if it represents an effort to preserve the political power of a declining hegemonic coalition, particularly when that coalition seeks to protect or enhance existing economic inequalities.

However, this does not mean we should oppose all attempts at judicial review creation if we have doubts about the motives of the political factions supporting it. If one insight unites the work of Scheppele, Hirschl, and all the recent scholarship discussed in the first section of this chapter, it is that judicial review is fundamentally political. This fact does not constitute a reason to oppose it. One potential impact of judicial review is that the political influence of a particular governing coalition might cast a longer shadow on future political leaders, but eventually, that shadow will potentially fade. Countries with longer histories of judicial review have seen the political preferences of the court change over time, with attempts to preserve regimes by packing the courts not necessarily proving successful.[86] If judicial review provides other valuable benefits to democracy, the drawbacks identified by Hirschl might be an acceptable price to pay, especially because their influence will not necessarily be long-lived.

Furthermore, Scheppele's work on judicial review in Hungary and Russia suggests that judicial review that allows for individuals to directly petition the court might serve to make judicial review a more effective contestatory institution. The Indian Supreme Court, for example, loosened standing requirements to facilitate the social mobilization that might make rights claims more viable.[87] While inevitably most cases will go unheard, the mechanism provides an avenue for potential contestation that requires few financial and organizational resources. In situations (such as post-communist Hungary) where civil society is weak and social movements or interest groups lack much capacity to influence policy debate, the opportunities for contestation are few and far between, especially for those most at risk of domination. Even in societies with robust and well-organized civil societies, many of the citizens most vulnerable to domination will have little access to interest group influence. Again, judicial review that allows direct petitions to a constitutional court is not a silver bullet certain to protect these people from domination—no institutional arrangement can assure that. However, democracy-against-domination does not hold proposed institutional innovations to such a high standard; if such an arrangement allows the possibility of successfully contesting domination, it would have a major point in its favor.

### *Judicial Review is Likely to be More Useful in Resisting Some Forms of Domination than Others*

In general, judicial review in modern constitutional orders is not well-suited to combat all forms of domination. Democracy-against-domination theorists must be deeply troubled by increasing economic inequality and the vulnerability

Beyond Countermajoritarian Difficulty **31**

created by desperate poverty. Such circumstances, by forcing people to beg for assistance, charity, food, or jobs, invite or perpetuate relationships of domination. Henry Shue was surely correct to include subsistence among what he called basic rights: those rights that undergird the very possibility of meaningfully holding and exercising the rest of our human rights.[88] However, even if Hirschl is correct that no "bills of rights, rights litigation, rights jurisprudence has ever been responsible for long-lasting, effective redistribution or resources and opportunities, let alone sustained equalization of basic living conditions," it does not necessarily follow that constitutionalization and judicial review will not contribute to a reduction in domination.[89] For one thing, Hirschl is at his least convincing in his account of judicial review's *independent* contribution to the global shift toward greater economic inequality in the 1980's and 1990's. He does not, for example, include a relevant comparison with countries that did not enact judicial review. If judicial review is an important independent factor in the move toward a more unequal neoliberal order, countries without judicial review should demonstrate greater equality.[90] In addition, in none of his cases have contemporary constitutional texts or cultures shown a tendency to permit courts, in a manner comparable to the *Lochner* era of the United States Supreme Court, to restrict the basic regulatory powers of the modern state in any but the most marginal ways. Scheppele's case study reminds us that it may be possible in some circumstances for courts to provide some measure of redress for economic injustices.

Even if one plausibly assumes that Hungary is an outlier, there are other forms of domination that judicial review might be better situated to resist. In responding to critics who take him to task for writing the struggle for women's rights out of his definition of "progressive social change,"[91] Hirschl largely agrees that "from a formal *de jure* standpoint, as well as a symbolic one, women, ethnic minorities, gays and lesbians, indigenous populations, and other historically disenfranchised groups are far better off in the constitutionalization era."[92] Hirschl goes on to argue that these advancements mean very little without progressive social change in his more narrow sense of outcome and wealth redistribution. He is right to stress the symbiotic relationship between positive and negative rights, but he emphasizes one direction of that relationship over the other. Democracy-against-domination theorists ought to be skeptical about the possibility of any institutional arrangement being sufficient to eradicate domination, especially in cases such as the groups under consideration here. To the extent that judicial review provides the possibility of lessening domination in the sphere of *de jure* formal rights, it may have potential democratic value, particularly given that the possibilities for mobilization presented by litigation may have payoffs in the political arena. Although some judicial review arrangements may facilitate democracy better than others, there is no way to assure that review by a constitutional court will always be democratic or immune to the risk that such review may become an agent of domination rather than a means to resist it.

**32** Part I

Such is the nature of just hierarchical institutions and arrangements—as noted earlier, Ian Shapiro suggests all just hierarchical institutional arrangements are in danger of atrophying into domination. As long as courts grant the state considerable latitude to address private economic domination, the ability of judicial review to increase protection of civil liberties and other formal rights is not a trivial contribution from a democracy-against-domination perspective.

## Scholarship on Interbranch Relations Reveals Both New Democratic Potential and New Dangers in Judicial Review

In many cases, courts have been empowered by and served the interests of other political actors. While this undermines the countermajoritarian difficulty as an empirical hypothesis, it is not at all reassuring from a democratic perspective. Judicial review can provide an opportunity for elected political actors to evade responsibilities or to pursue policies while evading electoral consequences. Such actions may enhance or enable domination by letting those actors pursue policies that might lead to domination without suffering electoral consequences. The possibility that judicial review can provide another outlet that permits legislators to "run from daylight"[93] and affect important policy changes with a minimum of public scrutiny is a serious concern, and may especially contribute to domination by powerful economic elites. An additional concern is that judicial review can have the perverse effect of making legislators *less* attentive to their constitutional responsibilities, as they may vote for legislation they believe to be unconstitutional under the assumption that the courts will correct their mistake.[94]

Yet the diffusion of responsibility that follows when courts are empowered to review legislative actions can work against domination, as well. In the example of the Bokros package cases in Hungary, judicial review allowed for a democratic outcome because the courts had the legitimacy and relative independence to stand up to IMF officials whereas the legislature did not. One can imagine other cases in which the vicissitudes of electoral coalitions might make legislative action unlikely, even though the normative end of reducing domination requires action: the reapportionment cases that Earl Warren considered the most important of his tenure present an obvious example.[95] In these cases, the courts may be positioned to make a positive contribution to democracy in circumstances when other political actors are not. Still, on balance, the fact that judicial review can allow political actors to evade responsibility for making difficult policy choices has to be considered a net negative for the democratic value of judicial review. In particular, as Mark Tushnet suggests, this problem speaks to the advantage of "weak-form" review that authorizes legislatures to override the constitutional rulings of courts in some circumstances.[96]

Finally, some of the insights of the innovative new literature on the relationship between courts and legislatures have uncertain effects from the perspective of a democratic theory focused on lessening domination. That judicial review may alter the construction of legislation or express the fact that the court represents a "particular constellation of ideas and interests . . . somewhat different from the constellation represented in the elected branches"[97] is not inherently problematic from a democratic perspective. Injecting a different set of priorities from within a broad mainstream of ideas can have domination-limiting consequences.[98] Prison reform, for example, may be privately acceptable to governing elites, but for political reasons, much more likely to be initiated by the courts.[99] Similarly, one "distorting" effect of the overhang of judicial review may be increased attention to civil liberties and other constitutional values as legislators pursue various ends. This is not to say, however, that these distorting effects will always have the effect of reducing domination. For example, responding to a Canadian Supreme Court decision striking down a "rape shield" law that prevented the introduction of a woman's sexual history at trial in most circumstances, parliament responded with legislation (ultimately upheld by the court) that made some sexual assault defenses "reverse onus," putting the burden of proof on the defendant.[100] It is arguable that the original policy was more successful at addressing the distorting effect of patriarchal domination at sexual assault trials while *also* being more protective of civil liberties. Hence, it is possible for even "medium-level" review in Shapiro's sense to undermine domination-reducing objectives. While we would tentatively speculate that in most contemporary constitutional contexts these effects of judicial review would tend to marginally decrease domination, on balance, we also recognize that this is very much an open question and the claim should be subject to revision should further empirical study indicate otherwise. The primary value of moving beyond the "countermajoritarian difficulty" is to facilitate better questions about judicial review rather than providing easy answers.

## 1.8  Conclusion

Our review of some major developments in democratic theory reinforces our argument that the "countermajoritarian difficulty" framework, despite how central it has been to both empirical studies of and normative theorizing about the courts,[101] is of limited usefulness. It overestimates the extent to which legislative outcomes represent majority preferences. The flaws in this assumption are obvious in the U.S. system, in which many countermajoritarian elements are explicitly built into the structure of the political branches. Even in more centralized political systems like Canada and the United Kingdom, there are many institutional elements that insulate political actors from majority opinion (even assuming that a coherent majority opinion exists in the first place). While legislative policy outcomes may represent a majority consensus, this cannot simply be assumed.

**34** Part I

Moreover, the framework exaggerates the extent to which courts are isolated from majoritarian pressures. Judicial theorists also have made the flawed assumption that when courts and legislatures disagree, the legislature (for better or worse) represents the majority's policy preference. All democratic institutions have countermajoritarian mechanisms and unintended consequences such as path dependencies[102] that create (or maintain) legislative outcomes that do not necessarily reflect contemporary majorities of either citizens or legislators. In addition, the focus on the "countermajoritarian difficulty" tends to overstate the coherence of legislative policy outcomes, which often represent the ambiguous results of compromises between *ad hoc* coalitions of minority factions. Many of the problematic assumptions that distort perceptions about the courts— the focus on judicial independence, the identification of false conflicts, and the alleged tendency of courts to generate more social divisiveness—trace their roots to some degree from the first premise that courts are inherently "countermajoritarian" institutions. Finally, even more sophisticated theoretical approaches to judicial review often pay insufficient attention to the nature of interbranch relations. Most importantly for our purposes here, judicial review often expands because of legislative action. The fundamental issue is that "the countermajoritarian problem is rooted in Bickel's definition of democracy, not in actual politics."[103] This empirically inaccurate abstraction is doubly problematic because it is theoretically impoverished, as well. Moving beyond this assumption allows many of these distorted lenses to be removed from the study of judicial power.

This is not to say that the practice of judicial review does not raise serious problems. In one sense, the inexorable linkages between courts and governing coalitions may make judicial review more democratically defensible: due to the linkages, judicial policy-making is not necessarily opposed to the interests of legislators or citizens. But this is also a potential source of problems of democratic legitimacy, as legislators use the courts (just as they sometimes use delegation to executive agencies) to shift responsibility for difficult policy decisions onto other actors. This can have the effect of diluting electoral accountability and can result in the failure to address issues that demand urgent attention.

To move beyond Bickel's framework does not require one to become an apologist for judicial review. It is possible, for example, to normatively critique decisions such as *Roe v. Wade* and *Bush v. Gore* without claiming that they "usurp" majority preferences. One may also decry the dilution of accountability created by judicial review, just as one might criticize bicameralism.[104] However, a more sophisticated method, particularly one that adopts the "democracy-against-domination" approach to democratic theory, does preempt certain types of critique. Simplistic, polemical attacks on the democratic status of the courts have become all too common. These attacks rely on two flawed assumptions—first, that the courts are countermajoritarian in a qualitatively unique way as compared to other branches of government, and second, that majoritarianism and democracy are more or less interchangeable. The former shows a lack of serious attention to the nature of both the legislative and judicial branches, and the latter shows a lack of serious thinking about the implications of democracy. If these errors were limited to the polemics of popular political discourse, the usefulness of our project would be limited. However, the same errors that plague our political discourse are replicated in the realm of democratic theory, as well. Starting with this frame causes theorists to work with simplistic assumptions about the nature of both political and legal institutions that virtually nobody would defend for any purpose other than to assess judicial review. Several theorists have shown that adopting both a sophisticated understanding of the empirical complexities of judicial review in practice and a theory of democracy that doesn't reduce to majoritarianism (in this case, deliberative democracy) can move the conversation forward in productive ways.

We have begun the process of doing the same for the "democracy-against-domination" approach to democratic theory in this chapter. The remainder of this book will build the case that this is a promising way forward for democratic theory, with respect to the project of evaluating judicial review's democratic valence in particular. This approach does not give us easy answers, nor can it say anything about judicial review's democratic value at high levels of abstraction. In conjunction with attention to new avenues in court scholarship, it provides us with a set of tools and questions that help us determine whether a particular judicial review regime will be likely to make a contribution to democratic politics in its specific context. While our analysis provides reason for concern, there are also good reasons to believe that judicial review might make a modest contribution to democracy under the right circumstances. It is also almost certainly true that judicial review is just one potential tool among many for reducing domination, and in particular, it is likely to be ill-suited under most circumstances to address domination that has primarily economic sources. If it is important not to assume that judicial review is an inherently "anti-democratic" institution, it is equally important not to conflate "judicial interpretations of constitutional texts" with "rights." Advancing rights and minimizing domination will remain projects that to be successful must rely on a joint effort of multiple institutions and political actors. Judicial review has the potential to make a modest yet positive democratic contribution, but it can only play a partial and limited role in securing democracy.

## Notes

1 See Michael Klarman, "Rethinking the Civil Rights and Civil Liberties Revolutions," *Virginia Law Review* 82:1 (1996): 1–67.
2 Alexander Bickel, *The Least Dangerous Branch: The Supreme Court at the Bar of Politics* (Indianapolis, IN: Bobbs-Merrill, 1962), 16–17.
3 Ibid., 18.

4 For example, in 1952, Eugene Rostow reported that his fellow legal scholars evince an uneasiness or even guilt about judicial review, widely understood to be "an undemocratic shoot on an otherwise respectable tree." Rostow, "The Democratic Character of Judicial Review," *Harvard Law Review* 66:2 (1952): 193–223, at 193.

5 Mark Tushnet, "The Jurisprudence of Constitutional Regimes: Alexander Bickel and Cass R. Sunstein," in Kenneth Ward and Cecilia Castillo (eds) *The Judiciary and American Democracy: Alexander Bickel, the Countermajoritarian Difficulty, and Contemporary Constitutional Theory* (Albany: SUNY Press, 2005), 23–30; Thomas Keck, *The Most Activist Supreme Court in History: The Road to Modern Judicial Conservatism* (Chicago, IL: University of Chicago Press, 2004), 61–64.

6 There are, of course, exceptions; see, e.g., Sanford Levinson, *Our Undemocratic Constitution* (New York: Oxford University Press, 2006).

7 Ian Shapiro, *The State of Democratic Theory* (New Haven, CT: Yale University Press, 2003).

8 Terri Peretti, "An Empirical Analysis of Alexander Bickel's: *The Least Dangerous Branch*," in Kenneth Ward and Cecilia Castillo (eds) *The Judiciary and American Democracy* (Albany, NY: SUNY Press, 2005), 140.

9 Robert Dahl, "Decision-Making in a Democracy: The Supreme Court as a National Policy-Maker," *The Journal of Public Law* 6:2 (1957): 279–295; Stephen Wasby, *The Impact of the American Supreme Court: Some Perspectives* (Chicago: Dorsey Press, 1970); Stuart Scheingold, *The Politics of Rights: Lawyers, Public Policy, and Political Change* (New Haven, CT: Yale University Press, 1974) and "Constitutional Rights and Social Change: Civil Rights in Perspective," in Michael W. McCann and Gerald L. Houseman (eds) *Judging the Constitution: Critical Essays on Judicial Lawmaking* (Glenville, IL: Scott Foresman, 1989), 73–91; Donald Horowitz, *The Courts and Social Policy* (Washington, DC: Brookings Institution, 1977); Bradley Canon and Charles Johnson, *Judicial Politics: Implementation and Impact*, 2nd ed. (Washington, DC: CQ Press, 1998); Peretti, "An Empirical Analysis," 130–133.

10 Or Bassok, "The Supreme Court at the Bar of Public Opinion Polls," *Constellations* 23:4 (2016): 573–584. Prior to the advent of scientific public opinion polling, defenses of majoritarianism as a desideratum for courts simply conflated it with deference to legislation. See, for example, James Bradley Thayer, *The Origin and Scope of the American Doctrine of Constitutional Law* (Boston, MA: Little and Brown, 1893), 22–26.

11 Lucas A. Powe, Jr., *The Warren Court and American Politics* (Cambridge, MA: Belknap Press, 2000).

12 Mark A. Graber, "Constitutional Politics and Constitutional Theory: A Misunderstood and Neglected Relationship," *Law & Social Inquiry* 27:2 (2002): 313. Of course, whether (or to what extent) the key decisions of the Warren Court are "majoritarian" depends to some degree on one's perspective. Some of the crucial decisions—such as *Brown, Griswold,* and *Gideon v. Wainwright*—represented national majorities prevailing over regional outliers. Some, such as the great reapportionment cases *Baker v. Carr* and *Reynolds v. Sims,* were majoritarian by any definition. Others, such as the court's school prayer and many of its criminal procedure decisions, were genuinely contrary to public opinion. None of the major decisions, however, were antithetical to the Democratic coalition that controlled the federal government during the 1960s. And, certainly, Bickel's framework is incapable of accounting for these differences.

13 Lisa Conant, *Justice Contained: Law and Politics in the European Union* (Ithaca, NY: Cornell University Press, 2002), 50–94.

Beyond Countermajoritarian Difficulty **37**

14 Bickel, *The Least Dangerous Branch*, 21.

15 Christopher E. Eisgruber, *Constitutional Self-Government* (Cambridge, MA: Harvard University Press, 2001), 93.

16 See, e.g., Conant, *Justice Contained*; Scheingold, *The Politics of Rights*; Frances Zemans, "Legal Mobilization: The Neglected Role of Law in the Political System," *American Political Science Review* 77:4 (1983): 690–703; Michael McCann, *Rights at Work: Pay Equity Reform and the Politics of Legal Mobilization* (Chicago, IL: University of Chicago Press, 1994); Charles Epp, *The Rights Revolution: Lawyers, Activists, and Supreme Courts in Comparative Perspective* (Chicago, IL: University of Chicago Press, 1998); Troy Q. Riddell, "The Impact of Legal Mobilization and Judicial Decisions: The Case of Official Minority-Language Education Policy in Canada for Francophones Outside Quebec," *Law & Society Review* 28:3 (2004): 583–610; Rachel A. Cichowski, *The European Court and Civil Society: Litigation, Mobilization and Governance* (New York: Cambridge University Press, 2007).

17 Tom Ginsburg, *Judicial Review in New Democracies: Constitutional Courts in Asian Cases* (Cambridge: Cambridge University Press, 2003), 64. Emphasis retained from original.

18 See, for example, Mark Tushnet, *The New Constitutional Order* (Princeton, NJ: Princeton University Press, 2003); Keith Whittington, *Political Foundations of Judicial Supremacy* (Princeton, NJ: Princeton University Press, 2007), 41–45.

19 Thomas M. Keck, "Party, Policy or Duty: Why Does the Supreme Court Invalidate Federal Statutes?" *American Political Science Review* 101:2 (2007): 321–338.

20 Jacob Hacker and Paul Pierson, *Off Center: The Republican Revolution and the Erosion of American Democracy* (New Haven, CT: Yale University Press, 2005); *Winner-Take-All Politics: How Washington Made the Rich Richer and Turned Its Back on the Middle Class* (New York: Simon and Schuster, 2011).

21 See, for example, Keith Whittington, *Constitutional Construction: Divided Powers and Constitutional Meaning* (Cambridge, MA: Harvard University Press, 2001); James Mitchell Pickerill, *Constitutional Deliberation in Congress: The Impact of Judicial Review in a Separated System* (Durham, NC: Duke University Press, 2004); Neal Devins and Louis Fisher, *The Democratic Constitution* (New York: Oxford University Press, 2004).

22 Geoffrey Stone, *Perilous Times: Free Speech in Wartime from the Sedition Act of 1798 to the War on Terrorism* (New York: Norton, 2004), ch. 2.

23 Howard Gillman, "How Political Parties Can Use the Courts to Advance Their Agendas: Federal Courts in the United States, 1875–1891," *American Political Science Review* 96:3 (2002): 511–524; Thomas M. Keck, "The Relationship between Courts and Legislatures," in Lee Epstein and Stephanie A. Lindquist (eds) *The Oxford Handbook of U.S. Judicial Behavior* (Oxford: Oxford University Press, 2017), 381–398; James Mitchell Pickerill and Cornell Clayton, "The Rehnquist Court and the Political Dynamics of Federalism," *Perspectives on Politics* 2:2 (2004): 233–248; Keith Whittington, "'Interpose Your Friendly Hand': Political Supports for the Exercise of Judicial Review by the United States Supreme Court," *American Political Science Review* 99:4 (2005): 583–596.

24 George I. Lovell and Scott E. Lemieux, "Assessing Juristocracy: Are Judges Rules or Agents?" *Maryland Law Review* 65 (2006): 100–114.

25 George I. Lovell, *Legislative Deferrals: Statutory Ambiguity, Judicial Power, and American Democracy* (Cambridge: Cambridge University Press, 2003).

**38** Part I

26 See, for example, William Forbath, *Law and the Shaping of the American Labor Movement* (Cambridge, MA: Harvard University Press, 1991) and Victoria Hattam, *Labor Visions and State Power* (Princeton, NJ: Princeton University Press, 1993).
27 Mark A. Graber, "The Nonmajoritarian Difficulty: Legislative Deference to the Judiciary," *Studies in American Political Development* 7:1 (1993): 35–73.
28 See, for example, Robert Nagel, *Constitutional Cultures: The Mentality and Consequences of Judicial Review* (Berkeley, CA: University of California Press, 1993); Christopher P. Manfredi and James B. Kelly, "Six Degrees of Dialogue: A Response to Hogg and Bushell," *Osgoode Hall Law Journal* 37 (1989): 513–528; Sujit Choudhry, "Worse Than *Lochner?*" in Colleen Flood, Kent Roach and Lorne Sossin (eds) *Access to Care, Access to Justice: The Legal Debate over Private Health Insurance in Canada* (Toronto: University of Toronto Press, 2005), 75–100.
29 Janet Hiebert, *Charter Conflicts* (Montreal: McGill/Queens University Press, 2002).
30 Mark Tushnet, *Weak Courts, Strong Rights: Judicial Review and Social Welfare Rights in Comparative Constitutional Law* (Princeton, NJ: Princeton University Press, 2008), 80–82.
31 Bickel, *The Least Dangerous Branch*, 16–18.
32 According to Josiah Ober, the conflation of democracy with majority rule is as old as the concept of democracy itself, but it isn't what was meant by democracy in Athens. Rather, the confusion of democracy with majority rule was a misreading of democracy's original meaning by elite critics of democracy hoping to discredit it as a form of government. See Josiah Ober, "The Original Meaning of 'Democracy': Capacity to Do Things, Not Majority Rule," *Constellations* 15:1 (2008): 3–9.
33 Lovell, *Legislative Deferrals*, 13.
34 Ronald Dworkin considers judicial review as a necessary and good antidote to democratic legislatures or executives whose laws and actions violate political equality; see, e.g., *Sovereign Virtue* (Cambridge, MA: Harvard University Press, 2000). William Riker suggests that judicial review is one of several features of government that can guard against attempts to slip into what he calls "populism" (defined as when the elected legislatures attempt to govern to the collective will of the people, which for Riker is both incoherent and dangerous). See his *Liberalism versus Populism: A Confrontation between the Theory of Democracy and the Theory of Social Choice* (Long Grove, IL: Waveland Press, 1988), 250. We return to Riker's defense of judicial review in more detail in section 5.3.
35 This view is common among both legal and political theorists. Prominent legal theory works that advance positions along this line include Mark Tushnet, *Taking the Constitution away from the Courts* (Princeton, NJ: Princeton University Press, 1999) and Larry Kramer, *The People Themselves: Popular Constitutionalism and Judicial Review* (New York: Oxford University Press, 2003). Political theorists who take a similar position with respect to judicial review's democratic status include Jeremy Waldron, Richard Bellamy, and John McCormick. See Jeremy Waldron, *Law and Disagreement* (Oxford: Oxford University Press, 1999); "The Core of the Case against Judicial Review," *Yale Law Journal* 115:6 (2006): 1346–1406; Richard Bellamy, *Political Constitutionalism: A Republican Defense of the Constitutionality of Democracy* (Cambridge: Cambridge University Press, 2007); "Republicanism, Democracy, and Constitutionalism," in Cecile Leborde and John Maynor (eds) *Republicanism and Political Theory* (Malden, MA: Blackwell, 2008), 159–189; "The Democratic Constitution: Why Europeans Should Avoid American Style Constitutional Judicial Review," *European Political Science* 7:1

Beyond Countermajoritarian Difficulty **39**

(2008): 9–20; "Rights, Republicanism, Democracy," in Andreas Niederberger and Phillipp Schink (eds) *Republican Democracy: Law, Liberty, Politics* (Edinburgh: Edinburgh University Press, 2013), 253–275; and John McCormick, "Republicanism and Democracy," in Andreas Niederberger and Phillipp Schink (eds) *Republican Democracy: Law, Liberty, Politics* (Edinburgh: Edinburgh University Press, 2013), 89–127.

36 In his discussion of Gallie's concept of "essentially contested concepts," William Connolly makes precisely this point with respect to democracy: "Democracy—and other concepts like it—display in our discourse over a normal range of cases a close connection between its criteria and its normative point. The relation is close enough to allow us to say that if that connection were somehow abrogated by a large number of people for a large number of cases of a long period of time, the concept would either fall into disuse or undergo fundamental change . . . both the points and the criteria of our concepts are sanctioned by convention. Logically these conventions could be altered in an infinite number of ways, but showing that something is logically permissible does not establish that it is also justifiable and reasonable," William Connolly, *Terms of Political Discourse* (London: Blackwell, 1993), 32. See also Walter Bryce Gallie, "Essentially Contested Concepts," in Max Black (ed) *The Importance of Language* (Englewood Cliffs, NJ: Prentice Hall, 1962), 121–145.

37 Carlos Santiago Nino, *The Constitution of Deliberative Democracy* (New Haven, CT: Yale University Press, 1998). Nino does note several exceptions to his rejection of judicial review on democratic grounds, including judicial review "that strengthens the democratic process" (199–203). Alternatively, the process of litigating rights can actually stimulate and promote popular deliberation on constitutional principles—particularly with respect to currently unpopular constitutional ideals not subject to serious public deliberation. An account of this process with respect to the ACLU's shift toward a litigation-centered strategy in the 1920's can be found in Emily Zackin, "Popular Constitutionalism's Hard When You're Not Very Popular: Why the ACLU Turned to Courts," *Law & Society Review* 42:2 (2008): 367–396.

38 For example, Cass Sunstein and Richard Burt use deliberative democracy to critically evaluate U.S. Supreme Court decision-making throughout history. See Cass Sunstein, *The Partial Constitution* (Cambridge, MA: Harvard University Press, 1996) and Richard Burt, *The Constitution in Conflict* (Cambridge, MA: Belknap Press, 1995).

39 Jurgen Habermas, *Between Facts and Norms: Contributions to a Discourse Theory of Law and Democracy* (Cambridge, MA: MIT Press, 1996), 167–168.

40 Christopher F. Zurn, *Deliberative Democracy and the Institutions of Judicial Review* (Cambridge: Cambridge University Press, 2007). Hand's paternalism objection to judicial review can be found in his *The Bill of Rights* (Cambridge, MA: Harvard University Press, 1958).

41 Zurn, *Deliberative Democracy*, 4–6. See also his related discussion about arguments that legal discourse is particularly well suited to moral arguments at 163–178.

42 Ibid., 254.

43 Ibid., 281.

44 See, esp., Cass R. Sunstein, *One Case at a Time: Judicial Minimalism and the Supreme Court* (Cambridge, MA: Harvard University Press, 1999) and Eisgruber, *Constitutional Self-Government*.

45 As Zurn notes, Habermas appears to have abandoned the "critical-utopian potential of his broader project in favor of a type of ameliorist 'justificatory liberalism' that

**40** Part I

merely intends to show why the way we do things around here is pretty much just fine as it is." Zurn, *Deliberative Democracy*, 244. See also 252.

46 Many deliberative democratic theorists acknowledge this point, but two sustained discussions of this feature of deliberative democracy and the challenges raised by it are Jack Knight and James Johnson, "What Sort of Political Equality Does Deliberative Democracy Require?" in James Bohman and William Rehg (eds) *Deliberative Democracy: Essays on Reason and Politics* (Cambridge, MA: MIT Press, 1997), 279–321, and Archon Fung, "Democracy before the Revolution: Towards an Ethic of Deliberative Democracy," *Political Theory* 33:3 (2005): 397–419.

47 In chapter four, we'll offer our own reconstruction of the logic and attractiveness of democracy-against-domination. We'll save the heavy lifting for there, and here simply review some key insights from two of its most important contributors, with an eye toward their relevance for assessing judicial review in democratic terms.

48 Shapiro, *The State of Democratic Theory*, 3.

49 Ibid., 4.

50 Ibid., 66.

51 In more recent work, Shapiro seems more pessimistic about judicial review's democratic value (while not rejecting it altogether), noting that its virtues have been "oversold" and it can have an elitist, status quo bias. See *Politics against Domination* (Cambridge, MA: Harvard University Press, 2016), 71–72.

52 John Hart Ely, *Democracy and Distrust: A Theory of Judicial Review* (Cambridge, MA: Harvard University Press, 1980).

53 Daniel R. Ortiz, "Pursuing a Perfect Politics: The Allure and Failure of Process Theory," *Virginia Law Review* 77 (1991): 723.

54 For further elaboration of these points, see, e.g., Mark Tushnet, "Darkness on the Edge of Town: The Contributions of John Hart Ely to Constitutional Theory," *Yale Law Journal* 89 (1980), 1037; Paul Brest, "The Fundamental Rights Controversy: The Essential Contradictions of Normative Constitutional Scholarship," *Yale Law Journal* 90 (1981): 1063; Ortiz, "Pursuing a Perfect Politics."

55 Indeed, more generally realistic assessments of judicial review almost certainly require accepting that nothing can compel courts consisting of multiple judges to apply similar interpretive theories, and therefore justifications of judicial review that are dependent on the use of particular interpretive theories are unlikely to be persuasive. See Adrian Vermeule, "The Judiciary Is a They, Not an It: Interpretive Theory and the Fallacy of Division," *Journal of Contemporary Legal Issues* 14 (2005): 549–584.

56 *United States v. Carolene Products* 304 U.S. 144 (1938), n4.

57 At this point, Shapiro's account and that of Jeremy Waldron, a prominent judicial review critic, are much less far apart than they might appear. Waldron allows that judicial review might be normatively justified in some "non-core cases" in which an unpopular and historically beleaguered minority is refused political rights. See Waldron, "The Core of the Case," 1403. Waldron's deployment of something like the countermajoritarian difficulty will receive sustained attention in ch. 5.

58 Consider here Rogers Smith's well-known argument about the liberal, republican, and ascriptive threads of American ideas and laws about citizenship in his *Civic Ideals: Conflicting Visions of Citizenship in US History* (New Haven, CT: Yale University Press, 1999). While Smith focuses primarily on these different approaches to the law, it is clear enough that these threads can coexist in the mind of particular individuals. While Smith argues the logic of these different threads is mutually exclusive, that

doesn't rule out their holding sway simultaneously and in potentially contradictory ways in people's political views. Indeed, ascriptive views about unpopular minorities can make denying their rights appear consistent with general liberal ideals of political equality.

59 Waldron, "The Core of the Case," 1404–1405.

60 As Shapiro points out, any just hierarchical arrangement remains in constant danger of devolution into a tool of domination. Shapiro, *The State of Democratic Theory*, 4. See also Ian Shapiro, *Democratic Justice* (New Haven, CT: Yale University Press, 1999).

61 Philip Pettit, *Republicanism: A Theory of Freedom and Government* (New York: Oxford University Press, 1997); *A Theory of Freedom: From the Psychology to the Politics of Agency* (New York: Oxford University Press, 2001); *On the People's Terms: A Republican Theory and Model of Democracy* (Cambridge: Cambridge University Press, 2012); *Just Freedom: A Moral Compass for a Complex World* (New York: Norton, 2014). Pettit's historiography, with its sharp division between republican and liberal conceptions of liberty, has recently been persuasively called into question—see, for example, Eric Ghosh, "From Republican to Liberal Liberty," *History of Political Thought* 29:1 (2008): 132-167. Our use of his approach relies on his analytical, not historical, account of republicanism, and we take no position on the accuracy of his historical narrative here.

62 Philip Pettit, "Republican Freedom and Contestatory Democratization," in Ian Shapiro and Casiano Hacker-Cordon (eds) *Democracy's Value* (Cambridge: Cambridge University Press, 1999), 163. See also Pettit, "Democracy, Electoral and Contestatory," in Ian Shapiro and Steven Macedo (eds) *Designing Democratic Institutions: NOMOS XXLI* (New York: New York University Press, 2000), 106.

63 Pettit, *A Theory of Freedom*, 153.

64 Philip Pettit, "Democracy, Electoral and Contestatory" and "Depoliticising Democracy," *Ratio Juris* 17:1 (2004): 52–65.

65 Philip Pettit, "Deliberative Democracy, the Discursive Dilemma, and Republican Freedom," in James Fishkin and Peter Laslett (eds) *Philosophy, Politics, and Society* (New York: Cambridge University Press, 2003): 138–162.

66 Pettit, "Democracy, Electoral and Contestatory," 115.

67 There are good reasons to regard effective political participation as a defense mechanism against both *dominium* and *imperium*.

68 Ran Hirschl, *Towards Juristocracy: The Origins and Consequences of the New Constitutionalism* (Cambridge, MA: Harvard University Press, 2004).

69 Ibid., 44.

70 Ibid., 43–44.

71 Ibid., 62–63.

72 Scheppele's relevant work has been primarily on the Hungarian and Russian constitutional courts. See Kim Lane Scheppele, "The New Hungarian Constitutional Court," *East European Constitutional Review* 8 (1999): 81–87; "Declarations of Independence: Judicial Reactions to Political Pressure," in Stephen B. Burbank and Barry Friedman (eds) *Judicial Independence at the Crossroads: An Interdisciplinary Approach* (Thousand Oaks, CA: Sage, 2002), 227–280; "Constitutional Negotiations: Political Contexts of Judicial Activism in Post-Soviet Europe," *International Sociology* 18:1 (2003): 219–238; "Democracy by Judiciary: Or, Why Courts Can Be More Democratic Than Parliaments," in Adam Czarnota, Martin Kreiger and Wojciech Sadurski (eds) *Rethinking the Rule of Law after Communism* (Budapest: Central European University Press, 2005), 25–60.

**42** Part I

73 When the court struck down the Bokros reform package on constitutional grounds, their decision was supported by 84% of those who voted for the ruling party, and 90% of those who had voted for the opposition. The ruling party at the time had a sufficient majority to change the constitution with a single vote (2/3 is needed and they made up 72% of parliament) but they chose not to challenge the rule directly (Scheppele, "Democracy by Judiciary," 49–50).

74 Scheppele, "Democracy by Judiciary." Many of the justices were called at home by World Bank officials lobbying them against striking down these laws.

75 An English translation of one of the key "Bokros package" cases that uses the principle of legal security can be found in Laszlo Solyom and George Brunner (eds), *Constitutional Judiciary in a New Democracy: The Hungarian Constitutional Court* (Ann Arbor, MI: University of Michigan Press, 2000), 322–332.

76 In a sense, the court was not so much empowered to act against parliament as much as they were uniquely empowered to act on behalf of the avowed interests of Hungarians against international meddling. The prestige and respect for constitutional courts among IMF officials was a mechanism of domination prevention they were uniquely positioned to wield.

77 Scheppele makes a similar case for the democratic *bona fides* of the Russian Supreme Court. See Scheppele, "Constitutional Negotiations," 227–234.

78 Waldron, "The Core of the Case," 1353.

79 See, especially, Waldron, *Law and Disagreement*.

80 Tushnet, *Taking the Constitution away from the Courts*, 154.

81 Mark Tushnet, "Abolishing Judicial Review," *Constitutional Commentary* 27 (2011): 281–289. It is worth noting that, unlike in *Taking the Constitution away from the Courts*, Tushnet here preserves the possibility of federal judicial review of the actions of state governments. There are plausible arguments that reject judicial review for coordinate branches of the federal government but maintain it for other levels of government, such as a desire for uniform national standards or a Madisonian belief that state governments representing smaller, more homogenous constituencies are more likely to violate individual rights, although Tushnet does not pursue the point in this essay. For example, Justice Oliver Wendell Holmes once famously declared that "The United States would not come to an end if we lost our power to declare an Act of Congress void" but "I do think the Union would be imperiled if we could not make that declaration as to the laws of the several States." Richard Posner (ed), *The Essential Holmes: Selections from the Letters, Speeches, Judicial Opinions, and Other Writings of Oliver Wendell Holmes, Jr.* (Chicago, IL: University of Chicago Press, 1997), 147.

82 Of course, all things are not necessarily equal. Some would argue that the consequences of inappropriate judicial interventions that constrain police officers are potentially very negative given the public safety issues at stake.

83 Seth Kreimer, "Exploring the Dark Matter of Judicial Review: A Constitutional Census of the 1990s," *William and Mary Bill of Rights Journal* 5:2 (1997): 427–526.

84 Ibid.

85 Scheppele, "Democracy by Judiciary," 35–37.

86 See, for example, Mark A. Graber, "The Passive-Aggressive Virtues: *Cohens v. Virginia* and the Problematic Establishment of Judicial Power," *Constitutional Commentary* 67 (1995): 12.

87 Epp, *The Rights Revolution*, 86.

88 Henry Shue, *Basic Rights: Subsistence, Affluence, and U.S. Foreign Policy*, 2nd ed. (Princeton, NJ: Princeton University Press, 1996). The three categories of rights Shue argues

are "basic" are subsistence, security, and participation. The notion that freedom from poverty should be understood as a foundational right has a long history. See, for example, Cass Sunstein's discussion of FDR's "Four Freedoms" speech: *The Second Bill of Rights: FDR's Unfinished Revolution and Why We Need It More Than Ever* (New York: Basic Books, 2004). Thomas Jefferson also understood poverty as a threat to republican self-government, which led him to prioritize access to property (for subsistence without subservience and domination) and education. He articulated the relationship between subsistence rights (delivered through access to land), poverty, and citizenship in his 1776 constitution draft for the state of Virginia and created a property requirement for voting of 25 acres, but later in the same document, he advocated that "Every person of full age neither owning nor having owned [50] acres of land, shall be entitled to an appropriation of [50] acres." Julian P. Boyd (ed), *The Papers of Thomas Jefferson, Volume I: 1760–1776* (Princeton, NJ: Princeton University Press, 1950), 358.

89  Hirschl, *Towards Juristocracy*, 153.

90  This point is made by Leslie Goldstein, "From Democracy to Juristocracy," *Law & Society Review* 38:3 (2004): 626.

91  Linda McCain and James Fleming, "Constitutionalism, Judicial Review and Progressive Change," *Texas Law Review* 84:4 (2005): 833–870.

92  Ran Hirschl, "Constitutionalism, Judicial Review, and Progressive Change: A Rejoinder to McCain and Fleming," *Texas Law Review* 84:4 (2005): 871–907, at 895.

93  Hacker and Pierson, *Off Center*, 93–100.

94  For an elaboration of this argument, see Frederick Lee Morton and Rainer Knopff, *The Charter Revolution and the Court Party* (Orchard Park, NY: Broadview, 2000).

95  See *Baker v. Carr* 369 U.S. 186 (1962).

96  Tushnet, *Weak Courts, Strong Rights*, 81. In this book, Tushnet argues throughout that "weak-form" judicial review (systems with legislative override provisions such as the "notwithstanding clause" in Canada) offer advantages over "strong-form" judicial review for the protection of social and economic rights. The reason he identifies here is that strong-form review places the responsibility for constitutional interpretation entirely on the constitutional courts, whereas the responsibility is shared with the legislature in "weak-form" judicial review systems.

97  Keck, "Party, Policy, or Duty," 321.

98  A similar argument regarding the potential democratic value of bicameralism is made by Jeremy Waldron, "Bicameralism and the Separation of Powers," *Current Legal Problems* 65:1 (2012): 31–57. We'll return to Waldron's defense of bicameralism and the problems with the way he differentiates the democratic value of different veto points in chapter six.

99  Malcolm Feeley and James Rubin, *Judicial Policy Making and the Modern State: How the Courts Reformed America's Prisons* (New York: Cambridge University Press, 2000).

100  Hiebert, *Charter Conflicts*, 92–96; Christopher P. Manfredi and Scott E. Lemieux, "Judicial Discretion and Fundamental Justice: Sexual Assault in the Supreme Court of Canada," *The American Journal of Comparative Law* 47 (1999): 489–514.

101  For a history of the countermajoritarian difficulty as an "academic obsession" that dominated both the normative justifications of judicial review and constitutional interpretation as well as the empirical study of courts in post–World War II American legal scholarship, see Barry Friedman, "The Birth of an Academic Obsession: The History of the Countermajoritarian Difficulty, Part Five," *Yale Law Journal* 112:1 (2002): 153–260.

**44** Part I

102 See, for example, Paul Pierson, *Dismantling the Welfare State: Reagan, Thatcher, and the Politics of Retrenchment* (Cambridge: Cambridge University Press, 1995) and "Increasing Returns, Path Dependence and the Study of Politics," *American Political Science Review* 94:2 (2000): 251–267.
103 Graber, "Constitutional Politics and Constitutional Theory," 327.
104 We compare the democratic potential and dangers of these two veto points in chapter six.

# 2

# HOW NOT TO ARGUE ABOUT JUDICIAL REVIEW AND DEMOCRACY

## 2.1 Introduction

The democratic status of judicial review has been the subject of a good deal of recent work in legal and political theory. While there are exceptions, most arguments on this subject can be grouped into two categories. First, there are those that critique judicial review from a democratic standpoint, arguing it usurps important democratic decisions from the majoritarian institutions (such as legislators), where they belong. In contrast, others have argued that judicial review is justified precisely because of its countermajoritarian powers—that it constitutes a necessary and useful check on democratic majorities. In the preceding chapter, we argued that both of these lines of argument are flawed—that they rely on faulty normative assumptions about the relationship between democracy and pure majoritarianism on the one hand, and faulty empirical assumptions about the majoritarian nature of legislatures and the countermajoritarian nature of constitutional courts on the other. In this chapter, we take aim at another trend in this literature—a commonplace strategy for defending judicial review. Specifically, we will explore the practice of defending judicial review by giving an account of the ideal practice of judicial review and/or separating actual examples of the exercise of judicial review into "good" and "bad" categories—in other words, defending judicial review through an account of how constitutional judges should behave. The objective of our criticism is not the conclusion of these arguments—we also defend judicial review as potentially democratically justifiable. We will instead explore how this particular line of reasoning necessarily relies on some dubious implicit assumptions, all while evading, rather than engaging, the fundamentally political nature of judicial review. In short, it fails to constitute a *political* political theory of judicial review in Waldron's sense. This

**46** Part I

chapter will proceed as follows: In the first section, we'll offer a general overview of our critique of this strategy for defending judicial review, as well as a brief review of some recent work that follows this strategy. In the second section, we'll consider in more detail a recent effort to deploy this strategy in defense of judicial review, with reference to recent abortion jurisprudence in the U.S. In the third and final section, we'll give a sketch of our alternative to this approach, which incorporates political theories of institutional design alongside and in conjunction with agonistic democratic theory.

Before proceeding, we should note the limited scope of this critique. There is nothing inherently problematic about debating the boundaries of permissible legal reasoning in the exercise of judicial review, as a matter of political or legal ethics. Our critique is not of any of these arguments *per se*, but rather of the idea that such an argument or position can constitute a defense of the institution of judicial review. The defense of an institutional arrangement should be made independently of an idealized account of how actors empowered by these arrangements should exercise that power. At a minimum, if the two are to be linked, the link should be made through an account of how the institution can be constructed to incentivize the proper use of this power as a practical matter. This general point is broadly understood in other contexts—it is broadly understood that a defense of voting rights, for example, should be made independently of an ethical account of how citizens should vote,[1] or that it's reasonable to discuss positive and negative uses of executive pardons separately from an actual justification of that particular power.

## 2.2 "Instruct Judges" Theories of Judicial Review

In a recent article, Nicholas Buccola argues that the three leading theories of judicial review, which he, following Sunstein, labels "majoritarianism, originalism, and perfectionism," each elevate a corresponding virtue that judges should ideally have, which would direct and lead their exercise of judicial review.[2] Depending on which approach you defend, according to Buccola, your constitutional theory will emphasize the role of judges in the defense of popular sovereignty, the rule of law, or justice, respectively, and the chief virtue that will serve to promote proper exercise of the power of judicial review will be restraint in the first case, fidelity in the second, and justice in the third. The purpose of Buccola's intervention is to provide an additional contender for the central virtue of judicial review—prudence—and demonstrate that such a virtue would help better balance judges' conduct between the aforementioned goals of judicial review, as prudence is the virtue associated with constitutional pluralism. Near the beginning of this enlightening and thoughtful engagement with the utility and desirability of different judicial virtues, a warning for the reader is buried in a footnote: "judges do not always rely on 'theory' to guide their decisions. Many scholars of constitutional theory and theories of judicial review continue to believe, though, that whatever the descriptive truth of these theories, there is still a strong normative case for carrying on this discussion of what judges *should* do when confronted with hard cases."[3] The details or general character of that strong normative case held by many scholars is not shared with the reader. Our view is that a normative case for the conduct of such an investigation isn't needed; the ethics of judicial conduct is a topic clearly worthy of sustained scholarly attention. What such a discussion can't do, though, is serve as a substitute for a political theory (and especially a *political* political theory in Waldron's sense) of judicial review. Without an account of the institutional effects of judicial power, given the range of reasons and conduct we're likely to find in judges, we haven't made a democratic case for such a power, and an account of the virtues of a good president would stand in as an argument for the superiority of presidential over parliamentary systems. Buccola may not emphasize the limitations of the kind of project he's engaged in, but he does seem to recognize them. Too often, "instructions for judges" stands in as a substitute for a political theory of judicial review.

The flaws of this justificatory strategy are best illustrated through identifying the unspecified assumptions of this approach. Generally speaking, "instructions for judges" accounts of judicial review are meant to guide them to a proper balance of some relevant considerations. For example, they should rule to prevent outcomes that threaten the basis of the fundamental political equality of citizens (or persons) on the one hand, while also exercising restraint from undue interference in "normal" democratic decision-making on the other. In other words, judges are instructed to rule in such a way that judicial review will come to *solve democracy's problems*, or at least make a substantial contribution to a solution. This is evident in two recent works that take an "instruct judges" approach to defending judicial review by Ronald Den Otter and Corey Brettschneider.[4]

One of Brettschneider's central aims is to critique a purely procedural conception of democracy. He argues that in addition to a variety of majoritarian decision-making procedures, the concept of democracy also embodies substantive values that can, occasionally, come into conflict with the outcomes of procedural democracy. Democracy's three core values, according to Brettschneider, are political autonomy, equality of interests, and reciprocity. Brettschneider situates his own argument between pure democratic proceduralism and substantive liberal conceptions of justice for which actual democratic practice is irrelevant with respect to content. Unlike those who imagine judges as intervening in democratic outcomes to protect the liberal rights from majority tyranny, Brettschneider sees the purpose of judicial review as sorting out tensions internal to democracy, rather than tensions between democracy and liberal substantive values.[5] In what could be read as a partial concession to the "countermajoritarian difficulty" framework, he concedes that the exercise of judicial review over legislative decisions do constitute a violation of the "procedural integrity" of democracy, but if exercised properly, can make an overall net contribution to democracy.[6]

**48** Part I

In the first six chapters of his book, Brettschneider has little to say about democratic procedures and institutions. His focus is on defending and explaining his value theory of democracy, and demonstrating its capacity to shed light on perennial democratic controversies, such as privacy, the acceptable bounds of punishment, and welfare. In his final chapter, he turns to institutions and procedures to consider judicial review through the lens of the value theory of democracy. But instead of articulating why those who share his value theory of democracy should be inclined to appreciate this particular sort of veto point in the overall structure of democracy, he focuses his attention on how those who occupy this particular veto point should approach the task of exercising it. His defense of judicial review is structured around three imaginary justices: Justice Process, Justice Outcomes, and Justice Tension. Unsurprisingly, it is Justice Tension who recognizes the democratic loss in some judicial interventions, but proceeds anyway because those interventions are the most promising way to balance democracy's multiple commitments. Brettschneider argues that the choices and priorities of Justice Tension find reflection in the best of the U.S. Supreme Court's decisions (such as *Laurence v. Texas*,[7] *Loving v. Virginia*,[8] and *Reynolds v. Sims*[9]) and interpretive strategies (such as the application and use of the "rational purpose" and "compelling interests" tests in the appropriate contexts[10]).

Den Otter is less concerned with particular democratic values necessary to democracy, and more concerned with the nature and scope of democratic reasons.[11] Central to his argument is the concept of "public justification," which (he argues) is a requirement of exercises of public reason on the part of both judges exercising the power of judicial review and legislators making and defending laws—in other words, all public actors in a democratic community. Den Otter begins by laying out the core of his argument, explaining and defending the concept of public justification. "A theory of constitutional adjudication," he argues, "must distinguish between relevant and irrelevant reasons."[12] The central goal of his introduction and first several chapters is to make the case that a standard of public justification based on the practice of public reason, properly limited, must serve to "limit the interpretive latitude that judges have" in deciding cases and exercising judicial review.[13] Public justification is not a theory that is guaranteed to deliver the "correct" answer to constitutional questions, as "discretion is inescapable."[14] Public justification is necessarily "shallow" in that it must avoid any connection to any particular conception of the good life. It is also "rendered . . . less abstract" by being tied to the core values of freedom and equality.[15] Unlike most other normative approaches to judicial review, which emphasize the necessity for justification when judges invalidate legislative acts, normative demands of public justification is just as strong—perhaps stronger—when laws are upheld. The appropriate target audience of judicial reasoning in either case is to justify the decision to a "reasonable dissenter," explaining why this particular law (and any restrictions on the freedom and equality of the dissenter contained therein) are justified without reference to a conception of the

## How Not to Argue about Judicial Review    49

good life the reasonable dissenter may not share. Reasonable dissenters are characterized as "a person who is willing to be persuaded by the better argument, assumes that reasonable moral disagreement will characterize difficult constitutional cases, and will conclude that the legislation in question is publicly justified only when the state has produced sufficiently public reasons on its behalf."[16]

This leaves open, of course, the question of what constitutes a public reason, and to answer this, Den Otter turns to debates about the proper nature and boundaries of public reason. He considers but ultimately rejects the "laissez-faire" conception of public reason advocated by Habermas as too open and inclusive, thus rendering it "almost impossible for deliberators to find common ground."[17] He then considers exclusive theories of public reason, which categorically exclude all non-public reasons, and inclusive theories, which allow non-public reasons to be expressed alongside public ones, with priority for public reasons. While he is sympathetic to the inclusive approach, he ultimately argues for a version of the exclusive approach as the best option under conditions of moral pluralism. He is loath to allow any reasons based on conceptions of the good life into public reason because "the more that ordinary people introduce reasons based on their conceptions of the good, the more divided they will be."[18] However, he does not suggest that adhering only to public reason in political discourse is a general and universal duty of citizenship: only judges need to be held to the strict standards of public reason at all times. The strict prohibition on any non-public reasons is only needed for judges' reason-giving: they are agents of the state speaking to the reasonable dissenter, and as such have a duty to strictly adhere to public reasons.

One particularly refreshing feature of this book is Den Otter's avoidance of the frame that guides many analyses of the proper exercise of judicial review—namely, the question of which interpretive strategy should be used by judges in their rendering of the text of the Constitution. Den Otter notes that the concrete values he insists should guide judges—freedom, equality, and the separation of the right and the good—find expression in the Constitution itself and supporting documents, but this observation is not central to his defense of this approach.[19] Judges, he argues, inevitably must "look outside the law for normative guidance."[20] The question of the ideal interpretive strategy has for too long crowded out possible alternatives for framing the debate around the practice of judicial review, so it is promising to see a turn away from that frame. Den Otter offers an appealing image of the practice of how judicial review could be exercised to enhance freedom and equality in democratic societies.

That said, Den Otter's vision of judicial review, as appealing as it may be, remains just that—a vision. It is not in itself an argument for the institution. Unlike almost all others who employ this strategy to defend judicial review, however, Den Otter offers a concrete affirmative defense. Judges are needed, Den Otter argues, because of the failure of other actors; after all, if we used only public reasons connected to the values of freedom and equality in our political

**50** Part I

deliberation and law-making, judicial review would be redundant and unnecessary. However, politicians "do not exercise this kind of self-restraint" and citizens are unlikely to fare any better.[21] It is the evident, empirical failures of these actors to live up to the standards of public reason that trigger the need for the power of judges. However, just as citizens and politicians have a poor empirical track record, so too do judges. It is clear that Den Otter is aware judges often do not follow the stringent standards he has outlined in his book, as he notes on several occasions. His response to the empirical fact of judges' failures is manifestly different than his response to the failure of other political actors. For one thing, he is more charitable, suggesting that notable failures of judicial reasoning are cases of "judges who sincerely want to make the right decision mak[ing] good-faith mistakes."[22] Legislative failures of public reasoning are prone to be seen not as good faith mistakes, but as evidence of a pattern of thoughtlessness.[23] One of his stated purposes is to respond to failures in judicial reasoning by explaining in more detail and with more clarity and force what judicial reasoning ought to be. In contrast, the response to legislators' failures is to empower other institutions to correct for them. Judges, in Den Otter's view, are a kind of moral agents who are capable of being called to their duty to exercise and uphold standards of public justification. The rest of us, simply put, are not. To his credit, Den Otter does not shy away from the elitism inherent in this view. What this elitist account needs, at a minimum, is a more direct and persuasive account of precisely how those employed as judges come to be an entirely different kind of moral agent than the rest of the citizenry. Whatever explanation there might be for this fundamental difference in moral agency was neither identified nor defended. Waldron has explicitly made the alternative case, arguing against various justifications offered for the "Judges are Good at Morality" thesis.[24] Perhaps Waldron is mistaken, but the work needs to be done to demonstrate this. Skipping this step reveals a kind of functionalism at the heart of Den Otter's case, and "instruct judges" arguments more generally: the deficiencies of our institutions, or of human nature, mean that we need help staying the course. Judges are well-positioned to give us what we need. But politics in general and democratic politics in particular can't rely on such an easy out.

There are, in addition, serious issues with the workload Den Otter places on the back of the concept of "reasonable." The coherence and applicability of this concept are essential to his understanding of public reason and his argument as a whole, as he notes: "without a distinction between reasonable and unreasonable persons, it would be impossible for the state to meet any standard of public justification."[25] Den Otter has conceded that "public reason" is not a deterministic or mechanistic approach to reaching the one correct outcome, and that legitimately public reasons may well oppose one another. In light of this, his definition of the reasonable person as "willing to be persuaded by the better argument" seems overly demanding. If legitimate public reasons can take people in different directions, can acquiescence to "the better argument" really function as a

How Not to Argue about Judicial Review  **51**

mechanism to sort out the reasonable from the unreasonable? If reason X seems clearly more important than reason Y to me, it might be very tempting to dismiss those who cannot see this simple truth as unreasonable, even without rejecting the notion that Y is, in fact, a public reason. When one must give reasons that would be acceptable to any reasonable person, there is a strong tendency to sketch a reasonable person in a manner convenient to one's reasoning. Because the power to sort out the reasonable and the unreasonable lies solely in the hands of the reason-giver, this standard may be too malleable and open to abuse to accomplish its necessary work in Den Otter's theory. These two concerns about Den Otter's argument are part of a larger concern about his strategy of effective de-politicization of judges and the judiciary. If the standard for public justification is open enough to allow arguments for many different positions, it may be open and malleable enough for a skilled interlocutor to simply use public justification standards to defend a position they hold on non-public grounds. The human capacity for rationalization is surely great enough that this outcome does not require bad faith on the part of the actor. In other words, even if the standards argued for in his book are adhered to in public reason-giving, politics may still remain. However, in Den Otter's depoliticized view of the court, the political character of a courts' decision will necessarily remain invisible and therefore uncontested.

Before turning to Shapiro's deployment of this strategy, we will sum up our objections to this approach to defending judicial review. It represents a version of what Bonnie Honig has critiqued as an effort to "displace" politics in some fashion, rather than engage in it.[26] On Honig's account, "displacement" theories see the purpose of political theory as designing a way to contain, escape, or otherwise displace political conflict. This approach to justifying judicial review is another version of displacement, except the trick of escaping political conflict is now placed on a particular kind of actor. A consideration of the democratic value of a particular institutional feature should not turn on how that institution would work in an idealized sense. Most defenses of the full adult franchise, for example, do not turn on an idealized vision of how citizens should vote, nor is this justificatory strategy deployed for legislators.

It is our contention, drawing from the democracy-against-domination approach, that any democratic defense of a particular institutional arrangement should consider how that arrangement is likely to work. All political institutions are corruptible, and we cannot escape the dangers of politics by empowering the right actors in just the right way. Both Brettschneider and Den Otter have arguments more sophisticated than simple assertions that we need judges to save us from the tyranny of the majority, even if they build from that foundation. There is, as Brian Barry warns us, "no procedural alchemy whereby agents bent on injustice can be made to pursue justice instead."[27] We might furthermore add that there is no theory of judicial review, or any other political institution, that can solve the problem of the abuse or misuse of that institution. Contra

**52** Part I

Pettit, and to the frustration of many of its defenders, judicial review cannot be depoliticized, nor can it depoliticize democracy.[28]

Furthermore, while this non-ideal state of affairs may well be lamentable in certain respects, it is not entirely so. Democratic theorists should be open to creative, insurgent uses (and, indeed, misuses) of existing norms and institutions by those who find themselves excluded and ignored in the political process. The approach to justifying judicial review described in this chapter attempts to create a blueprint for acceptable democratic use of judicial review, presumably for judges to follow. Democracy's creative, insurgent side is thus ignored. What Honig calls "democratic takings"—appropriations of norms, rules, institutions, and spaces for the purposes of political contestation in ways beyond the currently acceptable—are an essential and necessary part of democratic politics.[29] Moreover, and crucially, the democratic value of a judicial ruling is not entirely, or even primarily, a product of the nature of the judicial reasoning deployed in the decision. Insofar as an act of judicial review is an exercise of power with social and political implications, its contribution to democracy must be evaluated in terms of its effect on both *imperium* and *dominium*. Certainly, if judicial review were exercised to prevent overwhelmingly popular legislative schemes designed to address social or political issues widely recognized as problematic, it would potentially be a source of domination as *imperium*—it would (in Pettit's terms) prevent the actions of the state from tracking the common avowable interests of the people. Generally speaking, this isn't how judicial review is used. Judicial review can potentially contribute to the struggle against *dominium* in important ways, both procedural and substantive: procedurally, it provides a route for democratic contestation; substantively, rulings may change the laws that make *dominium* of some populations more or less likely, or more or less intense. Such evaluation cannot simply be a matter of the right kind of reasoning: this approach fails to recognize the relationship between judicial review and social power. The remainder of this chapter seeks to illustrate this point further with a close examination of Ian Shapiro's democratic critique of *Roe* and celebration of *Casey*.

## 2.3   Abortion: Democratic Norms, *Roe*, and *Casey*

In place of a democratic theory that seeks a sanitized, non-dangerous conception of democracy via a judicial review "containment" strategy, we will make the case for a conception of democracy that finds democracy's value in opposition to domination. Ian Shapiro is one of the most prominent democratic theorists today working in the "democracy-against-domination" framework, so we take a particular interest in how he attends to this question. In *The Real World of Democratic Theory*, Shapiro considers judicial review's role in democracy through a demonstration of the democratic value of the abortion jurisprudence from the U.S. Supreme Court. Specifically, he compares the U.S. Supreme Court's landmark abortion opinion *Roe v. Wade* (1973) unfavorably with its decision in

*Planned Parenthood v. Casey* (1992) to uphold but modify *Roe*'s core holding.[30] In criticizing *Roe* from the standpoint of a particular democratic theory, Shapiro is hardly alone. Even among scholars sympathetic to the policy goal of decriminalizing abortion, cases such as *Roe v. Wade* are often seen as the courts operating (at best) at the farthest reaches of their justifiable authority. John Hart Ely developed the "representation-reinforcement" constitutional theory as a defense of substantively controversial Warren Court decisions, arguing that most Warren Court landmarks were justified because they corrected failures in the democratic process.[31] Ely, however, pointedly argued that *Roe* could not be defended in a similar fashion.[32] Cass Sunstein, whose theory of "minimalism"[33] has some important commonalities with Ely's in terms of goals if not doctrinal methodology, has also critiqued the broad scope of the opinion (albeit without arguing that the Texas statute in question should have been upheld).[34] According to this line of critique, while the landmark Warren Court decisions had corrected glaring defects in the democratic processes, most notably but not exclusively related to the oppression and disenfranchisement of African-Americans under Jim Crow, *Roe* simply represented the substitution of the substantive preferences of legislators with the substantive preferences of judges. While such an outcome is not impossible to defend from a democracy-against-domination perspective, it presents a more difficult challenge. Shapiro shares these reservations, arguing that the sweeping nature of the Court's holding in *Roe* arguably "render[s] its legitimacy suspect."[35]

Some of *Roe*'s critics, however, see *Casey* as more consistent with democratic norms. Ely, probably the most prominent critic of *Roe* in the legal academy, wrote a letter to praise the three justices who wrote the plurality opinion in *Casey*.[36] Other scholars have argued that *Casey* strengthens democratic principles by reflecting the Court's adherence to principle in the face of political opposition or its tendency to reflect centrist political values.[37] Shapiro also sees *Casey* in a more favorable light, arguing that the "undue burden" standard for determining when abortion regulations violate the Constitution may be more consistent with a democracy-against-domination framework than *Roe*'s trimester framework. *Casey*, argues Shapiro, has the "potential to reinvigorate the egalitarian considerations sidestepped when he looked to *Griswold*'s privacy foundation as the foundation for his opinion in *Roe*."[38]

This section will attempt to apply democracy-against-domination principles to the abortion debate by evaluating this claim. Ultimately, we find the conventional wisdom that *Casey* is more consistent with democratic and egalitarian principles than *Roe* highly unpersuasive. In addition, we will argue that to the extent that democratic principles should counsel the judiciary not to entirely foreclose substantial abortion regulation, the Supreme Court of Canada's landmark abortion decision *R v. Morgentaler* provides a much more useful framework than *Casey*, which ultimately fails to take the responsibility of the courts to minimize domination seriously. We argue that Ely was wrong: properly understood, *Roe*

**54** Part I

was fundamentally consistent with the democracy-reinforcing landmarks of the Warren Court.

## 2.4   Evaluating the Democratic Credentials of *Casey*

Shapiro and other supporters of *Casey* make a number of arguments for why the Supreme Court's 1992 decision represents a better marriage of democratic principles and fundamental rights than *Roe v. Wade*. Because some are more relevant to a democracy-against-domination approach than others, it is worth evaluating them separately.

### *Casey as an Act of Judicial Statesmanship*

As noted earlier, despite the perception of the Supreme Court as, for better or worse, a "countermajoritarian" institution, Supreme Court opinions tend to track somewhat with public opinion[39] and quite consistently with the views of the mainstream political elite.[40] Ironically, the courts are sometimes able to establish effective compromises that legislators beholden to local constituencies and embedded in institutions with multiple veto points cannot. Because Supreme Court justices are appointed by the only American politician with a national constituency and must have sufficient cross-regional support to win Senate confirmation, this should not be terribly surprising, even if dominant theoretical approaches to the Court assume otherwise.[41] *Casey*, by preserving *Roe*'s most popular element (prohibiting outright bans on pre-viability abortions) while permitting more popular regulations to be sustained, is a classic example of the Court's typical role. As Lucas Powe observes, the results in *Casey* "almost perfectly tracked public opinion."[42]

One reason to prefer *Casey* from a democratic standpoint, then, is simply that the decision mirrored public sentiment more closely than either *Roe* or the blunter alternative of overruling *Roe* entirely.[43] From the standpoint of a democracy-against-domination approach, however, the simple congruence of *Casey* with national public opinion (while perhaps a point in the Court's favor) is insufficient to lend the decision greater democratic legitimacy than *Roe*. The courts must sometimes protect against undue domination by nullifying laws that are the results of a defective legislative process or have a greatly disproportionate impact on relatively powerless groups while arguably contravening a fundamental right.

### *Casey as a Sounder Work of Judicial Craftsmanship*

Shapiro, explicitly echoing arguments made by Robert Burt and Supreme Court Justice Ruth Bader Ginsburg, argues that *Roe* created an excessive backlash in part because of its inadequate constitutional foundations.[44] Shapiro cites Ruth

Bader Ginsburg's famous argument that "*Roe* . . . would have been more acceptable as a judicial decision if it had not gone beyond a ruling on the extreme statute before the Court."[45] In particular, Ginsburg argued that the Court should not have issued a broader ruling until equal protection doctrine had further evolved, allowing the Court to rule on abortion as a matter of gender equality rather than privacy.[46] Based on this line of reasoning, *Roe* is problematic from a democratic standpoint because by justifying a very broad holding on a controversial issue with an opinion lacking in judicial craftsmanship, it created more opposition than necessary in a way that was self-defeating.

We do not disagree that a decision based in larger measure on the 14th Amendment's prohibition on sex discrimination would be more normatively attractive. The argument that the quality of the Court's opinion or the constitutional provisions in which it found the right to an abortion substantially reduced public acceptance of *Roe*, however, is implausible in the extreme. As a general matter, very few people without a professional obligation to do so read Supreme Court opinions—their public legitimacy rests on results, not on the level of craft achieved by the opinion writer(s).[47] In the specific case of *Roe v. Wade*, the Supreme Court's ruling has consistently proven to be as or more popular than the underlying policy conclusion it reached.[48] *Roe* may have a "legitimacy problem" among major academics, but there is no evidence that this extends to the general public or explains the extent of the opposition to legal abortion in the United States.

### Does Casey Take the Disparate Impact of Abortion Regulations More Seriously?

If *Casey* is to be viewed as being more attractive than *Roe* from a democracy-against-domination perspective, then it must be because Shapiro is right that *Casey* "reinvigorate[d] the egalitarian considerations" that were largely absent from *Roe*. While this argument has a superficial appeal, we believe that it ultimately fails. Analyzed carefully, *Roe* has more egalitarian implications than is commonly assumed, while *Casey* conspicuously fails to perform the kind of careful evaluation of the impact of abortion regulations that democratic values demand.

The democracy-against-domination critique of *Roe* outlined by Shapiro is well-known, and contains little merit. Most obviously, Blackmun's opinion for the Court essentially ignored women's rights, as the former general counsel of the Mayo clinic placed his focus on the rights of medical professionals. The subsequent failure of the Court to invalidate the Hyde Amendment (which banned the use of federal Medicaid funds for abortion in most cases) in *Harris v. McRae* (1980) lends some credence to the idea that the failure to focus on women's rights would lead the Court to protect abortion rights in a manner that placed insufficient attention on the barriers to access faced by poor and

**56** Part I

rural women.[49] It was in part for this reason that Ely believed that *Roe* was an aberration inconsistent with previous Warren Court landmarks that attempted to broaden democratic participation and correct defects in the democratic process. To critics of *Roe*, the Court's intervention represented a straightforward judicial imposition of policy preferences onto legislatures rather than a democratic course-correction.

Viewed in its specific social and political context, however, *Roe* has much more in common with the landmark decisions of the Warren Court than this line of critique suggests. First of all, the assumption that the Court in *Roe* (outside a small number of outlying states) "usurped" committed legislative majorities is highly dubious.[50] In addition, the mere fact that a ban on abortion (at least on paper) affected a majority of the population is not decisive in settling the question about whether severe legislative defects were in play. Texas women were in fact entirely disenfranchised when the bill struck down in *Roe* was enacted—still very much a relevant fact, given the strong status quo bias in American legislative politics—and even in 1973, women in all 46 affected states, as well as in Congress, were severely underrepresented. In addition to this problem, the arbitrary enforcement of bans on abortion (under which affluent women generally had access to safe abortions performed in hospitals while poorer women were forced to the black market) presented a severe problem of domination that courts were arguably in the best position to remedy. The issue at stake was very effectively described by Justice Robert Jackson:

> I regard it as a salutary doctrine that cities, states and the Federal Government must exercise their powers so as not to discriminate between their inhabitants except upon some reasonable differentiation fairly related to the object of regulation. This equality is not merely abstract justice. The framers of the Constitution knew, and we should not forget today, that there is no more effective practical guaranty against arbitrary and unreasonable government than to require that the principles of law which officials would impose upon a minority must be imposed generally. Conversely, nothing opens the door to arbitrary action so effectively as to allow those officials to pick and choose only a few to whom they will apply legislation and thus to escape the political retribution that might be visited upon them if larger numbers were affected. Courts can take no better measure to assure that laws will be just than to require that laws be equal in operation.[51]

Especially in cases where grossly inequitable enforcement is critical to maintaining a law on the books, it may be beneficial from a non-domination perspective for judges to intervene. Indeed, there is perhaps no better candidate for a judicial intervention from a democracy-against-domination perspective than a law that

How Not to Argue about Judicial Review **57**

powerful majorities refuse to apply against themselves even when applicable. From this point of view, *Roe* fits perfectly into the landmark cases of the Warren Court rather than representing an exception.[52]

While the plurality opinion in *Planned Parenthood v. Casey* did have more discussion of women's rights, the reasoning used by the judges is less important than the actual *holding* of the case. In theory, *Casey's* essentially vacuous "undue burden"[53] standard could, in isolation, lead to a wide variety of future applications, including ones that would carefully scrutinize abortion regulations for their impact on relatively disadvantaged women. In terms of defining what constitutes an "undue burden," what's critical is how the Court actually assessed the statute in question. As Shapiro acknowledges,[54] the Court in fact upheld all but one provision of the Pennsylvania law, holding that mandatory waiting periods, parental consent, and "informed consent" requirements were constitutional. Of particular relevance from a democracy-against-domination standpoint is that all of these regulations would have a greatly disproportionate impact on poor and rural women.[55] To compound the problems with the newly articulated standard, the one regulation the Court found unconstitutional—a provision requiring women to notify their husbands—had the least disproportionate impact on classes of women with the least prior access to abortion, most notably women who were poor and/or lived in rural areas.[56] From the standpoint of other courts, including the lower courts, which must make the first decisions about new kinds of abortion regulations, the regulations that were and were not upheld is far more relevant than the precise wording the Court used to justify its ruling. Whatever the *potential* value of the "undue burden" standard, then, from a democracy-against-domination perspective, *Casey* must be seen on its face as a major step backward.

The case that *Casey* is nonetheless superior from a democratic perspective must rest, then, on one of two grounds. The first is that because of its plasticity and its greater surface attention to the impact of abortion regulations on women, the "undue burden" standard has more potential than *Roe's* "trimester framework" to be consistent with democratic values, even if the initial applications have not been. The problem with this argument is that there is little reason to believe that the *Roe* framework was not similarly adaptable. In *Akron v. Akron Center for Reproductive Health* (1983)—overruled by the Court in *Casey*—the court struck down waiting period and parental notification provisions similar to those upheld in *Casey*. While it is true that Lewis Powell's majority opinion continued to place perhaps disproportionate attention on the rights of physicians as opposed to the rights of women, the *outcome* of the case reflected much more attention to the potentially disproportionate impact of some abortion regulations on disadvantaged women. As the subsequent opinions of *Roe's* author make clear, there is no reason that *Roe's* trimester framework could not be defended with more explicitly feminist language. In his partial

**58** Part I

dissent in *Webster v. Reproductive Health Services* (1989), Blackmun discussed the consequences of overruling *Roe*:

> The plurality would clear the way once again for government to force upon women the physical labor and specific and direct medical and psychological harms that may accompany carrying a fetus to term. The plurality would clear the way again for the State to conscript a woman's body and to force upon her a "distressful life and future."
>
> [. . .]
>
> Every year, many women, especially poor and minority women, would die or suffer debilitating physical trauma, all in the name of enforced morality or religious dictates or lack of compassion, as it may be.

Blackmun also made similar arguments in his separate opinion in *Casey*.[57] There is ultimately no reason to believe that *Roe* could not accommodate future jurisprudence that was sufficiently attentive to the effect of abortion regulations on women.

The second argument defending *Casey* might be that democratic values prevent the Court (at least without more explicit textual authorization) from making decisions based on making particular judgments about the moral status of the fetus. Mark Graber, for example, argues that the proper constitutional standard should be "equal choice": that is, whether or not abortion is criminalized, all women must have the same opportunity to choose an abortion. *Roe* was correct in context only because abortion laws were not fairly enforced.[58] This perspective dovetails in many respects with the democracy-against-domination approach. However, it is possible to argue from this perspective that *Roe*'s preemption of all future abortion bans, irrespective of whether or not they could be fairly enforced, goes too far. In this sense, *Casey* could be an improvement—but the Court was too inattentive to the impact of the regulations under review to be consistent with an "equal choice" approach.

## 2.4  Conclusion

Democracy-against-domination is an approach that demands careful attention to practical outcomes as well as reasoning. This is something that Shapiro has clearly grasped in other contexts,[59] but not judicial review. However, this critique of a particular line of argument does not commit us to a democratic critique of judicial review in the "popular constitutionalist" mold.[60] We argued in chapter one that judicial review should be understood to have modest yet positive impact on democracy, broadly speaking, and we will argue in chapter five that it is likely to have more democratic value than most veto points commonly found in democratic political systems. So, how should judicial review's democratic content be evaluated and defended?

How Not to Argue about Judicial Review **59**

We're building toward a more complete answer to that question, but we'll close this chapter with two general thoughts. First, any democratic defense of a particular institutional structure, from a democracy-against-domination perspective, will always be contingent. Domination comes from diverse and shifting sources and takes on new and unpredictable forms. The political-institutional arrangement that facilitates domination the least and best provide opportunities for the effective contestation and resistance of it is likely to be context-dependent, perhaps as much as the sources of domination are. So we must be attentive to the politics of judicial review on the ground. If judicial review is being enacted to extend the influence of a particular elite group over a longer time horizon, for example, it should be viewed skeptically (for a while, at least).[61]

Beyond that perhaps obvious but important point, judicial review's defenders should be attentive to theories of institutional design, but with a keen awareness that institutional design cannot solve democracy's problems or render democratic politics free of danger. It can, at best, be designed to facilitate politics of contestation and resistance to domination, but it cannot resolve the problem of domination alone. In chapter five, we ask the question: Is judicial review more or less likely than other veto points to empower already sufficiently empowered minorities (which might enhance their capacity for democratic domination) or otherwise unempowered minorities? We argue that, on balance, there's reason to believe the latter may be the case.

Because judicial review, like all institutional arrangements, cannot rescue or contain democracy, a theory of its value should also look to agonistic democratic theory. While some agonistic democrats hold that institutional arrangements and democracy are inherently at odds, and institutionalization is de-democratization,[62] others have adopted a more flexible take on agonistic theory. Institutionalization and insurrection are both necessary parts of the struggle for democracy, and the greatness and distinction of Arendtian political action need not be the primary aim of agonistic democratic theory. It is also about the search—through, around, or in spite of institutional orders—to find ways to resist and reduce domination in social and political life.[63] In this light, judicial review provides a potential, if problematic, outlet for democratic contestation, while also providing a possible path to deepen de-democratizing trends. It is on the importance and likelihood of these two trends that judicial review's democratic valence should be determined.

## Notes

1 One partial exception to this approach can be found in the work of Jason Brennan on the ethics of voting, but he properly restricts his concern to the ethics of deciding whether and how to vote, rather than institutional restrictions on voting. See his "Polluting the Polls: When Citizens Should Not Vote," *Australasian Journal of Philosophy* 87:4 (2009): 535–549; *The Ethics of Voting* (Princeton, NJ: Princeton University Press, 2011).

**60** Part I

2 Nicholas Buccola, "In Defense of Judicial Prudence: American Constitutional Theory, Virtue, and Judicial Review in Hard Cases," *The Journal Jurisprudence* 21:1 (2013): 49–72. The classification scheme comes from Cass R. Sunstein, *Radicals in Robes* (New York: Basic Books, 2005), with Buccola relabeling Sunstein's "fundamentalism" as "originalism."

3 Buccola, "In Defense of Judicial Prudence," 49–50 n3.

4 Corey Brettschneider, *Democratic Rights: The Substance of Self-Government* (Princeton, NJ: Princeton University Press, 2007) and Ronald C. Den Otter, *Judicial Review in an Age of Moral Pluralism* (New York: Cambridge University Press, 2009).

5 Brettschneider, *Democratic Rights*, 137.

6 Ibid., 6.

7 Ibid., 3, 80. Brettschneider suggests that those who defend the judicial intervention of *Laurence* are faced with the "countermajoritarian difficulty." This demonstrates the problems with that framework—it assumes that legislative action (or in this case, legislative inaction in removing an antiquated and very rarely enforced law) is automatically in some sense "majoritarian" and that courts overturning legislation are by definition countermajoritarian. For someone attuned to the difficulties of pure proceduralism, this is a puzzling, if common, presumption.

8 Ibid., 80–81, 155.

9 Ibid., 155.

10 Ibid., 149.

11 The following discussion of Den Otter's book draws from David Watkins, "Review of Ronald Den Otter, *Judicial Review in an Age of Moral Pluralism*," *New Political Science* 32:3 (2010): 435–438.

12 Den Otter, *Judicial Review in an Age of Moral Pluralism*, 5.

13 Ibid., 6.

14 Ibid., 52.

15 Ibid.

16 Ibid., 11.

17 Ibid., 117.

18 Ibid., 137.

19 Ibid., 27.

20 Ibid., 52.

21 Ibid., 11.

22 Ibid., 301.

23 Ibid., 77.

24 Jeremy Waldron, "Judges as Moral Reasoners," *International Journal of Constitutional Law* 7:1 (2009): 2–24.

25 Ibid., 83.

26 Bonnie Honig, *Political Theory and the Displacement of Politics* (Ithaca, NY: Cornell University Press, 1993).

27 Brian Barry, *Justice as Impartiality* (Oxford: Clarendon Press, 1995), 101.

28 Pettit, "Depoliticising Democracy."

29 Bonnie Honig, *Democracy and the Foreigner* (Princeton, NJ: Princeton University Press, 2001).

30 See Ian Shapiro, *The Real World of Democratic Theory* (Princeton, NJ: Princeton University Press, 2010), 236–245.

31 Ely, *Democracy and Distrust*.

32 John Hart Ely, "The Wages of Crying Wolf," *Yale Law Journal* 82 (1973): 920.

How Not to Argue about Judicial Review **61**

33 Sunstein, *One Case at a Time*.
34 See Cass R. Sunstein, "Concurring," in Jack M. Balkin (ed) *What* Roe v. Wade *Should Have Said* (New York: New York University Press, 2007), 148–151.
35 Shapiro, *The Real World of Democratic Theory*, 239.
36 John Hart Ely, *On Constitutional Ground* (Princeton, NJ: Princeton University Press, 1996), 304–305.
37 Ronald Kahn, "Social Constructions, Supreme Court Reversals, and American Political Development: *Lochner, Plessy, Bowers*, but Not *Roe*," in Ronald Kahn and Ken I. Kersch (eds) *The Supreme Court and American Political Development* (Lawrence, KS: University Press of Kansas, 2006), 67–115.
38 Shapiro, *The Real World of Democratic Theory*, 243.
39 For a strong version of the thesis, see Barry Friedman, *The Will of the People* (New York: Farrar, Straus and Giroux, 2009). See also Thomas R. Marshall, *Public Opinion and the Rehnquist Court* (Albany, NY: SUNY Press, 2008).
40 Lucas A. Powe, *The Supreme Court and the American Elite* (Cambridge, MA: Harvard University Press, 2009), 311.
41 For more on this point, see Mark A. Graber, *Dred Scott and the Problem of Constitutional Evil* (New York: Cambridge University Press, 2006), 91–172.
42 Powe, *The Supreme Court and the American Elite*, 311.
43 This is not necessarily to say that public opinion played a direct causal role in the outcome in *Casey*. One can certainly not discount the possibility that a plurality of justices did not want to explicitly overrule a popular, high-profile precedent. On the other hand, the outcome in *Casey* is precisely the outcome one would expect if moderate elite Republicans followed their ideological preferences, and moderate elite Republicans of course represented the median votes of the Supreme Court in 1992.
44 Shapiro actually refers to *Casey* as reflecting the "Burt/Ginsburg" approach. We decline to use this formulation because while (as we will subsequently discuss) Ginsburg had disagreements with the Court's reasoning in *Roe*, Shapiro's implication that Ginsburg prefers *Casey*'s holding to *Roe*'s trimester framework is without basis.
45 Ruth Bader Ginsburg, "Some Thoughts on Autonomy and Equality in Relation to Roe v. Wade," *North Carolina Law Review* 63 (1985): 385–386.
46 Ibid.
47 See, e.g., Jack M. Balkin, "What *Brown* Teaches Us about Constitutional Theory," *Virginia Law Review* 90:6 (2004): 1537–1577; Terri Peretti, *In Defense of a Political Court* (Princeton, NJ: Princeton University Press, 2001).
48 Ruy Teixeira noted that 2007 survey results indicating that the public "would not" want *Roe v. Wade* overruled by a margin of 62%–29% were "entirely typical." www. americanprogress.org/issues/2007/04/opinion_abortion.html (Site last accessed February 24, 2017). The most recent major national survey as of this writing, conducted in April 2010, shows that 59% of the public believes that *Roe v. Wade* should be "upheld," while only 38% believe it should be overturned. www.pollingreport.com/abortion2. htm (Site last accessed August 14, 2017).
49 It should be noted, however, that three members of the *Roe* majority, including Blackmun, dissented in *McRae*, arguing that the Hyde Amendment was unconstitutional. It is far from obvious, therefore, that the upholding of the Hyde Amendment was an *inevitable* outcome of *Roe*, rather than a contingent one based on the specific personnel of the Court.
50 Scott Lemieux and George Lovell, "Legislative Defaults: Interbranch Power Sharing and Abortion Politics," *Polity* 42:2 (2010): 210–242. This raises an intriguing possibility

**62** Part I

with respect to democratic systems with multiple and competing veto points; namely, that veto points may, in fact, be majoritarian to the extent that they counter the effects of less democratic veto points. Certainly, post-*Roe* abortion policy was closer to public opinion than the pre-*Roe* consensus.

51 *Railway Express Agency, Inc. v. New York* 336 U.S. 106 (1949), 335–336 (Jackson J. concurring).

52 For further elaboration of this point, see Scott Lemieux, "For Richer or Poorer," *The American Prospect* January 22, 2007. www.prospect.org/cs/articles?article=for_richer_or_poorer (Site last accessed June 12, 2017).

53 *Casey* adopted the test long-advocated by Justice Sandra Day O'Connor that abortion regulations were constitutional unless they constituted an "undue burden" on a woman's right to choose an abortion.

54 Shapiro, *The Real World of Democratic Theory*, 243.

55 See, e.g., Melody Rose, *Safe, Legal, and Unavailable? Abortion Politics in the United States* (Washington, DC: CQ Press, 2006) and Helena Silverstein, *Girls on the Stand: How Courts Fail Pregnant Minors* (New York: New York University Press, 2009).

56 This is not to say that the spousal notification provision was not problematic in its democratic impact. As the plurality opinion noted, the provision "embodies a view of marriage consonant with the common-law status of married women but repugnant to our present understanding of marriage and of the nature of the rights secured by the Constitution." *Casey* (opinion of O'Connor, Kennedy, and Souter JJ), 898.

57 See *Casey*, Blackmun J. concurring in part, dissenting in part ("A State's restrictions on a woman's right to terminate her pregnancy also implicate constitutional guarantees of gender equality. State restrictions on abortion compel women to continue pregnancies they otherwise might terminate. By restricting the right to terminate pregnancies, the State conscripts women's bodies into its service, forcing women to continue their pregnancies, suffer the pains of childbirth, and in most instances, provide years of maternal care. The State does not compensate women for their services; instead, it assumes that they owe this duty as a matter of course.")

58 Mark A. Graber, *Rethinking Abortion: Equal Choice, the Constitution, and Reproductive Politics* (Princeton, NJ: Princeton University Press, 2001).

59 Ian Shapiro, "Enough of Deliberation: Democracy Is about Interests and Power," in Stephen Macedo (ed) *Deliberative Politics: Essays on Democracy and Disagreement* (New York: Oxford University Press, 1999), 28–38.

60 Waldron, *Law and Disagreement*; Bellamy, *Political Constitutionalism*.

61 This is Ran Hirschl's claim about judicial review in *Towards Juristocracy*.

62 Sheldon Wolin, "Fugitive Democracy," *Constellations* 1:1 (1994): 11–25.

63 The broad contours of the turn in agonistic theory we're sketching here are given more detail in Jean-Philippe Deranty and Emmanuel Renault, "Democratic Agon: Striving for Distinction or Struggle against Domination and Injustice?" in Andrew Schaap (ed) *Law and Agonistic Politics* (Burlington, VT: Ashgate, 2009), 43–56. The relationship between democracy-against-domination and agonistic democratic theory will receive greater attention in chapter four.

# 3

# THE REVOLUTION WILL BE *SUB SILENTIO*

## The Roberts Court and Judicial Minimalism

### 3.1 Introduction: Minimalism, Democracy, and Judicial Review

The previous chapter argued that we ought to be wary of any democratic theory that purports to explain judicial review's democratic value through the drafting of a "how to be good democratic judges" instruction manual. Judges are not unlike voters, bureaucrats, and politicians: they are human, all too human, and will use and abuse whatever institutional power they find themselves in possession of. The democratic value of judicial review can very much depend on the scope and design of judicial power, a topic we will address in more detail in the next chapter, but it cannot depend on a theory of judicial reasoning for two reasons: judges cannot be assumed to be uniquely compliant to the instructions of democratic and legal theorists, and domination can occur due to both exercises of political power and refusals to exercise it. The democratic valence of judicial review lies not in the particular character of the reasoning provided, but in the consequences of its exercise.[1]

Before we turn to the question of how we might better approach the topic of the democratic status of judicial review, as an illustration of this point, we will consider in some detail the problems of one particular theory presumably designed to enhance the democratic value of judicial review: minimalism. This approach is deserving of significant attention for two reasons. First, it has been embraced not just by a number of prominent legal scholars, but also by a number of judges, including most significantly the current Chief Justice of the Supreme Court of the United States. Second, this approach deserves attention because it purports to take democratic worries about the power of the courts, as understood through the countermajoritarian difficulty framework, quite seriously. As we

**64** Part I

shall argue, the steps taken in this theory to enhance judicial review's democratic value have, in fact had, if anything, the opposite effect.

Many of the scholars who take this approach understand judicial review as a potential threat to democracy in the abstract, but one that can be neutralized without dispensing with the core functions of the courts. It is in this light that legal theorists, as well as judges, have turned to judicial minimalism as a guide to the proper exercise of judicial review in democratic circumstances. This approach to the task of judicial review, according to its advocates, renders the practice most congenial to democratic politics. This chapter will critically examine this larger claim for judicial minimalism's democratic value, as well as a number of other secondary claims made regarding the virtues of minimalism, particularly in light of avowed minimalist John Roberts' elevation to the position of Chief Justice. We reach two central conclusions. First, the case for minimalism as a uniquely democratic approach to judicial review does not stand up to scrutiny. And we also argue that the form of argument made here is insufficient for a defense of judicial review, as an appealing theoretical approach is insufficient for a democratic defense of judicial review. The focus on judicial reasoning as a democratizing feature of judicial review is excessively deliberative and an insufficiently institutional way to think about the democratic value of institutions,[2] as the previous chapter argued. We need something more: not a theory of how to exercise judicial review, but a theory of how to situate it in a larger democratic system in such a way that it is most likely to promote contestatory non-domination. Through the critique of minimalism, we will gesture toward the framework for evaluation made explicit in chapter five.

## 3.2 The Minimalist Court

Shortly after his confirmation as the seventeenth Chief Justice of the United States, John Roberts told the graduating students at the Georgetown University Law Center the kind of opinions he would prefer his Court to issue:

> If it is not necessary to decide more to a case, then in my view it is necessary not to decide more to a case. Division should not be artificially suppressed, but the rule of law benefits from a broader agreement. The broader the agreement among the justices, the more likely it is a decision on the narrowest possible grounds.[3]

Roberts' statement suggests a commitment to the school of jurisprudence known as "minimalism." In the words of Cass Sunstein, its leading scholarly proponent, it consists of "saying no more than necessary to justify an outcome, and leaving as much as possible undecided."[4] This method of judging is often associated with a judiciary that has relatively chastened ambitions. Minimalism, argues Mark Tushnet, is the ideal jurisprudence of the "substantively modest" post-New Deal/

The Revolution Will Be *Sub Silentio* **65**

Great Society constitutional order.[5] When combined with the appointment of Samuel Alito—who also seemed to avoid broad pronouncements and demonstrated little interest in grand interpretive theories—the appointment of Roberts seemed likely to continue the frequently minimalist opinions of the late Rehnquist Court, despite the presence of two colleagues hostile to the approach in Justices Scalia and Thomas.

Due at least in part to his stated commitment to a minimalist jurisprudence, the confirmation of Chief Justice Roberts was supported by a number of law professors—including Sunstein himself—who one would not expect to be sympathetic to his general ideological orientation.[6] Indeed, many of the major decisions of the Roberts Court can be reasonably characterized as minimalist. The cautious approval the new Chief Justice received from scholars with largely antithetical views is in some measure reflective of a tendency to associate minimalism with judicial modesty: any justice appointed by President Bush will be a conservative, the argument may run, but a minimalist court will be much less aggressive about pursuing the legal goals conservatives support.

However, it should be noted that the defense of judicial minimalism by Chief Justice Roberts quoted in this section does not emphasize judicial modesty *per se*, but rather claims that minimalist opinions will enhance the reputation of the Court. A minimalist court may therefore be able to do *more*, not less. For example, consider the dissent by Chief Justice Roberts in a 2008 decision holding that state courts were free to retroactively apply a legal rule favoring defendants in state cases, even if the Supreme Court did not retroactively apply the rule in federal cases.[7] The result of the case "is contrary to the Supremacy Clause and the Framers' decision to vest in 'one supreme Court' the responsibility and authority to ensure the uniformity of federal law," Roberts argued, and "the Constitution requires us to be more jealous of that responsibility and authority."[8] Although this particular admonition would restrict the power of state courts rather than legislatures if it had carried a majority of votes, Roberts' strong defense of the Supreme Court as the dominant arbiter of constitutional requirements (even when other actors wish to provide greater protection for minority rights than the Supreme Court has mandated) strongly suggests that he is unlikely to oppose the tendency toward ever-stronger assertions of judicial supremacy by the Supreme Court (including by its minimalists).[9] Judicial *minimalism* does not necessarily lead to a commitment to judicial *modesty*.

Indications that the new Chief Justice is unlikely to lead the Court into a new era of less aggressive exercises of judicial power are also evident in a number of the Roberts Court's major holdings. These cases raise important questions about the virtues of minimalism claimed by its proponents. Although the most important advantage claimed for the approach is its tendency to leave more discretion in the hands of the political branches and to promote more deliberative solutions to public policy problems, the Court's minimalist decisions have

**66** Part I

generally deferred to the political branches only insofar as deference was consistent with the substantive preferences of the majority of the Court. And in such cases, a more maximalist decision would have led to *greater* latitude for legislative action. In other cases, minimalist jurisprudence has proven to be perfectly compatible with making it more difficult for the political branches to expand the rights of American citizens. While minimalists often tout the extent to which the jurisprudence they favor can protect the reputation of the Court, the first terms of the Roberts Court raise the possibility that even if true, this effect comes with serious democratic costs, as the Court can affect substantial changes in the law while minimizing public scrutiny. The Court's treatment of precedents is also often consistent with minimalism, but is very difficult to defend in terms of democratic legitimacy, as the precedents nominally being upheld become increasingly devoid of meaningful content. The Roberts Court is also likely to build on the decisions of previous judicial minimalists—including the arch-minimalist Felix Frankfurter[10]—to assert broader conceptions of judicial supremacy, at least in areas where increased judicial power is not inconsistent with the substantive preferences of a majority of justices.

The positive values attributed to minimalism, this chapter argues, have been largely absent from the Roberts Court. This is not because the jurisprudence of the Roberts Court openly contradicts the claims he made to the students at Georgetown: the chief majority opinions of the Court have indeed shown a real, although certainly not uniform, tendency toward formal minimalism. Rather, these opinions suggest—as have numerous examples in past eras of the Court— that undertheorized, narrowly argued opinions can be put to the service of ends that are not particularly minimalist. The particular minimalism most common in the Roberts Court emphasizes the weaknesses of minimalism while undermining its most evident virtues.

Before proceeding to this evaluation of minimalism through some of the first major cases of the Roberts Court era, we will briefly outline the potential strengths of minimalism, as well as some theoretical objections to these claims on its behalf. We will then briefly discuss the rise of minimalism as an important element of the Rehnquist and Burger Courts, arguing in particular that it is important not to overstate the significance of the fact that these courts formally left most important Warren Court precedents untouched. Finally, we will argue that several important decisions of the early Roberts Court have refined the minimalist techniques of its predecessors. In doing so, they have advanced a particularly indefensible variant of minimalism: using formally minimalist holdings to conceal major substantive changes in legal doctrine. The apparent conflicts between conservative minimalists and maximalists in cases concerning abortion, campaign finance, voting rights, and jurisdiction in Establishment Clause cases have been largely illusory, with essentially arbitrary distinctions about whether precedents are being overruled masking underlying substantive agreements.

The Revolution Will Be *Sub Silentio* **67**

In addition, the use of minimalism by the Roberts Court suggests that defenses of minimalism that rely on its ability to preserve the prestige of the Court are especially problematic. From a democratic standpoint, it is better when major substantive changes are made explicitly rather than covertly. Excessive focus on the formal distinctions between more maximalist and minimalist conservative judges obscures what is likely to be a central feature of Roberts Court conservatism: modifying the New Deal/Great Society regulatory state not through the outright nullification of major statutes, but by reading existing laws narrowly and making the enforcement of both statutory and constitutional rights more difficult. The use of minimalism by the Roberts Court would serve Republicans in Congress who seek the maximum policy change with a minimum of public scrutiny very well, but whether it is similarly valuable to democratic governance in general is much less clear.

## 3.3 Deliberation and Reputation: The Claimed Virtues of Minimalism

As with any other jurisprudence, minimalism comes in any number of variants with subtle differences. The post–World War II grandfather of the minimalist approach was Alexander Bickel,[11] who argued that the Supreme Court should use the various procedural techniques at its disposal to avoid deciding politically divisive cases unless its intervention was absolutely necessary.[12] Without denying Bickel's influence, we will primarily focus on minimalism as it has been elaborated and defended by its most extensive and persuasive contemporary proponent, Cass Sunstein.[13] Evidently, not all defenders of minimalism have identical approaches. Neal Devins, for example, while broadly sympathetic, argues that Sunstein's minimalist approach would benefit from more attention to the use of procedural discretion advocated by Bickel.[14] And as Sunstein argues, the content of any minimalism will depend on a variety of underlying substantive assumptions that will vary depending on the theorist (or judge).[15] It should be noted as well that Sunstein does not claim that minimalist jurisprudence is appropriate in all contexts. Rather, he argues that it is useful for some types of cases, but not in others. When judges have a high degree of justified confidence about the effects of an opinion or a stable foundation for advance planning is required, a maximalist opinion will be preferable.[16] For our purposes, any jurisprudence with a preference for relatively undertheorized and particularized judicial opinions can be fairly classified under the "minimalist" rubric.

Sunstein identifies two axes along which decisions may be relatively minimalist or maximalist: narrowness/width and shallowness/depth.[17] The former refers to the effect of a holding on future cases. A "narrow" holding will resolve a case in a way that will have a relatively minimal impact on future cases, while a "wide" ruling will announce a rule that can be expected to control a substantial number of future cases as well. The latter axis refers to the type of reasoning

**68** Part I

used to defend an outcome. A "shallow" opinion will avoid reference to grand theories of interpretation or broad moral principles, and will instead focus on concrete details of the particular case at hand and emphasize points of agreement among otherwise divergent viewpoints. A "broad" opinion is more completely theorized and will try to derive individual case outcomes from more abstract principles.

One wrinkle of particular importance in analyzing the Roberts Court is Sunstein's treatment of *stare decisis*.[18] One might expect a minimalist court to place relatively little weight on precedent because strict *stare decisis* has the effect of retroactively broadening a previous holding. On the other hand, from a formal standpoint, a Court that frequently announces the overturning of precedents is likely to be writing deep opinions, saying more than is strictly necessary to resolve an individual case. By focusing on concrete details, a minimalist judge will usually be able to find distinguishing features that can render a precedent inapplicable to the case at hand without requiring it to be overturned. While Sunstein is not entirely clear about his conclusions on this point, in his most comprehensive analysis of minimalism, it seems fair to assume that a minimalist judge will be reluctant to explicitly announce the overturning of precedents in the manner of Justice Kennedy in *Lawrence v. Texas*,[19] but will also not give precedent a large amount of weight in resolving a particular case.[20] In a more recent book, he more forcefully identifies the robust application of *stare decisis* with a minimalist approach, but without addressing the retrospective breadth problem.[21]

Another way of putting the distinction is to distinguish between *formal* minimalism and *substantive* minimalism, where formal minimalism refers to the reasoning of the opinion (the shallowness/depth axis) and substantive minimalism refers not to the *reasoning* but the *result* (to some extent, the narrowness/width axis.) In evaluating the latter, it is important to address not only whether a rule will bind future cases, but also the impact of a decision on the other actors involved in a case (i.e., How much does this holding affect the range of action available to the legislative and executive branches? How will it affect the ability of citizens to participate in politics? How is the policy status quo affected?). Focusing on the likely extrajudicial effects of a holding is particularly important[22] because, as Sunstein notes, the ultimate breadth of a precedent is largely in the hands of future courts rather than the court issuing the original decision. A broad opinion means little if future minimalists can avoid applying it to concrete cases that superficially appear to be controlled by the broad rule by declaring the relevant parts of the prior case *dicta*.[23] As this choice of terms might imply, a central argument of this chapter is that in terms of democratic legitimacy, whether a decision is *substantively* minimalist is of far greater importance than whether a decision is *formally* minimalist.

To illustrate the distinction, consider two landmark abortion decisions. *Roe v. Wade*[24] might be the case of the last forty years most cited as a case of judicial

The Revolution Will Be *Sub Silentio* **69**

overreaching (and therefore as a strong potential exhibit in a brief for judicial minimalism), including by Sunstein himself.[25] And, indeed, whether or not one believes that the Court overreached with its holding in *Roe*,[26] it is difficult to argue against the "maximalist" label for the decision. The Court invalidated forty-six abortion statutes, and while the majority opinion inevitably left a few related questions unanswered—such as whether the government could withhold general medical funding for abortions[27] or what kind of regulations might be consistent with advancing a state's legitimate post-first-trimester interest in a woman's health[28]—it foreclosed a great deal of potential abortion regulation as well. And yet, according to Sunstein's typology, *Roe* was maximalist on one dimension but minimalist in another.[29] While it was certainly a "wide" decision, it was also a "shallow" one, saying very little about the relevant due process rights that were being applied and, famously, almost nothing about the implications of the holding for gender equality.[30] Indeed, using Sunstein's criterion that shallow decisions are "incompletely theorized,"[31] *Roe* is a nearly definitive example of a minimalist opinion. And yet, it seems clear that *Roe's* substantive breadth is of considerably greater legal and political import than its theoretical shallowness. The result in *Roe* had a clear and substantial impact on policy and politics. How these policy and political outcomes would have changed had Justice Blackmun written the opinion differently is unclear, but it is overwhelmingly likely that any such changes would have been minimal.[32]

*Planned Parenthood v. Casey*[33]—which reaffirmed *Roe* while considerably modifying it and narrowing its restrictions on the state's ability to regulate abortion—is a harder opinion to classify. The best option, though, is to categorize it as the opposite of *Roe*—a narrow but deep holding. The "undue burden" standard the plurality opinion used to evaluate abortion regulations is a highly vague one on its face, and was applied in a deferential manner to the regulations at hand in the case (finding all but a spousal notification provision constitutional). Particularly compared to the "trimester framework" the case replaced, the "undue burden" standard is a very minimalist one. The opinion was not entirely minimalist in substantive terms because two precedents were overturned, but these overrulings seem broadly consistent with a minimalist perspective because they came as an alternative to overruling a much longer-established landmark. While the plurality opinion for the Court was narrow, however, it was also deep in many respects, with broad, detailed pronouncements about *stare decisis*, the role of the Court in American society, and the evolutionary nature of constitutional liberties. For example: "Each generation must learn anew that the Constitution's written terms embody ideas and aspirations that must survive more ages than one."[34] Or, to use perhaps the most-often quoted (and criticized) passage: "At the heart of liberty is the right to define one's own concept of existence, of meaning, of the universe, and of the mystery of human life. Beliefs about these matters could not define the attributes of personhood were they formed under compulsion of the State."[35] The opinion also had considerably more content

**70** Part I

about the implications of reproductive freedom for gender equality than *Roe*. In striking down the spousal notification provision, for example, the plurality argued that the provision embodied "a view of marriage consonant with the common-law status of married women but repugnant to our present understanding of marriage and of the nature of the rights secured by the Constitution."[36] But again, the decision's substantively minimalist aspects seem much more conse-quential than its formally maximalist ones. The substantive holding permitted considerably more state regulation of abortion.[37] On the other hand, believing that (for example) the plurality's admittedly grandiose assertion that the "Court's interpretation of the Constitution calls the contending sides of a national con-troversy to end their national division by accepting a common mandate rooted in the Constitution" had a significant impact on the politics of abortion seems as implausible as the Court's confidence that it could end the abortion contro-versy itself.

When evaluating the minimalist nature of various opinions, it is important to be mindful of the different ways in which they can be minimalist because different manifestations of minimalism can have different implications for demo-cratic politics. The choice between substantive minimalism and maximalism is likely to have concrete, identifiable effects on the public policy and the powers of the state (and the relationship of citizens to the state), while the effects of formal minimalism are more speculative and likely to be much more modest where the impact of judicial decision-making is concerned. With this in mind, we may turn next to briefly outlining some of the key potential strengths and weaknesses of the minimalist approach.

### Democracy Promotion

The most important virtue claimed for the new judicial minimalism is its strengthening of democratic self-governance. Minimalism, according to Sun-stein, "attempts to promote the democratic ideals of participation, deliberation, and responsiveness" and "allows continued space for democratic reflection from Congress and the states."[38] While Bickel was primarily (although cer-tainly not exclusively) concerned with maintaining the legitimacy of the courts, Sunstein and other contemporary minimalists "defend minimalism almost solely as a way of deferring to and bolstering the legitimacy and efficacy of the political branches."[39] (In this way, these defenses of minimalism have important commonalities with Ely's "representation-reinforcing" juris-prudence, which operated under the premise that judicial review should generally focus on removing barriers to political participation rather than imposing substantive values.)[40] By minimizing the impact of judicial errors, as well as compelling legislatures to address flaws in their enactments while not necessarily denying them the ability to pursue particular ends, minimalist judges can contribute to democratic debate and the functioning of democratic institutions. This democracy-promotion does not consist of a mechanical deference to the political branches, but does involve a preference for striking down a statute when necessary on, for example, vagueness or non-delegation grounds rather than on the basis of a broad constitutional principle. Doing so forces political actors to give more convincing reasons for their actions or to craft legislation more carefully rather than forestalling legislative action altogether.[41] Sunstein's underlying conception of deliberative democracy is not only crucial to his defense of minimalism, but also to defining its limits. He identifies a set of core values that act as a crucial democratic background to constitutionalism, and generally justify a more maximalist approach from judges when they are enforcing them.[42]

The potential of minimalism to contribute to the functioning of democratic institutions, insuring that constitutional interpretation is a collaborative rather than a unilateral affair, is one of the strongest points in its favor. There are nonetheless several potential objections to this purported virtue of minimalism. The first is that it represents excessive deference to the legislature because courts have a significant comparative advantage when it comes to constitutional interpretation. One way of putting this argument is that minimalism undervalues the ability of courts to protect valued constitutional norms.[43] (As we will see, however, the extent to which minimalist form *actually* constrains judges from protecting values they consider important is likely to be very limited.)

A related objection is that minimalism throws out what is most distinctive and valuable about judicial interpretation of the Constitution: the requirement that judges defend their actions explicitly and be compelled to apply consistent legal principles.[44] The line between a "minimalist" and merely "unprincipled" decision can often be somewhat thin. This is one difference between contemporary minimalists and Alexander Bickel: while Bickel thought that, once the Court decided to take a case, it should decide according to a generally applicable principle, Sunstein is skeptical of grand theory when it comes to decisions on the merits as well.[45] This debate in part is about the rule of law. The Court's most prominent maximalist, Antonin Scalia, has argued that the rule of law in a democratic state requires clear, consistent rules.[46] Sunstein, conversely, has emphasized the centrality of the incrementalism and particularism of common law judging to the Anglo-American legal tradition,[47] and also correctly notes the importance of creative ambiguity in constructing constitutions for pluralistic societies.[48] For the purposes of this chapter, this debate about the rule of law is important primarily because Scalia's arguments have created some measure of tension among the Court's more conservative members as well as drawing fire from more liberal critics.

The second objection to arguments about the democracy-promoting value of minimalism is that—at least as practiced by the Supreme Court—minimalism frequently does not result in increased authority for the political branches and deliberative space for political actors but rather simply increases the authority of

**72** Part I

lower federal and state courts. Such "minimalist" balancing tests as the *Lemon* test[49] or the "undue burden" standard of *Casey* only allow as much authority for legislatures as lower courts choose to give them, and lower courts can plausibly justify a wide variety of outcomes (including those striking down legislative and executive acts) under such standards. In contrast, *Miranda v. Arizona*,[50] which famously set out a detailed standard for admissible confessions in an opinion with a patent "legislative quality,"[51] may be seen as the antithesis of minimalism. Nonetheless, the *Miranda* rule gave much *less* discretion to lower courts than the "totality of the circumstances" test it replaced, and not all state courts would necessarily interpret the more minimalist test in a way that gave more deference to public officials. Even if it reduces the authority of the Supreme Court, then, it is far from clear that minimalist jurisprudence removes power from the judiciary as a whole. The "extraordinary growth in the ratio of lower court to Supreme Court decisions" makes minimalism on the part of the Supreme Court particularly less likely to increase legislative deliberation and more likely to increase judicial power overall as lower courts gain a large amount of discretion in resolving cases.[52] And as we have already discussed, it is far from obvious that the greater discretion given to police officers prior to *Miranda* was democratically valuable.

A final potential objection to this justification for minimalism is its implicit assumption that judicial power exists in a largely zero–sum relationship with power in the political branches, with expanded judicial policy-making resulting in a diminution of legislative and/or executive power. In practice, however, judicial power is often exercised in response to legislative deferral or delegation,[53] and in the American system, a great deal of the power the judiciary possesses is the product of statutes passed by Congress.[54] Minimalist opinions, then, may not be consistent with the preferences of a majority of elected officials in some cases, as they may prefer that the judiciary resolve certain questions that they prefer not to. For example, Sunstein's claim that the Court in its infamous *Dred Scott* decision "wanted to take the slavery issue out of politics" fails to acknowledge that many prominent elected officials urged the Court to resolve the issue broadly,[55] and that it is highly implausible that a minimalist ruling would have forestalled the collapse of the Jacksonian Democratic coalition that led to the Civil War.[56] In other cases, there may be no meaningful current legislative majority for courts to contradict.[57] On the other hand, taking a more complex and realistic view of the sometimes symbiotic relationship between courts and legislatures can also be turned into another argument in favor of the minimalist approach. By issuing a minimalist opinion, the courts may thwart attempts by the political branches to avoid taking responsibility for important issues by returning the ball to the legislative court, and hence enhance democratic self-government in a way that a maximalist opinion that let the political branches evade responsibility (at least in the short-term) would not.

## Protecting the Reputation of the Courts

Another defense of judicial minimalism is that it can serve to preserve the public reputation of the courts, which is of particular importance because of the extent to which the courts require the collaboration or acquiescence of the other branches to maintain their capacity.[58] This factor was particularly central to Bickel's conception of minimalism. He believed that the courts should use the "passive virtues" of rejecting grants of *certiorari* and other procedural tools to dodge some politically difficult cases so that the court's capacity could be saved for cases in which its intervention was truly necessary.[59] Although he generally characterizes himself as a proponent of judicial restraint or "democratic constitutionalism" rather than a minimalist *per se*, Jeffrey Rosen's defense of cautious judging and opposition to judicial "unilateralism" shares important points in common with Sunstein's claim that minimalist judges enhance democracy by increasing deliberative space.[60] To a greater degree than Sunstein, he emphasizes the necessity of judges acting deferentially to preserve the Court's reputation, arguing that maximalist judges such as William O. Douglas and Antonin Scalia have damaged it while more minimalist judges have preserved it.[61] In a related argument, proponents also argue that the use of minimalism could also reduce the social conflict that can be created by a maximalist opinion.[62] By avoiding broad (and inevitably contestable) moral or political claims, courts on this account can emphasize agreement and minimize political conflict by resting on points of consensus between people with divergent views.

To be sure, there may be circumstances in which preserving judicial authority is a desirable political good. When a court's basic authority is in question, for example, avoiding excessive commitment to clear rules and being willing to tolerate a significant measure of inconsistency may be a price worth paying to ensure that the judicial branch maintains at least some level of autonomy from the political branches.[63] Given a sufficiently established court, however, it is not clear why preserving the Court's reputation is necessarily a good thing in itself. Bickel's goal of preserving the court's authority for the times in which it must intervene is only a worthy one to the extent that we can trust the Court to both save its interventions for the right cases and to resolve these cases correctly—and if we can reliably do so, it is hard to see why the constraints of minimalism are valuable at all. The chief problem with this defense for minimalist theory is that its emphasis on conflict reduction ends up conflating what's good for the *courts* with what's good for the *polity*. It is certainly in the interest of the judicial branch itself to minimize opposition from the political branches and the public, and it is possible that providing a minimum of explanation and framing decisions as being consistent with existing precedents whenever possible may create an impression among some informed observers that the courts are acting more moderately than they are. However, this is not always truly desirable for democratic politics. In many cases, it is surely preferable for conflicts to be stated

**74** Part I

openly so that the actions of the court can be more fairly evaluated: the policymaking power of the Court hardly vanishes merely because the Court isn't transparent about the implications of its actions. It is far from clear why the judiciary, any more than the other branches of government, should be entitled to a fixed degree of legitimacy irrespective of the nature of their actions. On balance, clarity and candor from the Court (when possible) is arguably more consistent with democratic values than opinions that claim to be of less importance than they actually are, as this will make the courts (and the actors responsible for judicial appointments) more accountable in the long run. In this sense, Sunstein's minimalism (with its focus on strengthening the political branches) is considerably more normatively attractive than Bickel's focus on preserving the legitimacy of the judiciary.

Another extension of the reputation argument is the claim that substantively and/or formally maximalist opinions create uniquely harsh backlashes against the judiciary. Leaving aside the question of whether such heightened conflict is a serious problem, with respect to substantive maximalism, the empirical support for this claim is weaker than is often supposed. Pro-life opposition to abortion legalization, for example, was much more well-organized and effective prior to 1973 than is usually assumed.[64] With respect to the potentially destabilizing effects of formal minimalism, the argument is implausible on its face.[65] The broader public has little knowledge about the specific reasoning in legal opinions and generally evaluates judicial opinions on their results rather than their justificatory reasoning.[66] Moreover, as previously discussed, the reasoning (as opposed to the result) of *Roe* was minimalist if not subminimalist. So in addition to the problems with the assumption that having a high reputation for the courts is good in itself, the backlash generated by judicial opinions can sometimes be overstated. There is also little reason to believe that the use of shallow opinions is an effective way of concealing underlying substantive conflicts. The formal minimalism of *Brown II*[67] was unable to produce anything but token integration in the Deep South[68] and also failed to forestall the radicalization of Southern politics.[69] There is little reason to think that formal—as opposed to substantive—minimalism has a significant influence on the political impact of judicial decisions. Even if one assumes that preserving the Court's legitimacy is generally desirable, the ability of formal minimalism to insulate the Court from decisions that arouse significant political opposition is likely to be highly limited.

### Pragmatic Considerations

A final defense of minimalism involves political self-interest. Minimalism can be argued to have a moderating effect on judicial opinions (both because minimalist opinions are less far-reaching and minimalist judges are more ideologically unpredictable) that protects the interests of electoral losers. In the crudest version, liberals would prefer minimalist courts when the median vote is conservative, and vice versa. (It should be noted that it would be unfair to see this as a crucial motivating factor for Sunstein; when he first introduced his theory in 1996 and expanded it in 1999, there was a good chance that a Democratic victory in the 2000 elections would shift the median vote of the Court to the left.) Stated this way, there would seem to be little to recommend this motivation for minimalism, but in more general terms, this moderating effect is related to serious democratic arguments for judicial review. Tom Ginsburg's study of judicial review in emerging democracies found that judicial review can contribute to democracy by providing "insurance" to political losers.[70] Parties that lose power are likely to be represented in the judiciary, allowing them to maintain some degree of representation within the state and hence promoting political stability. Minimalism may enhance this effect by both increasing the chances that holdover judicial regimes don't overreach and provoke a constitutional crisis and increasing the chances that a factional takeover of the court will not necessarily result in the immediate reversal of precedents valuable to the minority faction. Minimalism, if it has the effects assumed by its proponents, may also make the adjustments brought on by judicial personnel changes less dramatic than they might be otherwise, which would further facilitate smooth transitions, as losers will find the decisions of the new judiciary more acceptable.

There are two potential problems with this justification. First, as with the reputation-enhancing justification, it may be more relevant to states without established courts and party systems. In countries (such as the United States) in which a stable party system and peaceful succession are well-established, this moderating effect of minimalism is of less democratic value. In addition, even assuming this moderating effect is desirable, its existence is open to serious question, as courts can use formally minimalist opinions to displace long-standing doctrines. Justice Brennan regularly used minimalist techniques such as overbreadth and vagueness doctrines to advance fairly maximalist liberal positions.[71] Similarly, the Court's decision in *Brown v. Board*[72] limited itself to the specific facts of school segregation and did not explicitly overrule the "separate but equal" doctrine as it applied in other contexts, and yet, the Court simply issued a series of unreasoned summary judgments citing *Brown* in ruling segregation unconstitutional in beaches, golf course, bathhouses, and other non-educational contexts.[73] The Court has also used a series of narrow, incrementalist holdings to substantially increase state regulation of tribal territories while diminishing tribal judicial sovereignty over non-tribal individuals.[74] Additionally, in *Dennis v. United States*, the Court significantly watered down protections to political speech while nominally applying a standard that had been more restrictive of state power in prior applications.[75] This disjuncture between announced doctrines and results, moreover, has been present in First Amendment jurisprudence for a considerable period of time, as Justice Holmes failed to apply the standard in a case in which the presence of a "clear and present danger" was even less plausible than in *Dennis* (but subsequently construed the standard as placing much greater limits

**76** Part I

on state power).[76] As Geoffrey Stone puts it, Chief Justice Vinson's majority opinion (like Justice Holmes's in *Schenck*) declared that it was applying the "clear and present danger" standard for free speech, but "found the danger to be both 'clear' and 'present' although it was neither."[77] Nor does the Court need to announce the overturning of precedents to engage in innovative policymaking. For example, the Marshall and Taney Courts used the minimalist technique of construing statutes by assuming their constitutionality, rather than explicitly overruling statutes, to enforce maximalist property rights doctrines.[78]

The frequency with which courts have overturned doctrines *sub silentio* or plainly altered the meaning of broad balancing tests should raise questions about the moderating effects of formal minimalism. The Supreme Court can, at least in some cases, transform constitutional law without drawing undue attention to the precedents being characterized. This fact is relevant to the consideration of the Rehnquist and Roberts Courts to which we now turn. Given the extent to which the former was identified with minimalism, it is useful to briefly discuss the Court and its use of minimalism before proceeding to an analysis of the first year and a half of the Roberts Court. Evidently, this is not intended to be a comprehensive analysis of that Court's jurisprudence, but to provide a basic sketch of the trajectory of the Rehnquist Court and the tensions within it as background to an analysis of the first terms of the Roberts Court.

## 3.4 Minimalism and the Rehnquist Court

To the extent that the Supreme Court has turned toward minimalist opinions in major cases, the trend did not start with the Roberts Court. Sunstein's contention toward the end of William Rehnquist's tenure as Chief Justice was that "[t]he current Supreme Court embraces minimalism. Indeed, judicial minimalism has been the most striking feature of American law in the 1990s."[79] And there is considerable ammunition for claims both that the Court was minimalist and that this minimalism had a moderating effect that created an asymmetry with the more ambitious Warren Court. The Rehnquist Court failed to overturn a single one of the precedents that most outraged conservative opponents of the Warren and early Burger Courts: landmark decisions holding prayer in public schools[80] and bans on abortion[81] unconstitutional were upheld,[82] as was the Court's holding that affirmative action was constitutional in some circumstances.[83] The most prominent symbol of the Warren Court's liberalism—*Miranda v. Arizona*—was explicitly (if tepidly) reaffirmed in a 7–2 decision written by Chief Justice Rehnquist himself.[84] Given this history, it could have been argued that caution was in order when legal observers were considering what to expect from the Roberts Court.

There is a considerable amount of truth in this narrative; the rightward shift in the Court under Burger and Rehnquist was less than might have been anticipated. There is truth as well in Mark Tushnet's related claim that the "guiding principle" of the "new constitutional order" consolidated by the election of George W. Bush in 2000 "is not that government cannot solve problems, but that it cannot solve *any more* problems."[85] The fundamentals of the New Deal constitutional order—in particular, the modern regulatory state—survived the Rehnquist Court largely intact. In some areas, the Rehnquist Court's tendency toward formal minimalism was married to substantive minimalism as well, including in doctrinal areas in which much larger changes seemed in the offing. As we will explain, federalism is the most obvious example of formal minimalism being wedded to substantive minimalism in the Rehnquist Court.

On the other hand, on issues of particular interest to the Republican Presidents appointing justices between 1969 and 1992, formal minimalism sometimes led to results of substantive significance. For example, two major Supreme Court decisions (both 5–4, with all of Nixon's appointees in the majority) significantly narrowed previously pro-integration applications of *Brown v. Board* without formally overruling or even questioning the landmark precedent.[86] This narrowing of *Brown* has substantially limited the ability of courts to facilitate integration or redress fundamental educational inequities.[87] Similarly, although no major Warren Court criminal procedure decision was formally overruled, the precedents "have largely been gutted."[88] The formal minimalism that generally characterized the chief majority opinions of the Burger and Rehnquist Courts by no means always produced substantively minimalist opinions, and the disagreements between the conservative minimalists on these Courts were often as important as the more widely noted conflicts between conservative minimalists and maximalists.

## The Competing Minimalisms of William Rehnquist and Sandra Day O'Connor

The central reason why labeling the Rehnquist Court "minimalist" is plausible is the fact that in many areas, Sandra Day O'Connor was the median vote. O'Connor not only preferred incrementalist, undertheorized, and particularistic opinions, but often (although having a generally conservative orientation) advanced substantively minimalist positions as well. Certainly, she had an ideologically moderating impact on the Court, qualifying both relatively conservative and liberal holdings with narrow concurrences.[89] Sunstein writes about her limiting opinion in a landmark case on the right to assisted suicide in detail.[90] This tendency can also be seen in affirmative action[91] and sex discrimination cases.[92] Another O'Connor concurrence limited a ruling in an Establishment Clause case, upholding the display of a crèche by advancing as a standard whether the state had "endorsed Christianity by its display" rather than joining an opinion by Chief Justice Burger than might have given significantly greater leeway to the state.[93] (The more liberal minimalist Justice Breyer also authored a limiting

**78** Part I

minimalist concurrence in a major church and state case.)[94] Reproductive freedom, as we will detail later in this section, is another example.

Justice O'Connor was not the Court's only important conservative minimalist, however. Chief Justice Rehnquist is something of the odd man out in Sunstein's characterization of his namesake court. While he reasonably categorizes Justices Scalia and Thomas as originalists[95] (or, later, as "fundamentalists,")[96] and Justices Ginsburg, Souter, O'Connor, Breyer, and Kennedy as minimalists,[97] Rehnquist (like the idiosyncratic John Paul Stevens) is placed in neither category. Rather, Sunstein argues that Rehnquist "has often endorsed the rule of clear mistake,[98] and is probably the most consistent proponent of this view in recent decades," although in some cases (like affirmative action), "his method is more like a form of independent constitutional judgment."[99] Describing Rehnquist as a Thayerite—even in a qualified way—is highly misleading. As with the other justices on the Court, his deference to the political branches was highly selective and tightly related to independent substantive commitments. While it's true that from 1993–2004 he was less likely than any other justice to strike down a state law, he was above average in his propensity to join votes striking down federal legislation.[100] While Rehnquist (like virtually all justices when voting to uphold the acts of the political branches) would frequently use language advocating judicial deference and would also occasionally engage in originalist analysis,[101] at least in formal terms he is most accurately described as a minimalist. His minimalism was just more substantively conservative than that of O'Connor, Powell, or Potter Stewart.

An even bigger problem with referring (even in qualified terms) to Rehnquist as a Thayerite is that the description fails to capture a major feature of the Rehnquist Court: its strong assertions of judicial supremacy.[102] Rehnquist's formally minimalist opinion upholding (what remained of) *Miranda*,[103] for example, also entailed rebuking Congress for attempting via statute[104] to reinstate the "totality of the circumstances" standard that *Miranda* had replaced. "Congress," the Chief Justice declared, "may not legislatively supersede our decisions interpreting and applying the Constitution."[105] Even more important in this respect was Justice Kennedy's opinion (signed by the Chief Justice, although not by Justice O'Connor) in *City of Boerne v. Flores*, which repudiated an attempt by Congress[106] to assert its own interpretation of the free exercise clause, despite the fact that the legislature wanted to give *more* protection to minority rights than the Court had required.[107] Although the *Boerne* opinion overturned no precedents and was not notable for any connection with grand theories of interpretation, it represented the Court "fully exercising its power-maximizing capacity"[108] against the attempts of Congress to enforce constitutional rights. These decisions are representative of a general trend in Rehnquist Court jurisprudence, the end result of which was that "Congress ha[d] substantially diminished powers to conduct its internal affairs or to engage in fact-finding and lawmaking that the judicial branch will respect."[109] Not only does the Rehnquist Court's relationship

The Revolution Will Be *Sub Silentio* **79**

with Congress make it clear that classifying Rehnquist as a Thayerite is implausible, it also suggests that the conflation of formal minimalism and judicial modesty is highly problematic. Rehnquist's minimalism, like O'Connor's, is not particularly deferential to political branches, although O'Connor's assertions of judicial power are more likely to be extended to state legislatures.[110]

A good example of the dueling minimalisms of O'Connor and Rehnquist can be found in *Webster v. Reproductive Health Services*,[111] the major abortion case that preceded *Casey* and presented the Court with the opportunity to overturn *Roe*, but also permitted it to cut back at *Roe* by upholding a series of abortion regulations without overturning the prior opinion. Rehnquist announced a strategy to effectively do the former while apparently doing the latter when he started the conference discussion:

> The Chief opened the discussion with a shocker. Instead of reiterating his previous opposition to *Roe*, he stated that he now thought *Roe v. Wade* had reached the right result given the specific facts of the case. Texas had banned all abortions except in the narrow circumstance where the life of the mother was at stake. In Rehnquist's revised view, this was too restrictive. Although he remained sharply critical of *Roe's* trimester framework, he said that Missouri's law, much less stringent than Texas's had been, could be upheld in every aspect without explicitly overruling *Roe* itself.[112]

In place of *Roe's* trimester framework, Rehnquist proposed a new standard: any legislation that "reasonably furthered" the state's interest in fetal life (which he held to be constant throughout pregnancy) would be constitutional. Had this standard been applied, *Roe's* content would have been reduced to virtually nothing. Justice Stevens circulated a memo acidly pointing out that

> If a simple showing that a state regulation 'reasonably furthers the state interest in protecting fetal life' is enough to justify an abortion regulation, the woman's interest in making the abortion decision apparently is given no weight at all. *A tax on abortions, a requirement that the pregnant woman must be able to stand on her head for fifteen minutes before she can have an abortion or a criminal prohibition would each pass your test.*[113]

In an attempt to keep a majority coalition, however, the opinion Rehnquist wrote replaced the "reasonably furthers" standard with the subminimalist tautology that a regulation was constitutional if it "permissibly furthered" the state's interest in human life.[114] Ultimately, this opinion commanded only a plurality, as O'Connor yet again moderated the impact of the Court's judgment by advancing the "undue burden" standard that would ultimately prevail in *Casey*.[115] However, the difference in the outcomes O'Connor and Rehnquist preferred was not a product of O'Connor's formal minimalism *per se*; *neither* opinion was deeply or broadly

**80** Part I

reasoned, and neither sought to overturn *Roe* explicitly. Rather, it was a case of two minimalist opinions reaching different substantive conclusions, with one opinion trying to overturn *Roe sub silentio*, while the other would retain at least some constitutional protection for pre-viability abortions.[116]

There are other cases in which Rehnquist used or attempted to use minimalist techniques to push the law in a more conservative direction than O'Connor generally did. Rehnquist's opinion in *Rumsfeld v. Padilla*[117] is a classic example of using the "passive virtues" of discretion over jurisdictional questions to avoid an unfavorable precedent (although in this case, O'Connor joined Rehnquist's opinion). Had they reached the merits of the case, Justice Scalia's dissent in another case released on the same day[118] combined with the four dissenters[119] made it virtually certain that the Court would have determined that American citizens cannot be denied access to *habeas corpus* without an explicit act of Congress. By holding that Padilla had named the wrong defendant in his suit, however, Rehnquist was able to avoid a negative judgment on the merits.

A particularly direct contrast between Rehnquist and O'Connor can be seen in the University of Michigan affirmative action cases of 2003. O'Connor, repeating a trend of refusing to fully join her fellow conservatives (whether formally minimalist or maximalist) in advancing the idea of a "color-blind" Constitution that would forbid virtually all racial preferences,[120] wrote a minimalist opinion upholding the Law School's admissions system.[121] However, Rehnquist's majority opinion ruling the undergraduate admissions procedure unconstitutional[122] and his dissent to O'Connor's opinion[123] were also minimalist opinions: he did not call for any case to be overruled and based his rulings on the particulars of the cases. Given the outcomes of the cases, however, his formally minimalist holdings would seem to have been functionally indistinguishable from a clear ruling that the Constitution is "color-blind."[124] Similarly, his dissent in a key 2000 Establishment Clause case—although it would have clearly established a more substantively deferential standard—did not call for a precedent to be overturned and also advocated that the Court of Appeals be reversed because a facial challenge to the practice in question was inappropriate.[125]

No discussion about minimalism and the Rehnquist Court would be complete without some discussion of the case that ended the disputed 2000 election.[126] As Sunstein acknowledges, the decision reflected "some of the most severe vices of judicial minimalism."[127] The *per curium* opinion was a combination of a superficially broad equal protection rationale combined with the famous (sub)minimalist caveat that "[o]ur consideration is limited to the present circumstances, for the problem of equal protection in election processes generally presents many complexities."[128] On top of this was a remedy so inconsistent with the nominal holding as to be not merely subminimalist but to be inconsistent with basic principles of the rule of law.[129] Rehnquist's concurring opinion in the case, however, was minimalist without qualification; reversing the Florida Court based on a completely unprecedented reading of the provision in Article II regarding the appointment of electors[130] would not have had any significant precedential value to limit. *Bush v. Gore* provides another example of both Rehnquist's minimalism and the fact that minimalism is no bar to an aggressively interventionist court.

Of course, as *Webster* and *Casey* demonstrated, not every attempt by Rehnquist to firmly nudge the law to the right was entirely successful. Most notably, the "federalism revolution" that seemed to be portended by *U.S. v. Lopez*[131] turned out to be notably less revolutionary than advertised. As Mark Tushnet concludes, "scholars of real revolutions would be amused by the Rehnquist Court's federalism revolution. Not a single central feature of the New Deal's regulatory regime was overturned in that revolution, nor were central elements of the Great Society's programs displaced."[132] That this formally minimalist opinion turned out to have surprisingly little short-term impact can be seen as a point in favor of claims of the moderating effect of narrower opinions. However, it should be noted that it was not the arch-minimalist O'Connor (or Rehnquist) but the "fundamentalist" Scalia who cast a crucial vote and wrote a concurring opinion that signaled that *Lopez* would not be applied broadly.[133] The formal minimalism of *Lopez* did not in itself require its limited impact. Rather, the modest nature of the Rehnquist Court's federal powers jurisprudence suggests that a majority of justices do not support a substantial rollback of the modern regulatory state.

There are two points about the Rehnquist Court that are most relevant in terms of analyzing the Roberts Court. First, to the extent that the Rehnquist Court was ultimately less transformative than some expected, this was not primarily a product of minimalism so much as the ideological moderation of the median votes on the Court. A Court in which Chief Justice Rehnquist rather than Justice Powell or Justice O'Connor was the median vote would likely have been no less formally minimalist but considerably more substantively conservative. Second, it is important not to focus excessively on whether major Warren and early Burger Court precedents were formally overturned. Landmark decisions such as *Miranda, Engel,* and *Roe* were not overturned, but their content was substantially cut back. Such doctrinal shifts make clear that minimalism can be used to quietly achieve non-minimalist substantive changes. Decisions by the Court to explicitly overturn precedents or not can be largely arbitrary, and therefore the formal maintenance of precedents is often not a reliable means of assessing the direction of the Court.

## 3.5 Judicial Modesty or "Faux Judicial Restraint"? Minimalism and the Roberts Court

### A Split or Unified Conservative Bloc?

The appointments of John Roberts and Samuel Alito replaced at least one (and arguably two) minimalist justices with two more. As previously discussed, the formally minimalist approach of the new Chief Justice caused him to

**82** Part I

win broader support from the legal academy than might have been expected. Although he was replacing a more moderate justice, Alito's similar disdain for grand theory caused some Court observers (although not Sunstein)[134] to predict that committed legal conservatives may once again be disappointed by a Republican appointment. Wrote one Court watcher, "Alito will probably be to the left of Antonin Scalia, albeit with less of a libertarian streak. He will be well to the left of Clarence Thomas, and far more respectful of precedent."[135] Particularly crucial is the assumption of some observers that Alito's formal minimalism would lead him in substantively different directions than Scalia. Alito's minimalism, this argument seems to imply, will make for less conservative substantive outcomes than Scalia would prefer and is also likely to entail a more modest role for the judiciary. The claim that Alito's formal respect for precedent would be of substantive significance should also be emphasized.

After the full first term of the Roberts Court, Sunstein, while conceding that the new justices appointed by President Bush cast the same votes as their colleagues Scalia and Thomas "with stunning regularity,"[136] insisted that the differences between the new justices and the "fundamentalist" Thomas and Scalia remained significant:

> Despite this seeming consensus, however, an intriguing division is emerging among the Court's conservatives. Roberts and Alito are conservative minimalists. They prefer to preserve previous decisions and work within the law's existing categories. Their opinions avoid theoretical ambition and tend to be narrowly focused on the particular problem at hand. By contrast, Scalia and Thomas are conservative visionaries, parallel, in many respects, to such liberal predecessors as Hugo Black and William O. Douglas. They favor fundamental change, immediately, and their opinions are sweeping and broad, often calling for overruling longstanding precedents.[137]

There indeed can be little doubt that in a formal sense, Alito and Roberts are more "minimalist" judges than Scalia and Thomas. The key question, however, is whether this formal difference is of any *substantive* significance. Does this split represent a real difference in how the Court will evaluate the actions of other branches? Or does the split—like the nominal split between Rehnquist and Scalia in *Webster*—simply represent formally different paths leading to the same desired endpoint? To address this crucial distinction, we will evaluate several major areas from the Roberts Court in which an important opinion can be described as minimalist, with particular attention to some cases where there were superficial splits between minimalist and maximalist opinions within the majority coalition. As with the previous discussion of the Rehnquist Court, this analysis cannot be exhaustive, and will also give short shrift to the Court's more liberal minimalists because of their lesser influence under the new Court. In general, the Court's major opinions so far suggest that the formal differences within the Court's conservative bloc have been of very limited substantive significance.

## Abortion

The Roberts Court has so far issued two abortion rulings that shed light on the potential impact of minimalist arguments. The first was the final opinion written by Sandra Day O'Connor, *Ayotte v. Planned Parenthood*.[138] This unanimous opinion seems on the surface to be both formally and substantively minimalist. The case involved a parental notification regulation that—contrary to the Court's precedents[139]—did not contain an exemption in cases of a threat to a young woman's health. Rather than strike down the statute or overrule the precedents that required a health exemption, the Court remanded the case with instructions to issue a narrow remedy (presumably, a ruling that would render the law inapplicable in cases of a threat to a woman's health). The remedy is, however, somewhat puzzling. While reading legislation to assume its constitutionality is a generally sound minimalist principle,[140] to effectively "read in" a health exemption—although, as Justice Souter noted at oral argument, "there seems to be an ample record here that the legislature or a majority of the legislature made a conscious choice that they would rather have no statute than a statute with a health exception in it"[141]—is highly problematic. If the legislature specifically elected not to include such an exemption, it cannot be considered true deference to the legislature to read such an exemption into the statute. Surely, the more democracy-promoting remedy would be to send the issue back to the legislature and allow it to craft legislation consistent with the Court's requirements. Also important about *Ayotte* is its implication—which was a subject of considerable discussion at oral argument—that in some cases, a facial challenge to abortion legislation is inappropriate, and rather challenges should be on an "as-applied" basis. Although upholding legislation on this ground would be a typical formally minimalist technique, the substantive effect of making it more difficult to claim rights has the potential to be considerable.[142]

The second case from the early Roberts Court is also in many respects minimalist on the surface.[143] The court's decision in *Gonzales v. Carhart* (*Carhart II*) upheld the federal "Partial Birth Abortion Ban Act" while simultaneously declining to explicitly overrule *Stenberg v. Carhart*, although the latter decision had struck down a virtually identical state law.[144] Both deferring to the legislature in applying a vague judicial rule (in this case, *Casey's* "undue burden" standard) and avoiding the unnecessary overturning of precedents provide superficially good examples of formal minimalism. In substantive terms, however, the effect of nominally upholding *Carhart I* is virtually nil; unless a future legislature were

**84** Part I

to pass a law banning "partial birth" abortions using literally the same language as the Nebraska statute, it is unclear how nominally upholding the precedent has any constraining effect on the state's ability to ban the procedure (and because Justice Kennedy dissented in the first case, even a re-enactment of the Nebraska law voided in *Carhart* would presumably be upheld). A refusal to overrule a precedent is of little significance unless some of the substantive content of the precedent is retained, which is not the case with *Carhart II*. Declining to overrule a clearly conflicting precedent may have prevented headlines about the Court overturning a precedent in an abortion case but it does not affect the powers of the state in any discernible way.

### *Standing*

In discussing the differences among the Court's conservative bloc, Sunstein emphasized the competing opinions in *Hein v. Freedom From Religion Foundation*.[145] In his formally minimalist plurality opinion, Justice Alito (joined by Chief Justice Roberts and Justice Kennedy) held that plaintiffs in an Establishment Clause suit did not have standing. In reaching its conclusion, Alito argued that the landmark standing case *Flast v. Cohen*[146]—which had granted standing in an otherwise similar case—was inapplicable because the earlier case concerned a legislative enactment, while the case at hand concerned the spending of appropriated funds by the executive branch. The formal minimalism of the holding is clear: it distinguished rather than formally overturned a major precedent, and did not set a clear rule to govern a broader set of cases. In a concurring opinion, Justice Scalia (joined by Justice Thomas) took a more maximalist approach, urging that *Flast v. Cohen* was inconsistent with the Court's holding and should therefore be overruled.[147]

Substantively, however, this is likely to be a distinction without a significant difference. Whether the nominal retaining of precedent in this case matters will depend on whether lower courts interpret *Flast* as being overturned *sub silentio*. Some justices in the lower Court may permit lawsuits challenging legislative subsidies of religious organizations under the *Flast* standard to proceed. Certainly, given the patent illogic of having standing turn on the distinction between legislative and executive expenditures, lower courts will have strong ammunition if they decline to apply *Flast*, given that the majority of the Court suggested that the earlier case had been effectively overruled. In his concurrence, Justice Scalia argued that the plurality opinion relied on "the creation of utterly meaningless distinctions, which separate the case at hand from the precedents that have come out differently, but which cannot possibly be (in any sane world) the reason it comes out differently."[148] Similarly, Justice Souter (speaking for the four dissenting justices) concluded that "the controlling, plurality opinion declares that *Flast* does not apply, but a search of that opinion for a suggestion that these taxpayers have any less stake in the outcome than the taxpayers in *Flast* will come up empty: the plurality makes no such finding, nor could it."[149] Although it is impossible to be certain until the Court decides standing cases in the future, the most plausible outcome is that the Court's conservative majority will continue to severely restrict the ability of taxpayers to challenge potential Establishment Clause violations, even where legislation as opposed to executive action is concerned. As long as the Court maintains the same personnel, however, it is unlikely to grant standing under *Flast*[150]—at least to litigants advancing substantive claims to which conservatives are unsympathetic—whether or not the decision is formally overruled. As with the importance of the facial challenge issue in abortion cases, the minimalist narrowing of standing is important for another reason: it effectively gives the government considerably more latitude to fund religious organizations, while leaving existing Establishment Clause jurisprudence nominally undisturbed. Rights without a viable means of enforcement, however, might as well not be acknowledged by the Court at all.

## Campaign Finance

A very similar division between the Court's conservatives was evident in *F.E.C. v. Wisconsin Right to Life*,[151] in which the Court nullified a ban on third-party election advertising in the sixty days prior to an election. The decision seemed to conflict with the Court's recent ruling in *McConnell v. F.E.C.*,[152] which upheld most of the statute under which the advertising was banned. Again, however, Justice Roberts and Justice Alito declined to explicitly overrule *McConnell*, which once again provoked a biting reaction from Justice Scalia (this time joined by Justice Kennedy as well as Justice Thomas) questioning the use of formal minimalism in the plurality opinion:

> While its coverage is not entirely clear, it would apparently protect even *McConnell's* paradigmatic example of the functional equivalent of express advocacy—the so-called "Jane Doe ad," which "condemned Jane Doe's record on a particular issue before exhorting viewers to 'call Jane Doe and tell her what you think.'" Indeed, it at least arguably protects the most "striking" example of a so-called sham issue ad in the McConnell record, the notorious "Yellowtail ad," which accused Bill Yellowtail of striking his wife and then urged listeners to call him and "[t]ell him to support family values." The claim that §203 on its face does not reach a substantial amount of speech protected under the principal opinion's test—and that the test is therefore compatible with *McConnell*—seems to me indefensible. Indeed, the principal opinion's attempt at distinguishing *McConnell* is unpersuasive enough, and the change in the law it works is substantial enough, that seven Justices of this Court, having widely divergent views concerning the constitutionality of the restrictions at issue, agree that the opinion effectively overrules *McConnell* without saying so. This faux judicial restraint is judicial obfuscation.[153]

**86** Part I

Even more so than in *Hein*, it is difficult to argue with Scalia's characterization. It is unclear what substantive effect the refusal to explicitly overturn a directly conflicting precedent is likely to have on future jurisprudence. Again, the formal conflict within the conservative bloc does not seem to involve any substantive difference about what regulation of campaign finance law is permissible under the First Amendment. Given the substantive similarity that is discerned by the majority of the Court's members, it is hard to imagine lower courts applying *McConnell* as good law, and it is even more difficult to imagine a future application of the advertising restrictions contained in the Bipartisan Campaign Reform Act being upheld by the Supreme Court barring a change in personnel. It is also hard to see the democratic benefits of an as-applied rather than facial ruling of unconstitutionality when the premises of the majority future applications are almost certain to rule attempts to enforce the statute as unconstitutional. Elections demand an especially high premium on knowing which actions are legal and which are not before the fact: a losing candidate affected by a campaign finance provision later ruled unconstitutional will have no useful recourse after the election is over.

The Roberts Court would ultimately abandon its formal minimalism in campaign finance, making the disingenuousness Scalia identified in its earlier opinions more clear. In *Citizens United v. F.E.C.*,[154] in an opinion Chief Justice Roberts assigned to Justice Anthony Kennedy, the Court held that most limits on corporate campaign spending were unconstitutional. What is particularly striking is that the holding went not only well beyond what was necessary to resolve the case, but before the case was held over for re-argument, the Court was planning to issue an opinion that went well beyond what the *plaintiffs* were seeking.[155] Because of the rather unusual set of facts—the case involved not direct campaign spending but an order by the Federal Election Commission to prevent the showing of an anti-Hillary Clinton documentary during the 2008 campaign—the Court could have easily held that the FEC's actions were not authorized by the relevant statute or simply ruled that the FEC's actions violated the First Amendment without addressing other issues such as traditional campaign advertising.

From a substantive standpoint, we believe that a narrower decision would have been preferable,[156] although how to balance the centrality of spending to speech in contemporary elections on the one hand and obvious inequities that arise from unlimited campaign spending on the other is a question over which reasonable people can disagree. Because a majority of the Roberts Court clearly believed that virtually all restrictions on campaign spending were unconstitutional, from a democratic standpoint, it seems preferable that the Court state this explicitly rather than arriving at the same destination piecemeal. To have required further litigation to reach the inevitable conclusion would be a pointless waste of resources, while also being less transparent. There may in some cases be democratic value in substantively minimalist holdings, but the value of masking maximalist substantive positions with deceptively narrow holdings is much less clear.

## Limits on Punitive Damages

One pragmatic defense of minimalism is that it will tend to make justices more moderate and ideologically unpredictable, and the jurisprudence of Justice O'Connor provides a compelling example. However, there are also cases in which it is primarily rule-bound judges who are more ideologically unpredictable, while a minimalist with strongly held substantive views need virtually never reach an outcome inconsistent with them. At least in cases that are not central to their substantive values, maximalist judges may reach unpredictable outcomes in individual cases to advance broader legal values. Examples of both effects can be seen in *Phillip Morris v. Williams*.[157] Narrowly, the case involved the question of whether a jury could consider harm inflicted on third parties when determining punitive damage awards. The case also required the application of a previous line of cases in which the Court had held that the Due Process Clause of the Fourteenth Amendment should be interpreted as limiting the amount of punitive damage awards by juries.[158] On the one hand, Justice Breyer—arguably the liberal on the Court most associated with minimalism—wrote a majority opinion rejecting the jury's award of punitive damages based on third party harm. This may be seen as an example of minimalism producing ideological unpredictability, as one might expect a more liberal justice to be more sympathetic to upholding punitive damage awards (although, given that the Chamber of Commerce "was especially enthusiastic" about Breyer's nomination because of his reputation for being a pro-business moderate, the extent to which his minimalism led to a conflict with his substantive values is far from clear).[159] The opinion from the Court was joined by the Court's two clearly minimalist conservatives, Chief Justice Roberts and Justice Alito, as well as by Justice Kennedy.

On the other hand, however, Justices Scalia and Thomas dissented in the case. These dissents are representative of their consistently applied rule that the Fourteenth Amendment should not be interpreted as constraining punitive damage awards.[160] This case illustrates that the application of clear ideological rules can create as much or more ideological unpredictability than a more minimalist jurisprudence. Justice Scalia's preference for rule-bound jurisprudence makes him more likely to differ from the policy preferences one might expect from a Republican-appointed judge.[161] For this reason, it is highly misleading to claim that Alito or Roberts' "greater respect for precedent" should be seen as putting them to "the left" of Scalia or Thomas. In some cases this will be true, but in others it will not. Broad and/or deep rulings, no less than minimalist ones, can produce ideological unpredictability and moderate a judge's vote.

**88** Part I

## 3.6 Assessing the Claims for Minimalism's Democratic Value

George W. Bush's two nominees to the Supreme Court established some clear formal differences with their conservative colleagues Thomas and Scalia. They have proven themselves more reluctant to formally overturn precedents and have little interest in linking case outcomes to originalism or another grand interpretive theory. *Substantive* differences between the justices, however, are much less evident. While they frequently disagree about how to characterize precedents, they seem to have very little disagreement about the scope of rights or how power should be apportioned among the branches and levels of government. To the extent that there is a substantive contrast between the two pairs of conservatives, if anything, one could argue that the minimalism of Roberts and Alito allows them *greater* leeway to reach substantive outcomes consistent with the preferences of the governing coalition that appointed them. If one returns to the various virtues ascribed to jurisprudence described earlier, is there reason to see value in this kind of formal minimalism?

### Democracy Promotion

The minimalism that is evident in numerous major Roberts Court opinions presents particular difficulties for democratic justifications of minimalism. The Roberts Court's rulings do not (for better or worse) demonstrate a particularly strong relationship between minimalism and judicial modesty toward the political branches. (This could also be seen in the late Rehnquist Court; in terms of the number of state and federal statutes justices voted to strike down, the arch-minimalist Justice O'Connor ranked 3rd with 63, tying with Justice Stevens.)[162] In some cases, such as reproductive freedom and religious subsidies, minimalism produced greater deference and arguably left more room for political deliberation. But in these cases, a maximalist opinion would have led to even more deference, as the state would be permitted to act with less constraints (or none at all). In the case of *Ayotte*, it's difficult to argue that the Court's suggested minimalist remedy—essentially reading a health exemption into a statute although the legislature declined to include one—promoted democratic deliberation. In this case, striking down the bill and compelling the legislature to craft its own narrower health exemption would arguably promote democratic values more effectively. In the case of affirmative action, the Roberts Court's new minimalists reached the same non-deferential conclusions as the Court's conservative maximalists, taking away from local governments their ability to develop policies to facilitate school integration. And in the case of punitive damages, the conservative maximalists favored a more deferential outcome, and would have left it to legislatures to deliberate and determine a remedy if they believed that excessive punitive damages were a problem. There is no obvious trend within these decisions of minimalists promoting deliberative democracy. Whether or not one believes the judicial interventions to be justified, then, has little to do with the formal framing of these opinions and much more to do with whether one finds the more conservative substantive outcomes of the Roberts Court desirable.

Even more problematic is the relationship between the minimalism of Roberts and Alito and the rule of law. On this score, Justice Scalia's critique of the unwillingness to overturn precedents that directly conflict with the Court's holdings is compelling. There are good arguments for staying within established precedents when possible, but nominally upholding precedents while refusing to apply their core reasoning to the case at hand is a different story. While there may be a good case for not basing a decision on broad philosophical principles when they can be based on narrower points more justices and citizens can agree on, when substantive outcomes clearly reflect a coherent substantive worldview, failing to acknowledge the underlying basis for an opinion is of negligible value. Additionally, while formal minimalism is potentially valuable (and certainly inevitable) when attempting to assemble a majority coalition among judges with divergent worldviews, in the case of the Roberts Court, there seems to be broad agreement about a large number of substantive core principles among the Court's majority bloc. Particularly from the standpoint of deliberative democracy, in such cases, transparency is preferable to obfuscation. The Supreme Court clearly stating the principles that underlie its opinions when the majority has reached a consensus makes it easier for public officials, scholars, and reporters, and the informed public, to evaluate the Court's actions and consider whether they approve of the Court's direction or not.

## Reputation Enhancing

With respect to this defense of minimalism, it is still too early in the life of the Court to know if its use of formal minimalism will enhance the reputation and authority of the Court. As previously discussed, given that the minimalism of the Roberts Court has been much more formal than substantive, it seems unlikely that it will have much effect on the Court's reputation in the long run either way, but this will not be known for certain for several years. Although no single minimalist opinion is likely to have a significant impact on the public, it could be that a general refusal to overturn precedents even when making substantial changes in the law will reduce criticism of the Court. It is conceivable that overturning seven or eight precedents in one term would have, for example, become an issue in the 2008 presidential campaign even if no one individual case would attract much public attention. If this were the case, however, the reputation-protecting effect of minimalism would hardly be desirable from a democratic perspective. If the same major opinions issued by the Court were written by Justice Scalia or Thomas and grounded in grand theories, while squarely addressing conflicting precedents instead of being written in an incrementalist fashion, it probably would not significantly alter the policy effect of the Court's holdings. If the Court's reputation would decline if the same outcomes were couched in different formal terms, it would not be consistent with democratic accountability for the Court to preserve its authority through obscuring its substantive ends. We cannot know how the Roberts Court would be judged by the public if they issued more maximalist rulings—but if their reputation is preserved or enhanced, it should be because people approve of their actions, not because people fail to understand what they are doing. Several Roberts Court opinions are examples of Sarah Krakoff's point that "judicial opinions that are shallow, whether narrow or not, may in fact conceal the assumptions underlying their outcomes in a manner that actually stifles democratic deliberation."[163] Information is the lifeblood of democratic deliberation; this kind of minimalism obscures important information from public view for reasons that might be desirable from the standpoint of the Supreme Court and its political allies, but are much less so from the standpoint of democratic deliberation.

## Pragmatic Considerations

The more pragmatic defenses of minimalism rely on two factors sometimes associated with the jurisprudence: unpredictability and moderation. The minimalism of Justices Roberts and Alito, however, suggests that these characteristics may not be as closely associated with minimalism as one might assume. To perhaps an even greater extent than William Rehnquist, Roberts and Alito have remarkably consistent votes; according to prominent Court observer Martin Lederman, in his Court's first full term, "the Chief Justice voted for the more conservative result (by most observers' lights) in 24 out of the 24 cases decided by a 5–4 vote."[164] While there have been two major exceptions to the Chief Justice's alliance with conservatives—his opinions upholding most of the Affordable Care Act[165] and rejecting an interpretation of the statute that would have made providing tax credits on the health insurance exchanges established by the federal government illegal[166]—Roberts has been a very consistent vote for Republican policy preferences on a wide range of issues. Conversely, the more consistent application of broad theories by Scalia and Thomas in some cases made them *less* predictable than judges with strong ideological commitments but with less interest in broad theorizing. There has also been little substantive difference between the Court's more maximalist and minimalist judges. Even if one assumes *ceteris parabis* that minimalist judges are more likely to be moderate, this is beside the point when evaluating any individual judge. To this point, claims that their minimalism would make the justices nominated by George W. Bush significantly more unpredictable or moderate than their more maximalist colleagues have proven unfounded. Whether this is a good or bad thing, of course, depends on whether one substantively approves of their jurisprudence.

## 3.7 Conclusion: Rethinking Minimalism in the Wake of the Roberts Court

Several of the crucial minimalist opinions of the Roberts Court raise serious questions about the ability of minimalism to promote democratic values. It is important, however, to qualify our general argument. First of all, our goal is not to urge the replacement of minimalism with another grand theory of jurisprudence. All grand theories of constitutional interpretation have problems and potentially negative side-effects for democracy,[167] and extant judges never apply grand theories with perfect consistency in any case.[168] More importantly, our criticisms are not so much directed at minimalism *per se* as at a specific kind of minimalism: the use of formally minimalist opinions to achieve substantively broad results. To criticize this application of minimalism is not to claim that minimalist opinions are never sometimes wise and democracy-promoting, and certainly both formal and substantive minimalism will sometimes result from the need to assemble majority coalitions. A significant amount of minimalism in majority opinions is inevitable, therefore, and is not necessarily problematic when this minimalism is the result of genuine substantive dissensus within a majority coalition.

Nonetheless, in many of its important opinions, the Roberts Court has tended to emphasize the flaws and minimize the strengths of the minimalist approach. While minimalism is a sound approach when it is necessary to find some measure of consensus between people with divergent theoretical perspectives, it is much less defensible when used to mask the implications of judgments reached between judges who seem to share fundamentally similar substantive convictions. The first full term of the Roberts Court particularly exposed minimalism's treatment of *stare decisis* as problematic, precisely because the majority's treatment of precedent in cases like *Carhart II, F.E.C. v. Wisconsin Right To Life*, and *Hein v. F.F.R.F.* seem fully consistent with a minimalist approach. Certainly, the Roberts Court in such cases can be accused of neither retroactively broadening rules nor aggressively reaching out to explicitly overturn precedents. But keeping precedents as Potemkin façades while fully gutting their content seems like the worst of all worlds: the thin form of minimalism attempting to cover significant substantive changes. This is a recurrent pattern; the minimalist form of Alito and Roberts has not generally led to a systematic increase in judicial modesty. It is the relatively maximalist Justice Scalia and Thomas, not the Court's new minimalists, who have continued to resist reading limits on punitive damages into the due process clause of the Constitution.

To be sure, whatever one thinks of the normative outcomes, it is perfectly legitimate and inevitable for a governing party to use its appointment powers to alter the substantive direction of the Court.[169] Although one can argue that, for example, the Court's narrow readings of antidiscrimination statutes and reliance on anachronistic conceptions of gender are in conflict with democratic

**92** Part I

values, the fact that the Roberts Court has affected major changes in a number of important doctrinal areas is not for the most part a democratic problem in itself. However, if the Court decides to overturn important, long-standing precedents, it ought to do so explicitly; it owes public officials and informed voters the most information possible. While it is true that many members of the relatively small audience for judicial opinions won't be fooled, the Court is failing to perform an essential function: its requirement to justify outcomes with transparent reasons available for public scrutiny. Even if this illusion of stability protects the public reputation of the Court—which is empirically unclear—it does so at too high a price. Like any other institution, the judiciary is not entitled to a fixed level of public esteem irrespective of how it performs its functions.

Another of the key lessons of the Roberts Court is that formal minimalism should not be conflated with substantive moderation. The many years during which the median seat on the Court was occupied by Sandra Day O'Connor and Lewis Powell—both cautious moderates on many issues and quintessential formal minimalists—makes the two kinds of minimalism seem logically intertwined, but the jurisprudence of Alito and Roberts demonstrates (as, arguably, did the jurisprudence of Roberts' predecessor) that formal minimalism can coexist with less than moderate substantive commitments. It is important, therefore, for scholars of the Court to pay more attention to how a judicial opinion evaluates an enactment of the legislative branch or executive action or what scope of individual rights remains rather than how a Court characterizes the relationship between a case outcome and past precedents. The substantive effect of a decision should be considered apart from its formal packaging when the latter amounts to political posturing rather than legal substance.

Of course, the importance of evaluating courts in a larger institutional context means that the ultimate political effect of the Roberts Court's minimalism is unclear: the limited effect of formal minimalism on judicial power cuts both ways. As long as the lower federal courts remain very conservative, the substantively conservative minimalism of Roberts and Alito is likely to be a *very* effective way of quietly pushing the law to the right, arguably more effective than formally maximalist opinions would be. If a series of Democratic administrations significantly changes the ideological makeup of the lower courts, however, the strategy could backfire by leaving more leeway for lower courts to resist the rightward drift of the Supreme Court, even if Democratic presidents are unable to immediately change the Court's ideological makeup. Also, as history has already shown, there's no reason that a future majority of liberal minimalists can't treat precedents as cavalierly as Roberts and Alito have. If the ultimate impact of the particular form of minimalism that has emerged from the Roberts Court is uncertain, however, its democratic value is even more so. Democratic self-governance is not always well-served by courts creating broad rules, but it is even less well-served when courts create broad rules under the nominal cover of formally narrow opinions.

# Notes

1 This is not to say that the demand that constitutional courts explain themselves has no relevance whatsoever to the question of judicial review's democratic value. In chapter five, we will argue that this requirement is a point in judicial review's favor from a democratic perspective, but it is just one small part of the question of judicial review's democratic valence.

2 Shapiro, "Enough of Deliberation."

3 Hope Yen, "Roberts Seeks Greater Consensus on Court," *The Washington Post* Sunday May 21, 2006. www.washingtonpost.com/wp-dyn/content/article/2006/05/21/AR2006052100678.html (Site last accessed June 8, 2017).

4 Cass R. Sunstein, "The Supreme Court 1995 Term: Foreword: Leaving Things Undecided," *Harvard Law Review* 106:6 (1996): 6.

5 Tushnet, *The New Constitutional Order*, 130.

6 For a summary of some of the liberal law professors who supported Roberts' confirmation, as well as their reactions after the first full term of the Roberts Court, see Emily Bazelon, "Sorry Now?" *Slate* June 28, 2007. www.slate.com/id/2169344 (Site last accessed February 16, 2017).

7 *Danforth v. Minnesota*, 128 USC 1029 (U.S. 2008).

8 Ibid., 878.

9 Keck, *The Most Activist Supreme Court in History*, 285–293.

10 *See Cooper v. Aaron* 358 U.S. 1 (U.S. 1958) at 20–23.

11 Bickel, *The Least Dangerous Branch*.

12 For an analysis of the relationship between Bickel and Sunstein, see Tushnet, "The Jurisprudence of Constitutional Regimes."

13 Sunstein, *One Case at a Time*.

14 See Neal Devins, "The Courts: The Democracy-Forcing Constitution," *Michigan Law Review* 97:6 (1999): 1971–1993.

15 Sunstein, *One Case at a Time*, ch. 4.

16 Ibid., 57–60.

17 Ibid., 10–14.

18 Ibid., 19–22.

19 "*Bowers* was not correct when it was decided, and it is not correct today. It ought not to remain binding precedent. *Bowers* v. *Hardwick* should be and now is overruled." *Lawrence v. Texas* 539 U.S. 558 (U.S. 1986) at 578.

20 Sunstein also argues in his discussion of *Romer v. Evans* 517 U.S. 620 (U.S. 1996) that it "would certainly not have been minimalist" to reject "a precedent that is fairly long-standing and that has helped stake out on important position on the meaning and future of the due process clause." See Sunstein, *One Case at a Time*, 152.

21 Sunstein, *Radicals in Robes*, 28–29.

22 The impact of the invalidation of a statute, for example, will depend on such factors as whether the statute is being seriously enforced or whether it can be fairly said to represent a current legislative majority as opposed to a never-repealed legislative majority that is several generations old and whose past legislation is protected by the multiple veto points of Madisonian political institutions, which make it much easier for minorities to block the repeal of old legislation than to get new legislation passed. See Lovell and Lemieux, "Assessing Juristocracy," 105–109.

23 Sunstein, *One Case at a Time*, 20.

24 *Roe v. Wade* 410 U.S. 113 (U.S. 1973).

**94** Part I

25 Sunstein, "Concurring."
26 Our position is that, at least in the context of laws that either lack a strong connection with legitimate state objectives or are arbitrarily enforced, *Roe* was not excessively broad. Scott Lemieux, "For Richer or Poorer," *The American Prospect* January 22, 2007. http://prospect.org/article/richer-or-poorer (Site last accessed May 1, 2017).
27 *Harris v. McRae* 448 U.S. 297 (U.S. 1980).
28 *City of Akron v. Akron Center for Reproductive Health* 462 U.S. 416 (U.S. 1983).
29 Sunstein, *One Case at a Time*, 17.
30 See, for example, Catherine Mackinnon, "Roe v. Wade: A Study in Male Ideology," in Jay Garfield and Patricia Hennessey (eds) *Abortion Moral and Legal Perspectives* (Amherst, MA: University of Massachusetts Press, 1984), 45–54; Ginsburg, "Some Thoughts on Autonomy and Equality," 375–386; Jack M. Balkin, "Roe v. Wade: An Engine of Controversy," in Jack M. Balkin (ed) *What* Roe v. Wade *Should Have Said* (New York: New York University Press, 2005), 3–30; Reva Siegel, "Sex Equality Arguments for Reproductive Rights: Their Critical Basis and Evolving Constitutional Expression," *Emory Law Journal* 56:4 (2007): 815–842, at 826.
31 Sunstein, *One Case at a Time*, 11.
32 It could be argued that a more carefully written due process opinion would have limited the subsequent development of the Court's substantive due process jurisprudence, but this seems implausible. Focusing on the particulars of the invasion of the marital relationship in *Griswold* did not prevent the court from extending the right to use and obtain contraception to unmarried couples, and then from extending this to the case of abortion. It may have made some difference to subsequent cases had Blackmun located the right to obtain an abortion in the equal protection clause and emphasized issues of gender inequity, but 1) the failure to mention gender rights at all itself suggests any mention of gender rights would not have been particularly robust, and 2) heightened scrutiny was applied to gender before the end of the decade in any case. See *Craig v. Boren* 429 U.S. 190 (1976).
33 *Planned Parenthood of Southwestern PA. v. Casey* 505 U.S. 833 (U.S. 1992). For a more detailed analysis of this case from a democracy-against-domination perspective, see section 2.3.
34 Ibid., 901.
35 Ibid., 851.
36 Ibid., 898.
37 Rose, *Safe, Legal, and Unavailable?*
38 Sunstein, *One Case at a Time*, x.
39 Christopher J. Peters, "Assessing the New Judicial Minimalism," *Columbia Law Review* 100:6 (2000): 1454–1537.
40 Ely, *Democracy and Distrust*.
41 Sunstein, *One Case at a Time*, 27–28.
42 Ibid., 61–74.
43 See, for example, Devins, "The Courts,"; Peters, "Assessing the New Judicial Minimalism."
44 Ronald Dworkin, *A Matter of Principle* (Cambridge, MA: Harvard University Press, 1985).
45 For further elaboration, see Christopher Peters and Neal Devins, "Alexander Bickel and the New Judicial Minimalism," in Kenneth Ward and Cecilia Castillo (eds) *The Judiciary and American Democracy* (Albany, NY: SUNY Press, 2006), 45–70, at 46–47.

The Revolution Will Be *Sub Silentio* **95**

46 Antonin Scalia, *A Matter of Interpretation: Federal Courts and the Law* (Princeton, NJ: Princeton University Press, 1998).
47 Sunstein evaluates Scalia's theory at length in *One Case at a Time*, 209–243.
48 Sunstein, *One Case at a Time*, 11–12.
49 *Lemon v. Kurtzman* 403 U.S. 602 (U.S. 1971). The most crucial element of the three-pronged test the opinion created for Establishment Clause cases held that a government subsidy must not represent an "excessive government entanglement" with religion.
50 *Miranda v. U.S.* 384 U.S. 436 (U.S. 1966).
51 Powe, *The Warren Court*, 395.
52 Only 0.12% of eligible cases were reviewed by the Supreme Court in 2003. Richard A. Posner, "Forward: A Political Court," *Harvard Law Review* 119:1 (2005): 35–36.
53 Lovell, *Legislative Deferrals*.
54 Martin Shapiro, *Who Guards the Guardians? Judicial Control of Administration* (Athens, GA: University of Georgia Press, 1988); Charles A. Shipan, "The Legislative Design of Judicial Review," *Journal of Theoretical Politics* 12 (2000): 269; Gillman, "How Political Parties Can Use the Courts"; Whittington, *Political Foundations of Judicial Supremacy*.
55 Graber, *Dred Scott*, 33–35.
56 Ibid., 35–45.
57 Graber, "The Nonmajoritarian Difficulty."
58 Horowitz, *The Courts and Social Policy*; Gerald Rosenberg, *The Hollow Hope: Can Courts Bring about Social Change?* (Chicago, IL: University of Chicago Press, 1991), 10–21.
59 See esp. Bickel, *Least Dangerous Branch*, ch. 4–5.
60 Jeffrey Rosen, *The Most Democratic Branch: How the Courts Serve America* (Oxford: Oxford University Press, 2006).
61 Jeffrey Rosen, *The Supreme Court: The Personalities and Rivalries That Defined America* (New York: Times Books, 2007).
62 See, for example, Sunstein's treatment of *Roe*, *One Case at a Time*, 251–252.
63 The self-protecting doctrinal shifts of the Marshall Court provide a good example of this; see Graber, "The Passive-Aggressive Virtues."
64 Scott E. Lemieux, *Constitutional Politics and the Political Impact of Feminist Litigation: Legal Challenges to Abortion Law in Comparative Perspective*, Ph.D. Dissertation, University of Washington, Seattle, WA (2004), ch. 6. For an extensive discussion of the relationship between minimalism and backlash, see Robert Post and Reva Siegel, "*Roe* Rage: Democratic Constitutionalism and Backlash," *Harvard Civil Rights-Civil Liberties Law Review* 42 (2007): 401–407.
65 One example would be Ruth Bader Ginsburg's argument that *Roe* would have been better received had the Court waited for gender equality jurisprudence to develop. See Ginsburg, "Some Thoughts on Autonomy and Equality."
66 Peretti, *In Defense of a Political Court*, 161–188.
67 *Brown v. Board of Education* 349 U.S. 294 (U.S. 1955).
68 Rosenberg, *The Hollow Hope*, 49–54.
69 Michael Klarman, *From Jim Crow to Civil Rights: The Supreme Court and the Struggle for Racial Equality* (Oxford: Oxford University Press, 2004), 389–421.
70 Ginsburg, *Judicial Review in New Democracies*.
71 Robert C. Post, "William J. Brennan and the Warren Court," in Mark Tushnet (ed) *The Warren Court in Historical and Political Perspective* (Charlottesville, VA: University of Virginia Press, 2003), 123–137.

**96** Part I

72 *Brown v. Board of Education* 347 U.S. 483 (U.S. 1954).

73 Powe, *The Warren Court*, 60.

74 Sarah Krakoff, "Undoing Indian Law One Case at a Time: Judicial Minimalism and Tribal Sovereignty," *American University Law Review* 50 (2001): 1177.

75 *Dennis v. United States* 341 U.S. 494 (U.S. 1951).

76 *Schenck v. United States*, 249 U.S. 47 (1919). *See* Scott E. Lemieux, "The Exception That Defines the Rule: Marshall's *Marbury* Strategy and the Development of Supreme Court Doctrine," *Journal of Supreme Court History* 28:2 (2003): 197–211.

77 Stone, *Perilous Times*, 404.

78 Mark A. Graber, "Naked Land Transfers and American Constitutional Development," *Vanderbilt Law Review* 53:1 (2000): 73.

79 Sunstein, *One Case at a Time*, xi.

80 *Engel v. Vitale* 370 U.S. 421 (U.S. 1962).

81 *Roe v. Wade* 410 U.S. 113 (U.S. 410).

82 The most explicit reaffirmation of *Roe* was in *Planned Parenthood Southeastern Pennsylvania v. Casey* 91 U.S. 744 (U.S. 505). On the Rehnquist Court's Establishment Clause jurisprudence, see Mark Tushnet, *A Court Divided: The Rehnquist Court and the Future of Constitutional Law* (New York: W. W. Norton & Company, 2005), ch. 7.

83 *Grutter v. Bollinger* 539 U.S. 306 (U.S. 2003), which again upheld *Regents of the University of California v. Bakke* 438 U.S. 265 (U.S. 1978).

84 *Dickerson v. United States* 530 U.S. 428 (U.S. 2000).

85 Tushnet, *The New Constitutional Order*, 32.

86 *San Antonio v. Rodriguez* 411 U.S. 1 (U.S. 1973) (upholding the financing of school districts through local property taxes no matter how inequitable the resulting funding), *Miliken v. Bradley* 418 U.S. 717 (U.S. 1974) (ruling that integration remedies could not include metropolitan areas if the initial discrimination occurred in the city proper). See Ryane McAuliffe Straus and Scott Lemieux, "The Two *Browns*: Policy Implementation and the Retrenchment of *Brown v. Board of Education*," *New Political Science* 38:1 (2016): 44–60.

87 See, e.g., Jonathan Kozol, *The Shame of the Nation: The Restoration of Apartheid Schooling in America* (New York: Crowne, 2005).

88 Powe, *The Warren Court*, 497. See, e.g., John Decker, *Revolution to the Right: Criminal Procedure Jurisprudence during the Burger-Rehnquist Court Era* (New York: Garland Pub., 1992) and Tinsley Yarbrough, *The Rehnquist Court and the Constitution* (Oxford: Oxford University Press, 2001), 215–242.

89 Nancy Maveety, "Justice Sandra Day O'Connor: Accommodation and Conservatism," in Earl Maltz (ed) *Rehnquist Justice: Understanding the Court Dynamic* (Lawrence, KS: University Press of Kansas, 2003), 103–139.

90 *Vacco v. Quill* 521 U.S. 793 (U.S. 1997); Sunstein, *One Case at a Time*, ch. 5.

91 See, e.g., *Wygant v. Jackson Board of Education* 476 U.S. 267 (U.S. 1986); *Johnson v. Transportation Agency* 480 U.S. 616 (U.S. 1987), O'Connor J. concurring.

92 *Price Waterhouse v. Hopkins* 490 U.S. 228 (U.S. 1989), O'Connor J. concurring.

93 *Lynch v. Donnelly* 465 U.S. 668 (U.S. 1984), O'Connor J. concurring.

94 *Van Orden v. Perry*, 545 U.S. 677 (U.S. 2005), Breyer J. concurring.

95 Sunstein, *One Case at a Time*, 8.

96 Sunstein, *Radicals in Robes*, ch. 2.

97 Sunstein, *One Case at a Time*, 9.

98 This is the idea, associated with James Bradley Thayer, that courts should overrule judgments of the political branches only in the case where no reasonable person could

The Revolution Will Be *Sub Silentio* **97**

see the action as consistent with the Constitution. James Bradley Thayer, "The Origin and Scope of the American Doctrine of Constitutional Law," *Harvard Law Review* 7 (1893): 129.

99 Sunstein, *One Case at a Time*, 8.

100 Lori A. Ringhand, "Judicial Activism: An Empirical Examination of Voting Behavior on the Rehnquist Natural Court," *Constitutional Commentary* 24:1 (2007): 43–102.

101 *Wallace v. Jaffree* 472 U.S. 38 (U.S. 1985), Rehnquist, J. dissenting.

102 See esp. *City of Boerne v. Flores* 521 U.S. 507 (U.S. 1997). Chief Justice Rehnquist's opinion upholding *Miranda* in the fact of an attempted legislative override is another good example. See also Mark Tushnet, *Taking the Constitution away from the Courts*, ch. 1; Kramer, *The People Themselves*, 225–226.

103 *Dickerson v. United States* 530 U.S. 428 (U.S. 2000).

104 Pub. L. No. 90-351, 82 Stat 197 (1968).

105 *Dickerson v. United States* 530 U.S. 428 (U.S. 2000) at 437.

106 42 U.S.C. § 2000bb (1993).

107 *Employment Div., Dept. of Human Resources of Ore. v. Smith* 494 U.S. 872 (U.S. 1990).

108 Tushnet, *Taking the Constitution away from the Courts*, 26.

109 Ruth Colker and James J. Brudney, "Dissing Congress," *Michigan Law Review* 100:1 (2001): 80–144.

110 Ringhand, "Judicial Activism."

111 *Webster v. Reproductive Health Services* 492 U.S. 490 (U.S. 1989).

112 Edward Lazarus, *Closed Chambers: The Rise, Fall, and Future of the Modern Supreme Court* (New York: Penguin, 2005), 399.

113 Ibid., 409–410.

114 Ibid.

115 U.S. 833 at 874. For an account of *Webster* from O'Connor's perspective, see Joan Biskupic, *Sandra Day O'Connor: How the First Woman on the Supreme Court Became Its Most Influential Justice* (New York: Harper Collins, 2005), 219–233.

116 Note that in addition to its famous criticisms of O'Connor, Justice Scalia's concurrence denounced the minimalism of the plurality opinion as well: "Of the four courses we might have chosen today—to reaffirm *Roe*, to overrule it explicitly, to overrule it *sub silentio*, or to avoid the question—the last is the least responsible." Even more scathingly, but no less accurately, Justice Blackmun's dissent also denounced the minimalism in Rehnquist's opinion: "Nor in my memory has a plurality gone about its business in such a deceptive fashion. At every level of its review, from its effort to read the real meaning out of the Missouri statute to its intended evisceration of precedents and its deafening silence about the constitutional protections that it would jettison, the plurality obscures the portent of its analysis."

117 *Rumsfeld v. Padilla* 542 U.S. 426 (U.S. 2004).

118 *Hamdi v. Rumsfeld* 542 U.S. 507 (U.S. 2004), Scalia J. dissenting.

119 See *Rumsfeld v. Padilla* 542 U.S. 426 (2004), Stevens J. dissenting, at fn. 8.

120 See Keck, *The Most Activist Supreme Court in History*, 230–231.

121 *Grutter v. Bollinger* 539 U.S. 306 (U.S. 2003).

122 *Gratz v. Bollinger* 539 U.S. 244 (U.S. 2003).

123 Grutter (539 U.S.), Rehnquist C. J. dissenting.

124 See, e.g., *Adarand v. Pena* 515 U.S. 200 (U.S. 1995), Scalia J. concurring; Thomas J. concurring.

125 *Santa Fe Independent School District v. Doe* 530 U.S. 290 (U.S. 2000), Rehnquist C. J. dissenting.

**98** Part I

126 *Bush v. Gore* 531 U.S. 98 (U.S. 2000).
127 Cass R. Sunstein, "Order without Law," *University of Chicago Law Review* 68:3 (2001): 757–773, at 767.
128 *Bush v. Gore*, 532.
129 Kim Lane Scheppele, "When the Law Doesn't Count: The Rule of Law and Election," *University of Pennsylvania Law Review* 149:5 (2001): 1361–1438.
130 Art. II, §1, cl. 2.
131 *United States v. Lopez* 514 U.S. 549 (U.S. 1995).
132 Tushnet, *A Court Divided*, 277.
133 *Gonzales v. Raich* 545 U.S. 1 (U.S. 2005), Compare Scalia J. concurring with O'Connor, J. dissenting.
134 Cass R. Sunstein, "On the Contrary," *The Washington Post* A25, Tuesday November 1, 2005.
135 Stuart Taylor, Jr., "Borking Alito," *National Journal* 37 (2005): 3423.
136 Cass R. Sunstein, "Split Decision: The Supreme Court's Conservative Divide," *The New Republic* Friday June 29, 2007. https://newrepublic.com/doc.mhtml?i=w07062 5&s=sunstein062907.
137 Ibid.
138 *Ayotte v. Planned Parenthood of Northern New England* 546 U.S. 320 (U.S. 2006).
139 For a summary of Supreme Court doctrine on parental involvement laws, see Silverstein, *Girls on the Stand*, 19–38.
140 In some cases, however, this type of statutory construction can yield major restrictions on state and federal power, as was the case during the Marshall and Taney Courts. See Graber, "Naked Land Transfers."
141 Transcript of oral argument at 25, Ayotte (U.S. 546).
142 Scott Lemieux, "Endangering Roe," *The American Prospect* December 2, 2005. http:// prospect.org/article/endangering-roe (Site last accessed August 15, 2017).
143 550 U.S. _____ (2007).
144 *Stenberg v. Carhart* 530 U.S. 914 (U.S. 2000).
145 127 S. Ct. 2553 (2007).
146 *Flast v. Cohen* 392 U.S. 83 (1968).
147 207 U.S. LEXIS 8512 (2007) at 450–1.
148 Hein (127 S. Ct.) at 56.
149 Ibid., 89.
150 Although Justices Scalia and Thomas urged the overturning of *Flast* and a very narrow interpretation of standing rules in church and state cases, they have supported much broader standing rules in cases where they are more sympathetic to the substantive rights claims, permitting affirmative action litigation to proceed even in the absence of evidence that plaintiffs suffered a direct injury as the result of the policy. See *Northeastern Fla. Chapter of the Associated Gen. Contractors v. City of Jacksonville* 508 U.S. 656 (U.S. 1993).
151 551 U.S. _____ (2007).
152 *McConnell v. Federal Election Commission* 540 U.S. 93 (U.S. 2003).
153 Ibid., Scalia J. concurring, fn. 7. Cites omitted.
154 *Citizens United v. Federal Election Commission* 558 U.S. 310 (2010).
155 Marcia Coyle, *The Roberts Court: The Struggle for the Constitution* (New York: Simon and Schuster, 2013), 250–251.
156 See Robert C. Post, *Citizens Divided: Campaign Finance Reform and the Constitution* (Cambridge, MA: Harvard University Press, 2014).

The Revolution Will Be *Sub Silentio* **99**

157 549 U.S. ___ (2007).

158 See, e.g., *State Farm Mutual Auto Insurance Company v. Campbell* 538 U.S. 408 (2003).

159 Jeffrey Rosen, "Supreme Court Inc.," *New York Times Magazine* 42, March 16, 2008: MM38. http://www.nytimes.com/2008/03/16/magazine/16supreme-t.html (Site last accessed August 15, 2017).

160 See *BMW of North America, Inc. v. Gore* 517 U.S. 559 (U.S. 1996), Scalia J. dissenting; *Cooper Industries v. Leathermantool* 532 U.S. 424 (U.S. 2001), Thomas J. dissenting.

161 See *National Treasury Employees Union v. Von Raab* 489 U.S. 656 (U.S. 1989), Scalia J. dissenting at 680–687; *Kyllo v. United States* 533 U.S. 27 (U.S. 2001); *U.S. v. Gonzales-Lopez* 548 U.S. ___ (2006).

162 Justice Kennedy and Justice Souter—also sometimes classified as minimalists—finished 1st and 2nd, respectively. See Ringhand, "Judicial Activism," 6, 13. For further discussion of activism in the late Rehnquist Court, see Keck, *The Most Activist Supreme Court in History*, 250–253.

163 Krakoff, "Undoing Indian Law," 1179–1180.

164 "It was the Supreme Court that conservatives had long yearned for and that liberals feared," *Balkinization*, June 30, 2007. http://balkin.blogspot.com/2007/06/it-was-supreme-court-that-conservatives.html (Site last accessed April 6, 2016).

165 *National Federation of Independent Business v. Sebelius*, 567 U.S. ___ (2012).

166 *King v. Burwell*, 576 U.S. ___ (2015).

167 See, e.g., Mark Tushnet, *Red, White, and Blue: A Critical Analysis of Constitutional Law* (Lawrence, KS: University Press of Kansas, 2015); Richard Posner, "Against Constitutional Theory," *New York University Law Review* 73:1 (1998): 1–22 and Daniel A. Farber and Suzanna Sherry, *Desperately Seeking Certainty: The Misguided Quest for Constitutional Foundations* (Chicago, IL: University of Chicago Press, 2004).

168 Even Clarence Thomas, the current Justice who is probably the most consistent about applying a grand theory, will sometimes decline to apply it if it cannot seem to justify results to which he is strongly committed, and other applications of his originalist theory are historically dubious. See Mark Graber, "Clarence Thomas and the Perils of Amateur History," in Earl Maltz (ed) *Rehnquist Justice: Understanding the Court Dynamic* (Lawrence, KS: University Press of Kansas, 2003), 70–102.

169 Howard Gillman, "Party Politics and Constitutional Change: The Political Origins of Liberal Judicial Activism," in Ronald Kahn and Ken I. Kersch (eds) *The Supreme Court and American Political Development* (Lawrence, KS: University Press of Kansas, 2006), 138–168.

# PART II

# 4

# DEMOCRACY-AGAINST-DOMINATION AND CONTEMPORARY DEMOCRATIC THEORY

## 4.1 Introduction: Toward Desiderata for a General Theory of Democracy: Reform, Opposition, Aspiration

The first part of this book focused on what has gone wrong in our thinking about judicial review: relying on the misleading framework of the countermajoritarian difficulty, pinning our hopes on judges applying the "right" theory or approach, and the misguided hope that a commitment to minimalism will guide judges to the right conclusion. The opening chapter to this book introduced a conception of democracy for which democracy's central purpose is to oppose and resist domination, serving as a counterforce and bulwark against it. This chapter will offer a fuller account of this approach to democratic theory, identifying several of its principle theorists, situating it among other contemporary approaches, and explaining why it offers important advantages as a general democratic theory over some leading contemporary theories. First, we want to consider what it is that we ought to be looking for in a general theory of democracy. By "general," we mean something more than a theory of a well-ordered democratic state or ideal democratic decision-making arrangements. A general theory accounts for not just the forms democracy takes, but the purpose of those forms. It doesn't merely allow us to describe democratic arrangements, but also to explain why they are democratic. A general theory of democracy offers an account of not just what democracy looks like, but also what democracy is for.

A general theory of democracy, we argue, should be able to operate, account for, and guide us in three distinct democratic modes. A democratic theory should be, at once, reformist, oppositional, and aspirational. In its reformist mode, a

**104** Part II

democratic theory must be able to provide direction regarding the alteration, in a democratic direction, of a wide variety of social and political orders, including those that fall quite far from a democratic ideal. Democratization is often an incremental process, and a democratic theory that cannot see its way toward democratizing existing power relations would be of little use in the vast majority of circumstances where radical democratic change is not presently possible.[1] At the same time, a general democratic theory should have an oppositional mode: sometimes a particular arrangement or form of social power must be categorically rejected for the violence it does to democratic values, even if the necessary social power to end it is not presently manifest. Oppositional democratic politics are important because they might weaken the institution being opposed, but they might also serve as a persuasive way to communicate to others the fundamental injustice of current conditions. Finally, democratic theory should be capable of being aspirational. It should do more than just identify reforms or practices that must be opposed: it should help us imagine a social and political order worth striving for. Aspirational democratic theory will, of course, not make the new aspired-to democratic forms appear, but has value in contributing to and shaping the democratic imagination, and beginning (or carrying on) a conversation about how we could collectively better govern ourselves, and what we might wish to begin laying the groundwork for in the longer term. Democracy cannot be content to just reform fundamentally undemocratic institutional arrangements and forms of social power, even if that makes up the bulk of the work it does. Democratic theory's aspirational feature need not take the form of utopianism or ideal theory—it can still be grounded in and informed by our understanding and critiques of the existing order—but it should provide some larger vision for where we'd like to see democratization processes take us in the long run.

To explain the three demands we have of democracy, we'll turn to an example that will be taken up at greater length later in this chapter: the democratic response to the institution of slavery. Any theory of democracy worthy of serious consideration must oppose slavery, of course, as it is an affront to democratic values in every possible way. However, in a society such as the United States prior to 1860, where the current configurations of social power do not yet allow for slavery to cease to be legally and socially permitted, the tasks of democracy might include reformist laws that limit slavery in some way (including banning the importation of slaves in 1807, passing local legislation that sought to resist the Fugitive Slave Act, setting up networks to help slaves escape and escaped slaves elude capture, and pressing for new states admitted to the Union to be free states), but also direct opposition (legal and political attacks on slavery itself, even if doomed) and aspiration (making the case that a slavery-free society, should the social and political power behind slavery ever prove contestable, is a deeply desirable goal, and that such a world could be a desirable and practical one, whether it appears to be possible in the short term or not). The last task was, arguably, largely neglected in the pre–Civil War U.S. at great expense to the prospects for post-emancipation democracy: that racial equality was unthinkable helped make Jim Crow possible, if not inevitable.

The reformist, oppositional, and aspirational moments of democracy often look quite different, and some efforts at a general theory of democracy fare better with some of these faces than others. Democracy-against-domination works well on all three, as domination can be marginally reduced in the short-term, while structures that better facilitate social relations without domination require significant ambition and imagination.

## 4.2 Democracy-Against-Domination

Democracy-against-domination is generally not recognized as an independent and distinct approach to democratic theory in the way that, for example, deliberative democracy, participatory democracy, or Schumpeterian minimalism have been. This is not surprising, as those who have advanced this conception have done so in isolation and in the context of a wide variety of larger theoretical approaches. This chapter will proceed as follows. First, in this section, we will introduce some ideas from important theorists along with ideas in the emerging democracy-against-domination tradition, emphasizing along the way what we take from these theorists. The next three sections will then turn to two other prominent approaches to democracy—deliberative and agonistic democratic thought. I'll develop an argument that they're both better understood as occupying a place in a full account of democracy-against-domination, rather than a competing theory.

Ian Shapiro argues that democracy should be thought of as "a means of managing power relations to minimize domination"[2] and that the extent to which particular democratic institutions are likely to reduce domination should be the "yardstick of democratic legitimacy."[3] For Shapiro, the focus on domination is necessary to identify which sort of hierarchical arrangements are consistent with democracy. Just hierarchies are found in properly ordered, rule-following organizations in society including "armies, firms, sports teams, families, and schools."[4] While just hierarchies are normal and necessary social arrangements, they run the risk of atrophying into domination and should therefore "generally be presumed suspect."[5] On the one hand, Shapiro sets out an ambitious and demanding task for democracy, which is persistent and unavoidable. Domination is always to be minimized, as eradication is an overly utopian goal. New forms of domination will inevitably arise from changing patterns in human social relations, even when the old forms have been successfully addressed with law.[6] Shapiro argues, however, that this is a more realistic goal for democracy than achieving ever-elusive "common good," which many democratic theories hold as democracy's central purpose.[7] The primary mechanism for democratic management of power relations is through institutionalized accountability mechanisms. This helps explain the clear, primary relationship between democracy and

**106** Part II

majoritarian electoral processes. The latter are treated as central to democracy not because they're asserted to simply be democracy, but because they exemplify democracy's central normative point in a very fundamental way—specifically, they manage the power relations between the government and the governed.

Unlike Shapiro, Philip Pettit's interest in democratic theory is secondary to his larger project, which is to explicate and defend a distinctly republican conception of freedom (for both individuals and political societies) in which freedom is explicitly defined as the absence of domination.[8] Eschewing Shapiro's reluctance to give a precise analytic definition of domination, as new forms and techniques of domination arise as social relations evolve and change, Pettit presents a clear analytic understanding of what domination is—a kind of power that is a) arbitrary with respect to the subject's interests, and b) immune to influence or control mechanisms that can bring that power in line with the avowed interests of the subject. The central feature of the absence of domination is not non-interference, but an absence of arbitrary interference (actual and possible). Arbitrary interference, for Pettit, is defined as interference that does not track the avowed or avowable interests of the interferee.[9] For Pettit, democracy is fundamentally understood as opposed to domination because it is the way a society can collectively be free. His account of democracy is not only derived from his theory of freedom, and is demanded and valued only in support of his theory of freedom—without tracking the avowable common interest of the citizenry, state action would be arbitrary and constitute *imperium*; that is, domination of its citizens. On the other hand, a capable and interventionist state is often required to prevent *dominium*—domination by non-state actors. According to Pettit, democracy has two stages or "moments," both of which are necessary to achieve the goal of tracking avowable interests of the citizens. The first function is democracy's generative or "authorial" one. It is the legislative act of translating the common avowable interests of the citizenry into concrete plans of action. Ideally, in a properly functioning parliamentary or legislative system, "the generative mechanism (that) will help insure that all policies whose implementation might advance common, recognizable interests will get a hearing."[10] The second part of democracy is characterized by Pettit as a "scrutinize and disallow" function, designed to minimize "false positives" in the search for the common good.[11] Institutional arrangements such as national or constitutional courts with the power of judicial review exemplify this essential feature of democracy. For Pettit, the association of democracy with non-domination (mediated through the value of freedom) helps shed a light on how the institutions that are structurally distant from simple majoritarianism might fit within a theory of democracy, instead of placing them outside of it, as the widespread "countermajoritarian difficulty" approach routinely does.

Pettit and Shapiro are probably the two most important political theorists working today on the project of articulating a democratic politics centered on anti-domination, and they both influence our project here to a considerable degree. Where they differ, we find ourselves in agreement with each of them on some key points. One difference where we find ourselves in some sympathy with both Pettit and Shapiro, seeking a compromise position, is the desirability of a low-veto point, broadly majoritarian political order. Pettit rightly emphasizes the value and importance of contestatory institutions in democratic politics for the reasons previously outlined. Shapiro, on the other hand, worries about the status quo bias produced by a high-veto-point environment. We'll return to this dispute in the next chapter (section 5.3) but here just note that, broadly speaking, we endorse Pettit's case for the necessity of some contestatory institutions and arrangements, while also sharing Shapiro's concerns about their collective effects. While we find Pettit's conceptual mapping of different forms of domination and their sources useful, we agree with Shapiro that domination's particularist, emergent nature can't be fully theorized, and anti-domination theorists should be prepared to address forms of domination not previously understood or prepared for (and, we would add, a desideratum for democratic theory is that it should be attuned to identifying and addressing new forms of domination). One place where we differ from Shapiro as well as Pettit, conceptually, is with respect to his understanding of democracy as nothing more than a quality of states. Democratic politics might effectively emerge in ways that avoid state actors altogether, and they shouldn't be written out of our theory.[12] Because we address state-level institutional mechanisms here, this point can be largely set aside— nothing in the account presented in the remainder of this book hinges on agreement with that point.

While Shapiro and Pettit have moved the ball the furthest on the development of a conception of democracy-against-domination, an ideologically and methodologically diverse group of theorists have also contributed to this project in various valuable ways, even if they have not identified their approach as "democracy-against-domination" explicitly. Michael Goodhart, for example, has advanced an innovative theory of democracy in response to the challenges (conceptual and empirical) that globalization presents for democratic theory. He terms his approach "democracy as human rights," and classifies it in a larger tradition of "emancipatory" theories of democracy—a tradition that includes liberal movements (such as the Levellers and the Chartists) as well as socialists and feminists.[13] Goodhart ties democracy to emancipation and confesses that although emancipatory theorists are "hostile to domination," they are not non-domination theorists in the Republican sense of the term because of republicanism's historical skepticism regarding rights and emphasis on public virtue.[14] Goodhart's mistake here is that he associates non-domination theory narrowly with neorepublicanism. This error has two components: first, it fails to recognize the multivocality of conceptions of democracy-against-domination; second, it does not recognize the extent to which Pettit's approach breaks ties with certain historical features and presumptions of republican theory, particularly the centrality or emphasis on virtue.[15] Indeed, Goodhart's account of the emancipatory tradition is quite useful

**108** Part II

in demonstrating that democracy-against-domination is not solely the domain of republicanism. The nature of the anti-domination stance is different than Shapiro's in an important way. Emancipation is defined by Goodhart as "both a state of non-subjection and the act of freeing or being released from subjection."[16] It is associated with a specific moment in the amelioration of domination, where a certain threshold is crossed such that we can now label the subject as "free." This contrasts to Shapiro's approach, which focuses on the minimization of domination, suggesting that democracy is about marginal improvements in the removal of domination, rather than being focused on a particular threshold-crossing moment in that process.[17] Goodhart's contribution to democracy-against-domination is valuable for several reasons—he names and attaches this approach to a tradition already present in political theory, and he shows how connected this approach to democracy is to the politics and theory of human rights in the contemporary world.

Michael Walzer's *Spheres of Justice* is not generally read as a work of democratic theory.[18] It does, however, contain a democratic theory, as democracy is one of Walzer's "spheres" and a particularly important one at that. The central claim of Walzer's book is that justice requires walls of separation between different spheres of human activity, such that success in one sphere, presumably following the proper and legitimate path to success in that sphere, defined through social and legal rules built on shared understandings, cannot be used as a shortcut to success in another, circumventing the rules of acquisition of the "goods" in that other sphere. Sufficient maintenance of these walls of separation provides us with what Walzer calls "complex equality." The degree to which each social good is distributed equally or unequally is entirely determined by the logic of distribution suggested by the shared meanings surrounding that social good. Illicit acquisition of social goods by means of wall-breaking is, in Walzer's terms, "dominance." For Walzer, a just society is one in which "no social good serves or can serve as a means of domination. . . . Domination is ruled out if and only if social goods are distributed for distinct and 'internal' reasons."[19] He doesn't describe it this way, but this bears a family resemblance to Pettit's conception of arbitrary power, if distinct in certain ways. Rather than focus on the avowed interests of the person over whom the power is asserted, Walzer's conception of domination focuses on adherence to the logic of the social good or social rules in question. But the difference here is not as great as it might seem. If the government uses the takings clause to purchase and tear down my home because it is in a crucial location for an important public project, I have not been dominated on Pettit's terms because while that might run afoul of my avowed interests, it does not run afoul of my relevant avowed interests, which do not include an exemption to be treated specially. If I was indeed treated, under the law, as any property owner would have been in that situation, I was not dominated. Similarly, for Walzer, the logic was internal to the political/legal rule at work here. However, if I suffered an unwanted taking because the local government officials had

Democracy-Against-Domination **109**

been bribed by other homeowners to pursue the public project on my property rather than theirs, that's domination on both Walzer and Pettit's terms—I was targeted arbitrarily according to Pettit, and a wall between spheres was breached on Walzer's account. Walzer identifies the location of democracy here—it is the only plausible logic of distribution for political power, and must be protected from undue influence from wealth, religion, and various other spheres. While he doesn't emphasize it, this theory sets out two challenges for democracy. First, political power must be organized in such a way that it cannot directly be subjected to, or abused on behalf of, sphere-crossing dominance. The second challenge is more difficult: the wielders of political power must strive, through law, to construct a political society in which the various relevant spheres can be free of incursion, but without creating a state too powerful and intrusive to not be too easily transformed into a tool of domination itself. Walzer doesn't develop a democratic theory along these lines, but his background assumptions, and what he needs from democracy to create a just society, place him squarely in the democracy-against-domination camp.

My final example of democracy-against-domination is found in the work of the late Iris Marion Young. In *Justice and the Politics of Difference*, Young argued that justice should be understood as a response to and strategy against practices and structures of oppression and domination.[20] While this is primarily a work concerned with justice, justice and democracy are for Young deeply conceptually entwined. Justice, for Young, is about much more than "distribution"—it is also about how the very structures that shape the distribution of wealth and power in society are composed. In a nutshell, justice demands more than just how much we get, but how who gets what gets decided in the first place—in other words, justice demands widespread participatory democratic power. In her later work, Young further uses the concept of non-domination to explain the value and necessity of self-determination.[21] Young draws explicitly on Pettit's conception of freedom as non-domination as a framework for thinking through the value of self-determination for different peoples in a densely interdependent world. Self-determination as non-domination helps us think about the democratic value of self-determination for peoples in a way that doesn't rely on notions of sovereign interdependence (by characterizing the necessary relations with other political collectivities in terms of non-domination rather than non-interference) and even territoriality.[22] Whereas Pettit applies freedom as non-domination primarily to individuals and polities, Young considers how non-domination is applied to other collectivities, such as "peoples (who) dwell together within political institutions that minimize domination among them."[23] Non-domination is also what ties self-determination to democracy for Young, as self-determination is a tool to avoid domination from outsiders, but it also must be applied to the group internally.[24]

One reason democracy-against-domination has rarely been recognized as a "school" or "approach" to democratic theory should now be evident. They do

**110** Part II

not obviously or easily fit together. The theorists who treat democracy's opposition to domination as central to its purpose do so in a wide variety of ways, and with distinctive theoretical assumptions and commitments. It is beyond our scope to offer a unifying conception of democracy-against-domination, showing how all these theorists do in fact share a common commitment. In general terms, though, the theories discussed here share a few common features. For one, they treat regularly held popular elections of public officials as (among other things) a useful tool to prevent domination of the general public by political actors. More than that, though, they all lead to potentially complex models—contestatory tools or amendments to strict majority rule, insofar as they prevent domination of individuals or groups in society, are consistent with democracy as well. Majority rule is a crucial tool for democracy, perhaps the most important one, but it is not synonymous with, or exhaustive of, democracy.

## 4.3 Democracy-Against-Domination, Agonism, and Deliberative Democracy

Rather than offer a straightforward defense, we will show how viewing democracy in this manner sheds light on some confusions and controversies in contemporary democratic theory. Two of the most prominent strands in contemporary democratic theory, deliberative democracy and agonistic democratic theory, appear to be in considerable tension with each other. The remainder of this chapter will be devoted to showing that this tension provides an opportunity to re-orient our thinking about democracy, demonstrating that both of them make more sense as examples of democracy-against-domination applied to a particular set of circumstances, rather than a general democratic theory. Deliberative democratic theory identifies democracy strongly with a particularly circumscribed set of conditions and rules, whereas agonists find democracy's essence in democratic movements that abjure institutional containment and rationalist rules of engagement. The differences between these two theoretical approaches have attracted considerable attention recently.

Accounts of the differences between these two democratic theories generally pursue one of three approaches. Some argue for the theoretical or practical superiority of deliberation or agonism.[25] Others have argued that the differences are overstated, and one theory should be properly understood as a particular version of the other.[26] Finally, some have argued that each makes a distinctive contribution to our understanding of democracy, and their distinctness is valuable and should be retained.[27] Here we take the latter approach and extend it. To explain how—and why—deliberation and agonism should be understood as complementary but limited democratic theories, we need another layer of democratic theory above them to offer an account of how each approach fits into the larger democratic project. We argue that deliberation and agonism should not be understood as general theories, but instead as democratic responses to (or, perhaps, strategies for) specific democratic contexts. The value of each of these theories must be viewed through the lens of their usefulness as a potential tool against domination—which they each have the potential to do, under certain circumstances. More concretely, agonism best captures the democratic politics of the broadly excluded or ignored, often but not necessarily in oppositional mode. Deliberative democracy, on the other hand, provides a democratic theory for sorting our differences among (relatively) non-dominated and autonomous democratic subjects. They are both properly understood as subsets of democracy-against-domination. We have introduced this theory in chapter one, and seek to further develop it here by exploring the way it clarifies the value—and limits—of deliberative and agonistic democratic theory. Democracy-against-domination offers a vision of democratic theory in which agonism and deliberation are important and complementary parts—placing each of them in the contexts in which they make democratic sense, but not overextending them. Neither one defeats or subsumes the other: democracy-against-domination contains both and gives an account of why they do not offer a general theory on their own, but remain an important part of democracy.

The next section of this chapter demonstrates that deliberative democracy and agonism have in common one important feature: they cast democracy as a form of struggle. But they characterize the kind of "struggle" that we should understand as democratic in distinctly opposite ways. The following section explores in further detail the sort of context that calls for deliberative democratic politics and the kind that calls for agonistic politics. Substantively, deliberation is appropriate for balancing competing goals—such as fairness and equality—whereas agonism is likely to seem more appropriate when fairness and equality are denied in tandem. Relatedly, deliberative democracy (as noted by many deliberative theorists) makes most sense between citizens granted full inclusion and status. Agonistic democratic politics, on the other hand, is particularly well-suited to those situations when such a shared status or baseline equality does not exist.

## 4.4 Democracy-as-Struggle

Here we seek to identify common ground between these two approaches to contemporary democratic thought that are often believed to be directly opposed to each other. It has become increasingly common to see the conflicts and controversies dividing these approaches as the preeminent controversy in contemporary debates in democratic theory,[28] so grouping them together is bound to raise some eyebrows. These approaches are different in a number of crucial ways, but as we'll begin to argue here, democratic theorists should pay particular attention to their similarities as well. Both deliberative and agonistic democratic theorists emphasize struggle in some significant way as the central activity of democratic politics. For deliberative democratic theorists, struggle achieves democratic status when it meets a specific set of conditions, constrained by the correct

**112** Part II

institutional arrangements and rules of debate. For agonistic democratic theorists, struggle achieves democratic status when it transcends, or aspires to transcend, those precise institutional arrangements and "ordinary" politics. Some agonists have focused on political struggle as a democratic moment in identity expression and formation,[29] while others have focused on moments of radical collective action that challenge or disrupt institutional arrangements through the people acting in concert.[30]

Deliberative democratic theory finds democracy in a particular kind of struggle; namely, the struggle that takes place within particular institutional locations and following particular argumentative procedures.[31] Habermasian accounts of communicative action[32] have been among the most significant theoretical touchstones for contemporary deliberative democratic theory, but it is hardly a new idea. Rousseau's insistence, for instance, that we submerge our particular wills to the general will when debating democratic politics and that we strive for consensus through persuasion leading to agreement rather than simple majority rule suggests that his democratic theory might be understood as proto-deliberative. Deliberation is both a theory of political democracy and an ethic for living together and addressing life's challenges in a democratic and egalitarian manner. Leading deliberative democrats treat proper deliberation as a requirement of legislative bodies, but also as a descriptive feature of democratic societies as well. While one of Gutmann and Thompson's first collaborations on deliberative democracy is explicitly an effort to devise a theory of legislative ethics,[33] they have clearly moved on to a theory of deliberative democracy that encompasses both public discourse in democratic societies and legislative ethics.[34] Habermas is also an advocate of "discourse ethics," a theory that has different but significant implications for both legislative political discourse and public democratic discourse.[35]

Why classify deliberation as a form of democracy-as-struggle, rather than a procedural theory of democracy? The procedure of deliberation—the particular ways in which deliberation is arranged and organized in society and government to best advance the practice of democracy and the search for the common good—can be understood as a way to contain democratic struggle in an orderly and organized manner, to capture what is ideal about it while avoiding potentially undesirable consequences. Deliberative democratic theorists are sometimes compared to participatory theorists like Pateman and Macpherson, but in a more weakened and constrained sense.[36] Participatory democrats included a wide array of popular activities that were not strictly deliberative in nature in their conception of valuable democratic action.

Why does the form of struggle and political participation that is the central procedural and normative moment in democracy require the sorts of constraints they place on it? For one thing, this is the form of political action that meets the standards of political equality and equal respect. We ought not to treat our fellow democratic citizens instrumentally, and we owe them public reasons for our preferences. We ought not try to manipulate them or otherwise trick them.[37] Deliberative democrats assume political disagreement is a logical and inevitable consequence of the free exercise of reason in an open society. The rules of democratic deliberation spell out the more substantive implications of political equality beyond equal voting rights.[38]

Why characterize democratic deliberation as a "struggle"? It is the forum in which different visions of the political good compete in the public sphere. The norms of mutual respect are the acceptable grounds of the struggle. In other words, deliberativist assumptions about the background conditions of democracy, mutual respect, political equality, and what some Habermasians have referred to as his "ideal speech situation" are assumed in understanding and constructing the rules of democratic struggle. This stands in sharp contrast to the approach of agonistic democratic theory. While agonistic democratic theory also begins with democracy-as-struggle, this approach contains few of deliberative democratic theory's efforts to contain democratic struggle within a set of precise institutional rules and arrangements.

Agonistic democratic theorists are reluctant to place limits on the sorts of struggle that constitute democracy.[39] One prominent agonistic democratic theorist, Bonnie Honig, identifies the desire to contain struggle with a "displacement of politics" in democratic theory.[40] In a more recent work, Honig argued that the key moment of democratic agency is that of "taking"—demanding a right or privilege above and beyond what the current rules or structure suggest the "taker" is entitled to have.[41] For Honig, democratic agency is often marked by stepping outside the official and institutionally sanctioned boundaries of political action, and disrupting and enlivening the political order with an unauthorized but compelling claim to political agency, access, and voice.

Another prominent agonistic theorist, Sheldon Wolin, emphasizes democracy's "fugitive" character—democracy for Wolin is always fleeting and temporary, and gains made in a moment of revolutionary democratic struggle are stripped of their democratic character by ossification into an institutional structure and arrangement.[42] In another essay, Wolin identifies both revolutions and constitutions as necessary and crucial parts of democratic practice. Revolutions are efforts at often radical constitutional (re)construction, but once the revolution is at an end, so too is the democratic moment. Democracy is a moment of both remembering and recreating the sphere of the political.[43] It is fundamentally in tension with institutionalization, and the nation-state in general, as the revolutionary moment becomes institutionalized and bureaucratized.[44] Revolutionary moments are those rare, fleeting, political moments when the political is open; not dominated by the power of the state.[45] A formal constitution represents a freezing of the authentic democratic moment—a removal from the people of their ability to seize power in a productive, provocative, and democratic manner. A theme running throughout much agonistic democratic theory is an unwillingness to accept previously agreed upon boundaries of politics and political action. It is,

**114** Part II

they insist, not merely the details of particular policy arrangements that must be subject to democratic contestation, but the bounds of politics themselves.

Wolin's inclusion in the category of agonistic democracy is controversial. This is largely because he writes about the actions of "the people" in these rare moments of democratic action. Other agonistic democrats focus more directly on the actions not of "the people" *per se*, but of political actors and groups in a society. Most agonists are pluralists. Indeed, for Chantal Mouffe, it is her pluralism that motivates her agonism. Mouffe is highly critical of both Habermasians[46] and Rawlsians[47] for their efforts to find neutral politics, practices, or procedures for the purposes of governing norms. Agonistic democracy is characterized by participation through conflictual action and struggle. To try to contain this into a particular institutional arrangement or ideological boundary, whether through political powers or political domination, is to (following Honig[48]) deny full political equality and status to these would-be participators in the political. Also central to Mouffe's theory of agonistic democracy is a letting go of the dream of a compromise in which the core problems and conflicts of a plural society are solved. It is possible (but not required) to read Habermas as if he wishes to do exactly that. For Mouffe and other agonists, to hope for a rational/institutional solution to the problems of politics is to misunderstand the nature of political action and engagement.

These two prominent approaches to democracy-as-struggle provide a striking dichotomy. On the one hand, deliberativists seek to contain democratic struggle not only to the realm of speech and debate, but also within a particular set of rules to govern the forms of speech and argument within a specific set of contexts. On the other hand, agonists remain suspicious of any attempt to contain democracy in an institutional context, suggesting that a willingness to question and challenge all that has been previously settled is of central importance to democracy. For deliberative democratic theorists, the institutionalization of democratic action is the end of the democratic moment. Our contention is that both these approaches to the relationship between democratic struggle and institutionalization are less than satisfying, and reflect a lack of attention to the diversity of contexts and situations to which democratic action is responding. This leaves us at something of an impasse. Those who view democracy as a struggle needn't choose between these two approaches. Deliberative democracy may be a suitable institutional arrangement in some cases, but not necessarily as a procedural norm for politics broadly speaking. The next section considers in more detail the kind of circumstances that might be well-suited for democracy as a deliberative struggle and democracy as an agonistic struggle.

Before considering the contexts of these different modes of democracy-against-domination, we want to clarify a few things about democracy-against-domination in general, and the relationship of this theory to other central democratic values. Democracy-against-domination can be understood as giving an account of the democratic content of particular democratic contexts and settings. Representative democratic institutions provide, among other things, an avenue for citizens to resist domination by the state. Democracy-against-domination also helps account for the democratic value of civil society (making the domination-by-the-state resisting properties of representative democracy stronger), as well as a variety of state interventions into social and economic life. The state, on the democracy-against-domination account, is both a source of potential domination (*imperium*) and a crucial counterweight against domination by non-state actors (*dominium*). Markets, as well, offer tools to resist domination (by the state or by other powerfully situated social actors) while remaining a potential source of *dominium* themselves.[49] The challenge of the democratic state becomes being sufficiently empowered to meaningfully stop domination in society, while remaining controllable through ordinary democratic means, thus limiting the state's ability to become a dominating force.

What about democracy-against-domination's relationship to other political values associated with democracy? As we aim to demonstrate in the next sections, democracy-against-domination requires the promotion of two central democratic values—fairness and equality—as well as sensitivity as the two are balanced. The relationship between non-domination and equality should be clear: some forms of equality are (as many deliberative theorists have noted) necessary for democratic representation to be meaningful. Excessive inequality is one way in which we might find ourselves open to domination. This point has been made by many, including advocates of democracy-against-domination theorists as well as democratic equality theorists.[50] But what of fairness? Fairness demands proper treatment in response to specific circumstances rather than treatment as an equal citizen. Fairness can work with equality—it is an indispensable part of equal treatment—but it can also come into tension with equality. By serving as a kind of counterweight to equality, a focus on fairness can limit a potential danger associated with the state becoming dominative toward some sections of the population. The insistence on fair treatment alongside equality has democratic value as well. Both fairness and equality are important democratic goals, and both concepts—whether working together or in tension with each other—are an important part of a democracy-against-domination theory.

## 4.5   Agonistic and Deliberative Contexts

At this point, we can identify two broad sorts of practical circumstances for democratic politics. The first would be the struggle for the right balance—when the demands of fairness and equality appear to come into conflict with each other and efforts are made to sort out this conflict, either for one side or the other, or for a new way of balancing the two. The second sort of democratic struggle would be working toward greater fairness or equality (or both) in the face of social practices or forces that manifestly defend unacceptable levels of

**116** Part II

unfairness or inequality. The struggles against apartheid, slavery, autocratic regimes, and many other sorts of manifest injustices would be of the latter sort. They are both important, of course, but the latter category is a far more urgent concern. Despite this, many approaches to contemporary democratic theory, including deliberative democracy, seem far more geared to the first sort of democratic challenge identified here.

Let's return to the most complete and thorough form of domination imaginable: slavery.[51] Every country, democratic and non-democratic, has arrived at the conclusion that slavery is unjustifiable and indefensible, and has consequently made slavery illegal. The democratic struggle against slavery has succeeded in rendering the practice categorically illegal in both national and international law. Nevertheless, there are approximately twenty-seven million people[52] held in slavery today, a total higher than any other time in human history. The global economy no longer relies on slave labor; slavery's direct economic contribution is minimal. Kevin Bales estimates the profit from slave-made goods at thirteen billion dollars annually, in addition to thirty-two billion dollars from human trafficking,[53] which isn't much money in the context of the global economy. Despite the relative small economic value of modern slavery, it circulates widely in global economic and social life, such that the consumptive habits of many are touched by slavery. Slavery functions under current conditions of globalization as what Jeremy Waldron has called "a contagion of injustice."[54] The networked web of modern economic life ensures that our lives are touched by slavery and slave labor (even if epistemic privilege disguises this fact for many). For example, while the number of slaves held in West Africa is small by global standards, the nature of slavery in these countries taints the majority of the world's chocolate supply with slave labor.[55] Furthermore, slavery in its modern forms turns out to be profoundly difficult to eradicate. The most appropriate focal point for 19th-century abolitionist movements was obvious: the end of the use of the law to justify and uphold the practice of slavery. When confronted with this alliance of unfairness and inequality in its current law-evading form, how should democratic struggle proceed? It seems unlikely deliberative democracy is of much use for this particular obstacle to democratization. The kinds of arguments deliberative democratic theory compels us to make don't allow for a defense of slavery, and, moreover, slavery would destroy the "background equality" that makes deliberative democracy possible. Joel Olson makes a persuasive case that in the face of slavery, zealotry had a prominent place in the abolitionist movement, and rightfully so.[56] Defenses of slavery don't deserve the respect of deliberate democratic norms of argument, and such an engagement might lend the defense of the indefensible an air of respectability it doesn't deserve. Deliberative democratic norms are limited when faced with the problem of slavery as a legal and economically central practice. This tells us little about the struggle against slavery today, when the juridical and public[57] moral battle has been won and slavery still persists.

Slavery's status outside the law has created new challenges for the struggle against slavery. For one thing, the price of slaves has dropped considerably. Absent an open market for slaves, slaveholders typically resort to deceit in the capture of new slaves (after they have been enslaved, violence replaces deceit as the central mode of domination). The kind of problem slavery has become is less and less of a public matter.[58] While there are likely political solutions that might lead to the amelioration of slavery, a great deal of other effective anti-slavery struggles has little to do with the state: providing education and rehabilitation for former slaves is crucial but need not be provided by state agencies. Consumer boycotts of industries or producers who use slave labor aren't state activities. In other cases, the struggle against slavery necessarily must begin with rescue. Kevin Bales recounts the story of a rescue of slaves, mostly children, working looms in an Indian village.[59] In this instance, the relevant agents of the state were not only uninvolved in planning and organizing the raid, they were purposefully kept in the dark until the last possible minute. This is because many of the local police are on the payroll of slaveholders. A public debate about the problem of slavery in India, or even the passage of a new law regarding slavery prevention and rescue, is not likely to change the local dynamics of law enforcement and slaveholders. One of the greatest tools for the prevention and amelioration of modern slavery, Bales insists, is the simple combination of knowledge and vigilance: developing the capacity to identify slaves in our own communities and lives.[60] Another important element of the modern struggle against many of the worst atrocities committed against people (such as slavery, as well as genocide and torture) is the task of bearing witness and testimony to the acts and their aftermath, assuring that these acts, which are often meticulously hidden, don't escape the historical record. Fuyuki Kurasawa suggests that the work of bearing witness is one of the central tasks of advocates of global justice:

> [T]estimonial acts undergird and create the ethical and socio-political conditions under which other modes of practice . . . can exist. Indeed, without the labour of groups and persons struggling to give voice and respond to mass abuses of political and socioeconomic rights, the pursuit of global justice would rapidly grind to a halt.[61]

The act of bearing witness isn't a form of deliberative argument—in its purest form, it's not an argument at all. Indeed, part of the power of bearing witness to slavery is that actually seeing and hearing the stories of victims of slavery, torture, and the like militates against the need for argument against these practices. Actual arguments that such practices and conditions of slavery are unjust affronts to norms of fairness and equality become superfluous to those confronted with an unflinching account of the consequences of such practices for their victims.

**118** Part II

The point of this discussion of modern slavery is two-fold. First, it is to demonstrate that the nature of the problem for democracy to solve will shape the kind of response we should demand from democracy. Slavery's illegality has allowed it to retreat from the public eye and the political agenda. This doesn't change its democratic valence—it is, from the perspective of the slave, the same affront to fairness and equality as it was in the times of legally sanctioned slavery. Second, it is to illustrate the ways in which a kind of commonplace thinking about democracy has taken the most undemocratic social practices in the modern world off the democratic agenda. When democracy as a concept is associated with an idealized version of the decision-making in modern democratic states, the problems of democracy tend to be of the sort these states are more likely to focus on. This kind of democratic struggle is often (but not always) about the balancing of democracy's two central normative goals. The normative ideals of deliberative democracy are relatively well-suited to good-faith efforts to sort out proper boundaries between fairness and equality (or competing equality claims or competing fairness claims) in specific cases. They are notably less well-suited to tackle areas of social life in which fairness and equality are both effectively destroyed, and seemingly out of reach without some radical change to the status quo for some parties. This is particularly true for the victims of these great wrongs themselves, as they are denied access to deliberative forums, political representation, and in many cases, the formative resources to articulate and formulate arguments and claims in the way deliberative democracy requires. One might plausibly make the case that these struggles ought to be democracy's most urgent ones. However, as the case of slavery demonstrates, these struggles may go through the state, but they also may go around, above, and underneath the state, and sometimes work against parts of the state (usually parts of the state with a great deal of distance from deliberative decision-making bodies). We need a theory of democracy that encompasses both these versions of democratic struggle.

It would be a bit too simple to suggest that internal democratic struggles regarding the proper boundaries between fairness and equality belong to the institutionalized, rule-based realm of deliberative theories of democracy, while the fight against unjust inequalities and unfairness are perhaps better captured by the agonists in all cases. Nevertheless, while this delineation of modes of democratic struggle is too crude and schematic to tell the whole story, it is a good starting point in the process of matching particular democratic challenges to particular forms of struggle. The former seems to fit the deliberative demo-cratic model because both sides are advocating a theory of the public good using a value that their opponents share to some degree.[62] The latter is more of an existential struggle against those who, in practice if not in theory, are rejecting one (or both) of the values that form the core of democracy.[63] The reality of democratic struggle is certainly more complicated than simply these two catego-ries, of course. This overly simplified version of the divide captures something important about why we need a theory of democracy that maintains a more flexible/contextual attitude toward disagreement. Deliberative democratic theorists often concede as much; for example, Gutmann and Thompson concede that "deliberation cannot make incompatible views compatible,"[64] but they don't consider this a reason to question the centrality of deliberation to democracy. This leaves an important question unanswered: What do we make of those cases when one or more of the incompatible views are opposed to fairness and/or equality, and the other is a view in favor of them? Surely, democratic actors have and will continue to encounter these cases with some regularity. The exclusion and denial of rights to women and slaves has been, at times, justified by paternalism rather than any pretense to a fairness or equality-based argument.[65] This doesn't mean deliberation has no role—often, it is the persuasion of third parties to act that leads to a successful democratic outcome—but it alone is perhaps not the best or most imaginable form of political process to attempt to rectify this problem.[66]

That deliberation can often be an appropriate, wise, and democratic mechanism to address some democratic dilemmas isn't a reason to place it at the epistemic or conceptual center of democratic theory. Deliberation is best understood as a democratic strategy that might be appropriate and effective for some, but not all, democratic challenges. In a recent article on the subject of deliberative democratic strategies "before the revolution," Archon Fung makes a series of related arguments and points on this issue.[67] However, there are important differences that distinguish his account of these issues from ours. First and foremost, Fung remains convinced that while deliberation may not currently be the sole appropriate method for democratic change, he does view a particular form of the deliberative ideal as a guiding principle shaping our understanding of the desirable end-state toward which we should strive.[68] An end-state in which all the preconditions to deliberation as identified by Fung, Knight and Johnson, Habermas, Gutmann and Thompson, and others have actually been reached is decidedly appealing and we have no doubt it would be preferable to present circumstances in a host of important ways. Some have suggested this feature of deliberative democracy as evidence that it is, indeed, a form of radical democratic theory.[69] Where some see radicalism, however, we see utopianism. Theorizing democracy as a struggle demands that we theorize democracy as a struggle relevant to the improvement of our current conditions. Sketching what ideal or near-ideal conditions might look like is only valuable to the extent that it might contribute to democratic struggle in a meaningful way. To the extent that we're willing to connect utopian thinking and democratic theory, we suggest that such utopianism would best be expressed as the elimination of as many major sources of unfairness and inequality as possible, while finding and maintaining a workable compromise between these two goals. Again, this world may have a great deal of overlap with the deliberation-enabling world Fung mentions. We don't pursue the question of precisely how much overlap there might be because we

**120** Part II

have little interest in sketching concrete utopias—ours or his—as such a task is of little use for the democratic theorist.[70] The key difference, from our perspective, is that our quasi-utopian thoughts are directed toward the normative point of democracy, whereas Fung's are premised on the enabling of a particular set of democratic methods. He explains the contours of his argument:

> This account of deliberative activism is addressed to those who find deliberative democracy attractive as a political ideal—as an *end* to which our political institutions and practices should aspire. To what extent should those who are so inclined also be committed to persuasion, discussion, and reason giving as principal *means* of settling disagreements and arriving at collectively binding decision even under circumstances that are unfavorable to fair deliberation?[71]

There seems to us to be something backward about this. The end for Fung is the creation of a system in which his preferred method of democratic practice can flourish. However, the procedure isn't—or shouldn't be—the point. The point should be to create fairer and more equal conditions, and to limit domination in its statist and social forms as much as we can. It's possible, of course, that a significant improvement to the fairness and equality of social relations and lessening of domination would lead to a situation in which most—or even virtually all—democratic processes took place in ways that resembled a version of the deliberative democratic ideal, and that would be entirely consistent with our approach. Democratic theory should speak to the social, economic, and political circumstances of the here and now.

At this point, it may seem as though our differences with Fung are largely semantic. But he approaches "democracy before the revolution," as he calls it, as a tragic necessity—a second-best sort of democratic practice. The democratic actor, in Fung's view, is one who engages in non-ideal forms of democratic struggle with a heavy heart, wishing (and working) for the day she can abandon these practices and become a proper deliberator. An implication one could reasonably draw from Fung's approach is that the closer we are to the necessary amount of "background equality," the closer our political activism can approximate the deliberative ideal. This makes intuitive sense—think of the decidedly non-deliberative forms of resistance from impoverished and relatively powerless peasants discussed in the work of James Scott, for example.[72] These peasants are very far from a situation of sufficient background equality, and their primary resistance technique is neither deliberative nor persuasive. Among other strategies, they are practicing what Pettit calls "strategic deference," a show of respect toward the powerful that is cynical and entirely strategic.[73] From Fung's perspective, we should respect this resistance as a response to the unfortunate situation they find themselves in. However, his approach still suggests that such resistance techniques are, while necessary, fundamentally less democratic, and as such should be avoided whenever it is reasonably possible to engage in more democratic forms of resistance. The real core of democratic action for Fung is a deliberative ideal that is suited for some future time. This is an improvement over ideal theory, which fails to acknowledge that conditions of the present are not conducive to that ideal practice. Nevertheless, it is still in some sense a democratic theory for some use in some future set of circumstances rather than the present. Democracy is a way to make the world better, not how we'll govern ourselves once the task of making the world better is complete, or very nearly so.

At this point, the skeptical reader might point out that at least Fung's deliberative ideal provides a method for evaluating means. Because we have offered no specific boundaries or limits to the forms of struggle that count as democratic, or for that matter a hierarchy of preferred forms of democratic struggle, it could be plausibly inferred that we have adopted an "ends justify the means" approach that allows violent, deceptive, or otherwise objectionable forms of struggle to share co-equal democratic status with far less objectionable methods. This concern brings us back to the larger concern of this book: how to evaluate democratic institutional structures. This is not, however, the case. As all struggles, to count as democratic, ought to be geared toward greater fairness and equality, or a recalibration of the differences between them, the consequences of this struggle should be evaluated in terms not only of their likely efficacy toward their goals, but also of any other fairness/equality norms they might or might not violate. Consider the following hypothetical: a male manager in a workplace is predisposed toward more favorable evaluations and faster promotions for the men he supervises, compared to women. This could be framed as a fairness problem, as it violates the fairness of some notion of meritocracy or transparency of procedure, or an equality problem, as it violates the ideal of gender equality in the workplace. Either way, it is clearly a proper subject of democratic struggle to change this situation. One could imagine a host of potential methods to pursue this social change that would fit with our approach to democracy. One could document his errors for the purposes of a lawsuit or a report to human resources; one could simply attempt to persuade him of the error in his evaluation or appeal to his sense of fairness and see beyond his biases; one could attempt to shame him for his bad behavior; or one could organize a collective labor action by the female employees and their sympathetic male coworkers. There isn't one obvious democratic strategy in this case, but some are surely better than others on pragmatic grounds. The best strategy depends a great deal on the existing legal options, the character of the manager, the degree of solidarity among female employees under his management, the larger corporate culture's attitude and policies regarding gender equality, the ability to gather concrete and persuasive evidence of bias, and so on. This hardly exhausts the forms of struggle available, however. Another possibility is that the female employees (perhaps taking inspiration from the film *Nine to Five*) could kidnap and torture the manager until they received a commitment to more equitable treatment in the workplace. For

**122** Part II

the purposes of this discussion, let's make the dubious assumption that the kidnappers and torturers have good reason to believe, and are correct in their belief, that this technique would be quite effective. Why wouldn't this be an acceptable approach to democratic politics? After all, unlike Fung, we've provided no guidelines for evaluation of different approaches to democratic action.

The answer is that such a form of struggle, while perhaps advancing equality, fairness and non-domination in one area of life, would violate other principles of fairness and equality in the process—and create a new form of domination. If we look at fairness and equality more broadly, this strategy could be described as "one step forward, two steps back." How might we evaluate this in terms of fairness for the manager? On just about any conceivable account of human rights, it's held that torture, under any circumstances, violates the norm of equality by violating the inherent dignity of persons. The detention of the manager without due process of the law is a violation of the norm of fairness. Overall, the use of terrorism to achieve ends is an exceedingly egregious violation of the norms of both fairness and equality in a host of different ways, regardless of the democratic content of the ends this struggle means to seek.[74] Our approach to the boundaries of democratic struggle is driven by the evaluative framework provided by the substantive normative point of democracy, whereas Fung's is driven by a vision of how democracy ought to work in a different world than our own.

Another noteworthy difference between Fung's approach to democratic process and ours relates to the social ontology that provides the backdrop for our respective accounts. One might infer from Fung's argument that he thinks that a social state of affairs is possible in which one possible democratic technique—deliberation, properly calibrated—is able to maintain a steady-state of affairs and to deal with all political problems as they arise, without concerns about the applicability and appropriateness of the method. Fung—like many deliberative democratic theorists—seems to favor a position with respect to democratic procedure similar to Nozick's position regarding social relations more broadly: "whatever arises from a just situation by just steps is itself just."[75] This view is in stark contrast to that expressed by Shapiro: just hierarchies, in their current form and operation, might remain a threat to democracy because when "left unchecked," they might "atrophy into systems of domination."[76] The choice between Nozick's and Shapiro's positions on the connection between social change and its impact on justice is an important one for political theorists, even though it is rarely directly addressed. We choose Shapiro's view over Nozick's for a variety of reasons, although we can't give a full account of them here. Even if we were to concede that this state of affairs really only needed deliberative democratic procedures, the preconditions for fully democratic deliberation could still be eroded from many sources. Many of these sources might well be beyond the scope of deliberation. For example, a strong tendency in many complex societies is for

Democracy-Against-Domination **123**

social inequalities to ossify and persist in "patterned pairs"[77] over time and space. Thus, even if inequalities were distributed in a manner consistent with the relevant and operative norms of equality and according to the rules of fairness *at the time*, those inequalities might become less in line with those norms over time. Social change is inevitable, and can't (and probably shouldn't) be entirely constrained and directed through political intervention. Furthermore, in many instances, the implications of some forms of social change will not and cannot be predicted in advance. New technologies, evolving social and cultural practices, and environmental changes may produce schisms and inequalities that upset the background equality that had heretofore provided the conditions necessary for democracy. Even if we were fortunate enough to find ourselves in social, economic, and political environments of near-perfect levels of fairness and equality and entirely free of domination, it would still be mistaken to assume that a particular, single, idealized form of democratic contestation would be able to maintain that state of affairs indefinitely. We don't see any reason to believe that a particular method of democratic action can—even in a hypothetical possible future social world—ever hope to become all that is necessary for future struggles against domination and toward fairer and more equal social relations.

## 4.6 Conclusion

We have argued that democracy-against-domination helps us make sense of the proper roles of different democratic theories. Against those who see the "debate" between deliberativists and agonists as a dispute to be "won" by one side or the other, we have argued they are both miscast as general or complete democratic theories. This error has misdirected democratic theory substantially. Each are properly understood as particular, partial manifestations of a larger democratic struggle, each in their own way geared to reduce or diminish domination in specific contexts, rather than democratic theories in themselves. Democracy calls for responses to and defenses against domination, with fairness and equality as central tools against domination. If democracy is to be an effective response to the threat of domination, as well as currently existing domination, it surely must adopt a sufficiently wide variety of forms to meet these challenges. Agonism and deliberative democracy are each important yet partial and provisional democratic strategies. They find their role in democratic politics when considered as part of a democracy-against-domination approach. Seeing them through the lens of democracy-against-domination, we see them not as competing approaches to democracy, but as democratic strategies—responses to particular instances of unfairness and/or inequality that form circumstances of domination (or threaten to if left unchecked). Shapiro has shown that basic electoral democracy fits well under the logic of democracy-against-domination; Pettit's innovation is that contestatory institutions fit there as well. But democracy-against-domination can

**124** Part II

provide a greater sense of the map of contemporary democratic practices and strategies than what Pettit and Shapiro have shown, as we have tried to demonstrate here.

Seeing democratic theory in this light suggests new insights not just into how we might view other democratic theories, but also how we might view practical democratic politics—both inside and outside institutional structures. It gives us a series of conceptual and empirical questions to pose to every democratic strategy, from deliberation to elections to mass protest. It also gives us the conceptual tools to ask this question of judicial review in the contemporary world. The remainder of this book considers judicial review from the perspective of the democratic theory developed in this chapter, and in an explicitly comparative context. Judicial review's democratic value rests on our evaluation of the likelihood with which it promotes anti-domination relative to other institutional arrangements and constraints. It is to this topic we now turn.

## Notes

1 Indeed, our approach to democracy follows Charles Tilly in rejecting a static sorting strategy, delineating between democracies and non-democracies and treating democratization and de-democratization as discrete, specific events. Instead, Tilly argues that all societies should be understood as being constantly subject to various democratizing and de-democratizing forces, even when regime conditions appear more or less stable. See Tilly, *Democracy* (Cambridge: Cambridge University Press, 2007).
2 Shapiro, *The State of Democratic Theory*, 3.
3 Ian Shapiro, "*The State of Democratic Theory*: A Reply to James Fishkin," *Critical Review of International Social and Political Philosophy* 8:1 (2005): 79–83, at 83.
4 Shapiro, *The State of Democratic Theory*, 4.
5 Shapiro, *The State of Democratic Theory* and *Democratic Justice*.
6 Shapiro, *Politics against Domination*, 23–24. Shapiro's account of domination as deeply particular in such a way that it's difficult to fully theorize is in some ways at odds with Pettit's *dominium/imperium* scheme.
7 This is another key difference between Pettit and Shapiro; when Pettit ties domination to (political) freedom, and political freedom to the tracking of common avowable interests, he's tying our understanding of domination to at least a weak version of a common good theory. See Shapiro, *Politics against Domination*, 195n87.
8 Pettit, *Republicanism* and *A Theory of Freedom*.
9 Ibid., 55.
10 Pettit, "Democracy, Electoral and Contestatory," 115.
11 Pettit, *Republicanism*, 293–297. A fuller statement of his democratic theory can be found in *On the People's Terms*.
12 One of us makes this critical point with respect to Pettit's account in David Watkins, "Institutionalizing Freedom as Nondomination: Democracy and the Role of the State," *Polity* 47:4 (2015): 508–534. Extending the argument to Shapiro would not be difficult; if anything, his account of democracy is even more statist than Pettit's.
13 Michael Goodhart, *Democracy as Human Rights: Freedom and Equality in the Age of Globalization* (New York: Routledge, 2005).

## Democracy-Against-Domination 125

14 Ibid., 120.
15 Pettit argues that virtue-based republican theory is "neo-Aristotelian," whereas his approach is "neo-Roman."
16 Goodhart, *Democracy as Human Rights*, 137.
17 For a critique of threshold theories, see Elizabeth Anderson, "What Is the Point of Equality?" *Ethics* 109:2 (1999): 287–337.
18 Michael Walzer, *Spheres of Justice: A Defense of Pluralism and Equality* (New York: Basic Books, 1983).
19 Ibid., xiv, xv.
20 Iris Marion Young, *Justice and the Politics of Difference* (Princeton, NJ: Princeton University Press, 1990). In this book, Young makes a subtle conceptual distinction between domination ("structural constraints on self-determination") and oppression ("structural constraints on self-development") (38). My use of domination is deliberately less precise than hers, and encompasses domination as well as oppression as defined by Young. For an account of freedom that treats non-domination and non-oppression as conceptually distinct, necessary components of a 'plural' conception of freedom, see Sharon Krause, *Freedom Beyond Sovereignty: Reconstructing Liberal Individualism* (Chicago, IL: University of Chicago Press, 2015).
21 Iris Marion Young, *Inclusion and Democracy* (Oxford: Oxford University Press, 2000), 236–275; "Two Concepts of Self Determination," in Stephen Hay, Tariq Madood and Judith Squires (eds) *Ethnicity, Nationalism and Minority Rights* (Cambridge: Cambridge University Press, 2004), 176–198; "Self-Determination as Non-Domination: Ideals Applied to Palestine/Israel," *Ethnicities* 5:2 (2005): 139–159.
22 Young, *Inclusion and Democracy*, 261.
23 Ibid., 265.
24 Young, "Two Concepts of Self-Determination," 176.
25 For a consideration of the differences between these approaches that concludes both incommensurability and the superiority of deliberative democracy, see Allyn Fives, "Reasonable, Agonistic or Good? The Character of a Democrat," *Philosophy and Social Criticism* 35:8 (2009): 961–983; and Eva Erman, "What Is Wrong with Agonistic Pluralism? Reflections on Conflict in Democratic Theory," *Philosophy and Social Criticism* 35:9 (2009): 1039–1062. For a case for the superiority of agonism in the context of divided societies, see Andrew Schaap, "Agonism in Divided Societies," *Philosophy and Social Criticism* 32:2 (2006): 255–277. For an argument that agonistic democracy better captures the authentic dialogue surrounding contentious moralized political controversies, see Simona Goi, "Agonism, Deliberation, and the Politics of Abortion," *Polity* 37:1 (2005): 54–81.
26 See, for example, Andrew Knops, "Agonism as Deliberation: On Mouffe's Theory of Democracy," *Journal of Political Philosophy* 15:1 (2007): 115–126; "Integrating Agonism with Deliberation—Realising the Benefits," *Filozofija I Drustvo* 23:4 (2012): 151–170; Gulshan Khan, "Critical Republicanism: Jurgen Habermas and Chantal Mouffe," *Contemporary Political Theory* 12:4 (2013): 318–337; and Robert Sparling, "M.K. Gandhi: Reconciling Agonism and Deliberative Democracy," *Representation* 45:4 (2009): 391–403.
27 Fuat Gursozlu, "Agonism and Deliberation: Recognizing the Difference," *Journal of Political Philosophy* 17:3 (2009): 355–368.
28 Chantal Mouffe, "Deliberative Democracy or Agonistic Pluralism?" *Social Research* 66:3 (1999): 745–759; Robert W. T. Martin, "Between Consensus and Conflict: Habermas, Post-Modern Agonism and the Early American Public Sphere," *Polity* 37:3 (2005):

**126** Part II

364–388; Bonnie Honig, "Between Decision and Deliberation: Political Paradox in Democratic Theory," *American Political Science Review* 101:1 (2007): 1–17; Knops, "Agonism as Deliberation."

29 Chantal Mouffe, *The Democratic Paradox* (London: Verso, 2000).

30 Sheldon Wolin, "Hannah Arendt: Democracy and the Political," in Lewis Hinchman and Sandra Hinchman (eds) *Hannah Arendt: Critical Essays* (Albany, NY: SUNY Press, 1994), 289–306, and "Fugitive Democracy."

31 There is an enormous amount of deliberative democratic theory literature. Our brief discussion here draws on the work of both Habermas and Amy Gutmann and Dennis Thompson. See Habermas, *Between Facts and Norms*; Amy Gutmann and Dennis Thompson, *Democracy and Disagreement* (Cambridge, MA: Belknap Press, 1996); *Why Deliberative Democracy?* (Princeton, NJ: Princeton University Press, 2004).

32 Jurgen Habermas, *Theory of Communicative Action, Volume 1: Reason and the Rationalization of Society* (Boston, MA: Beacon Press, 1985) and *Between Facts and Norms*.

33 Amy Guttmann and Dennis Thompson, "The Theory of Legislative Ethics," in Bruce Jennings and Daniel Callahan (eds) *Representation and Responsibility: Exploring Legislative Ethics* (New York: Plenum Press, 1985), 167–195.

34 For example, Gutmann and Thompson's *Why Deliberative Democracy?* begins with a discussion of the public debates about the impending 2003 war in Iraq from the perspective of deliberative democratic theory.

35 Jurgen Habermas, *Justification and Application: Remarks on Discourse Ethics*, trans. Ciaran Cronin (Cambridge, MA: MIT Press, 1994), 19–112.

36 See, e.g., Frank Cunningham, *Theories of Democracy: A Critical Introduction* (London: Routledge, 2002), 167.

37 Archon Fung relaxes this requirement for deliberative democratic actors in an imperfect world. His approach to this topic is revealing of a conceptual flaw in deliberative democratic thinking; his argument will be taken up in more detail in the next section. See his "Democracy before the Revolution."

38 A discussion of the equality-derived rules of deliberation, elaborating on Habermas's norms, can be found in Seyla Benhabib, "Toward a Deliberative Model of Democratic Legitimacy," in Seyla Benhabib (ed) *Democracy and Difference: Contesting the Boundaries of the Political* (Princeton, NJ: Princeton University Press, 1996), 67–94, at 69–70.

39 Important statements of agonistic democratic theory include Honig, *Political Theory and the Displacement of Politics*; "The Politics of Agonism: A Critical Response to Dana Villa's 'Beyond Good and Evil: Arendt, Nietzsche and the Aestheticization of Political Action,'" *Political Theory* 21:3 (1993): 528–533; *Democracy and the Foreigner*; Wolin, "Fugitive Democracy"; "Hannah Arendt: Democracy and the Political"; and "Norm and Form: The Constitutionalizing of Democracy," in Josiah Ober, John R. Wallach and J. Peter Euben (eds) *Athenian Democratic Thought and the Reconstruction of American Democracy* (Ithaca, NY: Cornell University Press, 1994), 29–58; William Connolly, "Democracy and Territoriality," *Millennium* 20:3 (1991): 463–484; *Identity/Difference: Political Negotiations and Democratic Paradox* (Ithaca, NY: Cornell University Press, 1991); *The Ethos of Pluralization* (Minneapolis: University of Minnesota Press, 1995); James Tully, *Strange Multiplicity: Constitutionalism in an Age of Diversity* (Cambridge: Cambridge University Press, 1995); "The Agonic Freedom of Citizens," *Economy and Society* 28:2 (1999): 161–182; Chantal Mouffe, *The Return of the Political* (London: Verso, 1993); "Deliberative Democracy or Agonistic Pluralism?" *Social Research* 66:3 (1999): 745–759; *The Democratic Paradox* (London: Verso, 2000); and "The Limits of John Rawls's Pluralism," *Politics Philosophy and Economics* 5:2 (2005): 221–231.

Democracy-Against-Domination **127**

40 Honig, *Political Theory and the Displacement of Politics.*
41 Honig, *Democracy and the Foreigner.*
42 Wolin, "Fugitive Democracy."
43 Wolin, "Norm and Form," 55.
44 Ibid.
45 Wolin writes a great deal about "the political" but as Nicholas Xenos, "Momentary Democracy," in Aryeh Botwinick and William Connolly (eds) *Democracy and Vision: Sheldon Wolin and the Vicissitudes of the Political* (Princeton, NJ: Princeton University Press, 2001), 25–38, argues, there is little difference between Wolin's use of democracy and his concept of authentic political moments.
46 Mouffe, "Deliberative Democracy or Agonistic Pluralism?"
47 Mouffe, "The Limits of John Rawls Pluralism."
48 Honig, *Political Theory and the Displacement of Politics.*
49 Anti-domination theories vary considerably in their views on markets and domination. K. Sabeel Rahman, *Democracy against Domination* (Oxford: Oxford University Press, 2017), taking his cues from social movements and politicians in the progressive era, states that the capacity and willingness to regulate and control market activity is central to any worthy democratic effort to restrain domination. Robert Taylor, on the other hand, makes the case in *Exit Left: Markets and Mobility in Republican Thought* (Oxford: Oxford University Press, 2017) that republicans should be celebratory rather than acquiescent toward competitive markets, as they are a crucial and powerful element of any domination-avoiding strategy.
50 Anderson, "What Is the Point of Equality?" and Anne Phillips, *Which Equalities Matter* (London: Polity, 1999). In *On the People's Terms*, Pettit advances the position that in addition to not being actively dominated, citizens in a republican polity need to be sufficiently resourced to be free of the threat of domination, but he advocates a sufficientarian, rather than egalitarian, view of resources. For a critique of Pettit on egalitarian grounds, see McCormick, *Machiavellian Democracy.*
51 Our discussion of modern slavery draws heavily from the work of Kevin Bales, one of the foremost experts on modern slavery. See Kevin Bales, *Disposable People: New Slavery in the Global Economy*, 2nd ed. (Berkeley, CA: University of California Press, 2004); *New Slavery*, 2nd ed. (Santa Barbara, CA: ABC-CLIO Press, 2004); *Understanding Global Slavery: A Reader* (Berkeley, CA: University of California Press, 2005); "Non-State Actors and the Challenge of Slavery," in George Andreopoulos, Zehra F. Kabasakal Arat and Peter Juviler (eds) *Non-State Actors in the Human Rights Universe* (Bloomingfield, CT: Kumarian Press, 2006), 273–288; *Ending Slavery: How We Free Today's Slaves* (Berkeley, CA: University of California Press, 2007); and Joel Quirk, *Unfinished Business: A Comparative Survey of Historical and Contemporary Slavery* (Paris: UNESCO Publishing, 2009).
52 This is the figure given by Bales and Anti-Slavery International. Of course, because modern slavery is often hidden behind fraudulent contracts and false kinship claims, this figure is probably inaccurate, but is more likely to underestimate the extent of the problem than overestimate it. See Kate Manzo, "Modern Slavery, Global Capitalism, and Deproletarianization in West Africa," *Review of African Political Economy* 106 (2005): 521–534.
53 Bales, *Ending Slavery.*
54 Jeremy Waldron, "Superseding Historic Injustice," *Ethics* 103:1 (1992): 4–28. Waldron coins the phrase to refer to the broad scope across time and space of the injustices of land appropriation in settler colonies such as New Zealand. Our use of Waldron's phrase here is not, as his was, referring to injustice persisting over time. Instead, we

**128** Part II

mean to suggest that the injustice of slavery ripples throughout the conduits and networks of globalization, across the space of the global economy.

55 For an analysis of the regional and global aspects of the West African slave trade, see Manzo, "Modern Slavery."

56 Joel Olson, "The Freshness of Fanaticism: The Abolitionist Defense of Zealotry," *Perspectives on Politics* 5:4 (2007): 685–701.

57 We use the term "public" here because in many cases, slaveholders defend what they do as appropriate and ethical business practices. This psychology is often adopted by the slaves themselves as a way of coping with their situation (Kevin Bales, "The Social Psychology of Modern Slavery," *Scientific American* 286:4 (2002): 80–88). Nonetheless, despite widespread ignorance of and indifference to modern slavery, *actual public and principled defenses of slavery* are virtually unheard of.

58 The changing nature of modern slavery demands a new set of democratic strategies. Joel Quirk has helpfully theorized this shift as the move from legal abolition to effective emancipation. See "Ending Slavery in All Its Forms: Legal Abolition and Effective Emancipation in Historical Perspective," *International Journal of Human Rights* 12:4 (2008): 529–554 and *The Anti-Slavery Project: From the Slave Trade to Human Trafficking* (Philadelphia, PA: University of Pennsylvania Press, 2011).

59 Bales, *Ending Slavery*, 36–42.

60 Bales drives home the importance of this strategy with anecdotes about slaves living in affluent communities in the United States whose neighbors were completely unaware of their status, largely due to their lack of knowledge about modern slavery. (Ibid., ch. 1).

61 Fuyuki Kurasawa, *The Work of Global Justice* (Cambridge: Cambridge University Press, 2007), 23. Kurasawa's theoretical innovations in the service of the construction of a critical theory of global justice as practice or work fits nicely with the argument we make here for democracy-as-struggle against domination.

62 Of course, the deliberative approach to democratic process is potentially subject to cynical misuse by those arguing in less than good faith even in cases such as these.

63 To be clear, this approach to democracy does not authorize in any sense struggles explicitly against fairness and equality (although, of course, there will often be disagreement as to whether a particular struggle or goal fits this category). Still, we assume for obvious reasons that no democratic theory can afford to assume that such struggles won't be a persistent feature of social life indefinitely.

64 Gutmann and Thompson, *Why Deliberative Democracy?*, 11.

65 Paternalism, in some forms, bears a family resemblance to a certain kind of "fairness" argument—that applying a certain kind of equality to a certain group of agents will set them up for failure due to a particular characteristic of this kind of agent.

66 To be clear, we are suggesting that those excluded from the political process (slaves, women in strongly patriarchal societies) can find no benefit in deliberation. The terms of their deliberation must necessarily be quite different from the deliberative ideal, with its strong background assumptions of political equality.

67 Fung, "Democracy before the Revolution."

68 Fung cites prominent passages from Habermas, *Between Facts and Norms*, and an influential essay by Knight and Johnson, "What Sort of Political Equality," 279–320, on the important preconditions of a truly deliberative public sphere, which is, without doubt, well short of the amount of "background equality" extant in most, if not all, political communities in the world today. Many other deliberative theorists, including Gutmann and Thompson, have made similar observations about "background equality."

69 See, for example, Stephen Grodnick, "Rediscovering Radical Democracy in Habermas's *Between Facts and Norms*," *Constellations* 12:3 (2005): 392–408, at 399.

70 By suggesting that such a task is of little use for democratic theorists, we don't mean to suggest that utopian visions have no role in democratic politics. They can be quite useful in demonstrating a serious problem in today's social, political, or economic world by showing how much better the world would be without it. But utopian visions are in this sense serving a particular role in a particular social context; their value is not capturing the correct and true vision of the best possible world humanity could possibly construct for itself, but in persuasively and vividly highlighting and critiquing specific flaws in the shared world of the sketcher of utopias and her audience. In David Estlund's sense, we are utopophobes; see his *Democratic Authority: A Philosophical Framework* (Princeton, NJ: Princeton University Press, 2008). For a defense of an utopophobic approach to democracy congenial to our point of view, see Patrick Tomlin, "Should We Be Utopophobes about Democracy in Particular?" *Political Studies Review* 10:1 (2012): 36–47.

71 Fung, "Democracy before the Revolution," 399. Emphasis retained from original.

72 See James Scott, *Weapons of the Weak: Everyday forms of Peasant Resistance* (New Haven, CT: Yale University Press, 1987). We should note that Scott thought he was identifying resistance and not (necessarily) democracy. Given the nature of the social relations being resisted, the activities he identified clearly fit within this conception of democracy.

73 Pettit, *Republicanism*, 86–87. Strategic deference occurs when those dominated attend to their own freedom by "develop[ing] and exercise[ing] strategies for placating and anticipating the powerful" through, for example, "strategic flattery and avoidance" (87). For Pettit, the necessity of developing strategies of strategic deference is one of many deleterious consequences of living a life in which one is potentially subject to arbitrary influence and domination. Those who practice strategic deference regularly, due to a persistent and/or permanent dominative relationship, are limited in their choices and therefore freedoms even when the potential dominator is successfully placated, and furthermore they risk the development of a strategic disposition that might serve to limit their ability to function as an agent and live a life of freedom in the future, even without persistent interference.

74 Furthermore, our stipulation that this method would be effective is highly suspect as well. We added that condition to show that such an approach would be highly problematic under our conception of democracy even if it were successful.

75 Robert Nozick, *Anarchy, State and Utopia* (New York: Basic Books, 1974), 151.

76 Shapiro, *The State of Democratic Theory*, 4. See also Shapiro, *Democratic Justice*.

77 Charles Tilly, *Durable Equality* (Berkeley, CA: University of California Press, 1999). For example, man/woman, rich/poor, noble/common, and white/non-white, to list the most prominent examples. Tilly considers these patterned pairs because the nature of the inequality between the two categories assumes patterns that replicate, reproduce, and reinforce themselves across time and space.

# 5

# COMPARED TO WHAT? JUDICIAL REVIEW AS JUST ANOTHER VETO POINT

## 5.1 Introduction

Democracy-against-domination provides not just a compelling account of the concept of democracy and its value, but a set of conceptual tools for evaluating the democratic valence of mechanisms and institutional arrangements, such as judicial review. As we argued in the second and third chapters, minimalism, like other "instructions for judges" approaches, fails to provide a way forward in our effort to assess the institution's democratic value. In this chapter, we evaluate judicial review in general terms from a broad democracy-against-domination framework, but one more thorough, systematic, and comparative than Shapiro, Pettit, and other previous theorists working in this tradition have introduced. Both a key distorting effect of the "countermajoritarian difficulty" framework and a more promising way forward are identified in Barry Friedman's history of the importance of the idea of the countermajoritarian difficulty in legal scholarship:

> On the other hand, there is an interesting question of political theory concerning how judicial review fits into the fabric of majoritarian democracy, but . . . this is not what most constitutional theorists address either. The theorist truly devoted to problems of democratic theory would want to examine each and every institution of democratic governance on this basis, from the least representative—such as the Federal Reserve Board, or independent administrative agencies, or the Senate for that matter—to the seemingly most representative, such as the House of Representatives. Constitutional theorists rarely address these institutions or devote any sustained attention to the real questions of political theory they present, once again

demonstrating that academics are not focused on an enduring problem of political theory. Rather, the academic tradition examined here is court-obsessed.[1]

While the potential research agenda laid out by Friedman is, of course, beyond our scope here, the key point is important: evaluations of the democratic legitimacy of judicial review are meaningful only in the proper *comparative* institutional context. All liberal democracies diffuse power among numerous institutions and scores of actors, and (because all of these institutions have some measure of autonomy from public control and none of these institutions operate without constraint) these institutions in practice cannot easily be sorted into "majoritarian" and "countermajoritarian" categories. The important question about judicial review for democratic theorists is not whether it is "countermajoritarian" and therefore inherently "anti-democratic."

A more empirically minded approach ensures that easy answers to this question are not likely to emerge, and indeed makes clear that there cannot be any single answer. Judicial review functions differently both within individual polities and between polities. The judicial power to nullify acts of elected branches cannot be assumed to have the same democratic effects operating within a highly centralized Westminster system that it has in a decentralized, veto point-laden Madisonian system. Nor will judges applying an 18th-century constitutional text within 19th-century constitutional norms have the same political effects as judges applying 20th-century texts within 21st-century constitutional norms. Of course, this is true of other veto points in democratic systems as well—their function within the overall democratic system varies substantially, depending on numerous features of that system's institutional structure, not to mention the particular democratic (and non-democratic) norms in circulation.

In other words, the project of definitively determining the democratic status of a particular veto point in the abstract is doomed to fail, but asserting that nothing can be said about the democratic properties of a particular veto point without access to all the particulars of a given context is unsatisfying as well. Therefore, we adopt a middle-ground strategy here—we will consider the veto point of judicial review in an explicitly comparative context. More specifically, we will examine how a democracy-against-domination approach might evaluate courts as veto points, compared to others. Is judicial review more or less likely to reduce domination than other veto points? First, however, we will establish and demonstrate the shortcomings of the framing of the judicial review and democracy *problematique* in contemporary democratic theory, among both judicial review's defenders (5.2) and critics (5.3). A number of prominent critics of judicial review have couched their criticisms in the flawed terms of the countermajoritarian difficulty, and their critiques fail insofar as their criticisms of judicial review are logically applicable to other common institutional features of democracy whose legitimacy is not only not questioned, but assumed to be central to the affirmative alternative offered to judicial review. We then turn, in 5.4, to a

**132** Part II

consideration of how judicial review might be expected to differ from other veto points. We identify five criteria on which the democratic value of veto points might be measured, and briefly consider, in 5.5, the relative likely value of judicial review on these grounds, before turning to some case studies (5.6, 5.7, 5.8) to illustrate our position. Judicial review appears comparatively strong compared to other common veto points in contemporary democratic systems, although many concerns remain.

## 5.2 Judicial Review in Contemporary Democratic Theory I: The Libertarian Defense of Judicial Review

Schumpeterian minimalists[2] and "democratic irrationalists"[3] such as William Riker,[4] following in the wake of the work of Kenneth Arrow,[5] have both taken the position that judicial review, while essentially undemocratic, may nonetheless be normatively desirable precisely because of its undemocratic nature. This is because for these theorists, democracy is only normatively desirable in a highly limited and specific way. For Riker, attempted legislative action on behalf of the public good or general will is highly undesirable because majority preferences are inherently unknowable and irrational.[6] While Bickel and his followers tend to valorize democratic majorities, Riker and his adherents hold that both electoral and legislative majorities are arbitrary and easily manipulated, which creates an easy solution to the "countermajoritarian" difficulty. Riker suggests that the protection of an array of classical liberal rights[7] is desirable and helps preserve their conception of the normative point of electoral democracy, which is simply the random removal of elected officials. Majoritarian elections are important, but in a minimalist sense; it is merely important that elected officials who are egregious violators of liberty may be removed from office through electoral means: "Riker . . . maintains that the mere fact that there will be elections, no matter whether they must fail in aggregating the preferences of those in the majority, suffices to impede self-serving behavior on the part of elected officials."[8] Przeworski largely agrees (while remaining far more agnostic about preference aggregation or general will fulfillment than Riker), and adds an element of individual restraint as well. For Riker, Przeworski, and other scholars working in the wake of Arrow, the normative point of democracy is quite limited and decidedly Hobbesian: "it allows us to change governments peacefully."[9] This is doubly valuable—peace is valuable in and of itself, and the changing of governments is valuable because "the very possibility that governments may change can result in peaceful regulation of conflicts."[10] On this logic, the order-maintaining and violence-avoiding value of democracy is evident at two moments—first, at the moment of peaceful transition of power, and second, at the moment of the ordinary day-to-day political conflict, when the losers of that conflict comply with the undesirable policies of those currently in power because they hold out hope that one day, through a fair election and the peaceful transition of power, they will gain the political power necessary to change the objectionable policy.

For those who approach democracy in this manner, judicial review is at worst normatively neutral and irrelevant to a discussion of democracy, as it bears no direct relationship to democracy's normative point. At best, judicial review can be substantively valuable. For Riker in particular, judicial review is valuable as it potentially restrains "populist" electoral outcomes in favor of Riker's "liberal" view of the value of electoral institutions. In later writings, Riker demonstrates a strong libertarian streak and makes it clear he prefers markets and not elections to govern economic life.[11] From this perspective, the predatory majoritarianism of the mass-driven legislature requires judicial checks to maintain liberalism (in Riker's sense of the term) and avoid "populism."[12]

There are a number of empirical and logical inconsistencies in his democratic theory.[13] For example, Riker's theory that the random removal of officials will constrain them is transparently incoherent—as Mackie points out, if one may be punished regardless of whether or not they actually break the law, there is no added incentive to behave.[14] For democratic minimalists and irrationalists, the minimal interpretation of democracy's value is incumbent on a highly pessimistic account of the possibility of democratic action. Their conclusions are not normatively justified beyond this purported realism, which, as Mackie has thoroughly demonstrated, has not been effectively substantiated on empirical grounds.[15] More importantly for our purposes, Riker's "liberal" interpretation of the limits of democracy's desirability necessarily and substantially ignores a great deal of potential and actual domination. On such a conception, democracy is meant "to control officials, *and nothing more.*"[16] This may have the effect of limiting some forms of domination over some segments of the population (perhaps even a majority). However, it is unlikely to disrupt *dominium* (domination by private actors) at all and is likely to leave *imperium* (domination by state actors) intact. Riker's limited understanding of democracy's value means that limiting the power of legislatures to intervene in society is perfectly acceptable. One of the key insights we take from the democracy-against-domination school of democratic thought is that domination comes from many sources, and an effective theory of democracy will take these multiple forms and sources of domination into account. From a democracy-against-domination perspective, the Rikerian justification for judicial review is exactly wrong,[17] but from a more general perspective, Riker's democratic theory is no less problematic. He fails to offer a justification for why democracy's value should be understood in minimalist terms, and he fails to theorize judicial review's relationship to democracy in terms of other prominent veto points in democratic systems.

It should be noted that not all libertarian democratic theories rely on assumptions that democratic politics are inherently irrational. Some justifications for expansive judicial review of economic regulations, such as those made by Randy Barnett[18] and David Bernstein,[19] cast their arguments in explicitly anti-domination

**134** Part II

terms. There is a strong potential overlap between the two forms of libertarian justifications for expansive judicial review—Richard Epstein, for example, argues that most of the 20th-century regulatory state should be held unconstitutional by the courts on the grounds of both constitutional first principles and public choice assumptions of democratic irrationality.[20] But the two arguments are not identical, and more modest libertarian arguments have some resonance with an anti-domination approach. Bernstein, for example, defends Gilded Age liberty of contract jurisprudence because "by providing more room for civil society and markets and restricting coercive regulation," *Lochner* and similar decisions "were likely a net positive from the standpoint of their practical effects."[21] It is possible that a democracy-against-domination approach should consider that some judicial supervision of economic regulation might in some cases reduce domination. However, even when faulty assumptions about democratic irrationality are jettisoned, the other main problem with Riker-like public choice arguments remains: insufficient concern for and attention to the threat unchecked *dominium* poses for democracy.

## 5.3 Judicial Review in Contemporary Democratic Theory II: The Populist Critiques of Judicial Review

Jeremy Waldron has pioneered an approach to democratic theory that is broadly consistent with the "countermajoritarian difficulty" hypothesis. His recent work contains both a sustained defense of the democratic content of legislative processes and outcomes, as well as a sustained critique of judicial review on both countermajoritarian and consequentialist grounds. Waldron's appreciation for the "majority-procedure" feature of legislative action is based on what he takes to be the normative point of democracy—which is to give equal respect to persons under conditions of persistent disagreement.[22] While Waldron concedes that equal respect doesn't logically or necessarily require majority-procedure, he does suggest that such a procedure is warranted given that "the problems we face pose themselves urgently for us *in the circumstances of politics*, and in particular in the circumstance of disagreement about what would be just, a moral or at any rate an appropriate solution."[23] He is skeptical that any substantive requirement of political equality can be removed from the procedural requirements of majority rule, as even if political equality is a widely shared goal, disagreement will quickly reemerge when we try to determine the substantive meaning of political equality.

What does this all mean for judicial review? It begins at a democratic disadvantage for Waldron because courts do not, like legislatures, "internalize those disagreements [about social justice in society] by building them into the institutional structure of our assembly (with arrangements like government benches and opposition benches, majority and minority parties, debates, rules of order, whips, and roll-calls), indeed by making them part of our law-making."[24] But here Waldron incorporates some potentially countermajoritarian features of legislatures into his democratic theory by suggesting that they represent the importation of the specific nature of a particular society's disagreements about social justice.[25] The crux of his critique of judicial review is that the liberal fears commonly associated with majority rule without judicial review—specifically, fears about a Madisonian "tyranny of the majority"—are not unique to legislative supremacy. A form of tyranny is possible regardless of the details of the final moment in decision-making.[26] Therefore, legislative supremacy is superior to a system of constitutional judicial review for two reasons, one philosophical and one pragmatic. The philosophical reason is that it is the decision-rule most clearly consistent with equal respect.[27] The pragmatic reason is that Waldron suspects that judicial review will do no better at protecting the rights of minorities than legislative supremacy.[28]

The latter claim is, of course, highly contingent. Waldron correctly and appropriately notes many moments in American constitutional history when the Supreme Court has notably failed to protect minority rights. We agree with Waldron that judicial review isn't inherently *necessary* for liberal democracy,[29] nor is it a universally reliable and effective protector of vulnerable and unpopular minorities. Furthermore, we agree that judicial review would be an ineffective barrier against emergent tyranny in many if not most cases.[30] But contingent empirical examples cut both ways. The structure and rules of legislatures cannot be counted on to efficiently and effectively translate majority political preferences into legislative outcomes, and courts may at times do a better job of doing exactly that. Barring a more systematic approach to empirical matters, the empirical/consequentialist element of this dispute cannot be resolved in a satisfying manner.

With respect to Waldron's more philosophical account of the normative desirability of legislative supremacy, we turn again to the relationship between the normative point of democracy and its procedural manifestation. Waldron contends that the normative point of democracy is equal respect. But as Christopher Eisgruber notes, "majority rule" is but one possible interpretation of the procedural manifestation of "equal respect."[31] Furthermore, some of the reasons Waldron gives for preferring majoritarian decision-making (in particular, May's theorem) do not appear to justify ceding power to *representative* institutions.[32] The core problem here is that Waldron conflates ordinary legislative procedure and majoritarian decision-making.[33] Waldron asserts that "the people are entitled to govern themselves by their own judgments,"[34] an entitlement that is extrapolated from the core right to political participation, which is inexorably linked to our reliance on our own judgments, be they primary or secondary. Political participation, according to Waldron, occupies a special ontological status among existing recognized human rights due not to any normative priority but because "participation is a right whose exercise seems peculiarly appropriate in situations where reasonable rights-bearers disagree about what rights they have."[35] But here

**136** Part II

the epistemic move from "the people" to legislative bodies and legislative supremacy in particular is made far too easily. For precisely the reasons Waldron wants to embrace majority rule, we must question fully conflating majority rule with democracy. Unsurprisingly, Waldron fails to make the case that majority rule is neutral, and later in the book, he backs off this claim altogether.[36] Here, Waldron's insistence on taking disagreement seriously manages to undermine its own conclusions—one can easily imagine reasonable grounds for disagreement regarding which dispersal of political powers best promotes equal respect for citizens.

Waldron does not fully consider how judicial review functions within contemporary democracies, and in so doing, both overestimates the autonomy of courts and underestimates the many ways in which the other branches are able to diffuse democratic responsibility. It is not clear why judicial review, more so than the many counter- or non-majoritarian features of the modern regulatory state, requires special justification. Waldron assumes that liberal democracies include "safeguards" such as "bicameralism, robust committee scrutiny, and multiple levels of consideration, debate and voting."[37] All of these features—in addition to other common features of modern democratic states, such as independent agencies in charge of monetary policy—frustrate majority will and dilute accountability. (In the American political system, for example, the committee system and the structure and rules of the U.S. Senate were much more important to frustrating attempts to reform Jim Crow in the United States than the Supreme Court, and indeed are what required the Supreme Court to act first.)[38] Another example of the way in which his assumptions about relations between courts and legislatures is insufficiently complex can be seen in his discussion of Canada's "notwithstanding clause," which allows federal and provincial legislatures to override judicial review.[39] Waldron correctly points out that "[in] practice, however, the notwithstanding clause is rarely invoked," and for that reason considers Canada's regime of judicial review a form of "strong" review, like the U.S., for the purposes of his argument.[40] The fact that legislatures who could override substantive constitutional rulings with a simple majority in a centralized parliamentary system virtually never do so raises serious questions about Waldron's assumptions that judicial review operates in a presumptively countermajoritarian and "undemocratic" fashion. The legislature must, according to Waldron, "misrepresent its position on rights" to use the notwithstanding clause, and is impaired because "the legislature is always somewhat at the mercy of the courts' public declarations about the meaning of the society's Bill or Charter of Rights."[41] But this is an empirical claim, and a strange one for someone with Waldron's belief in the democratic legitimacy of legislatures to assume, unquestioningly, to be accurate. Why would the demos automatically side with an unelected court over an elected legislature in a conflict over the nature of rights? The fact that Canadian legislators disdain the use of powerful weapons to oppose the exercise of judicial review (as do American legislators, who rarely use the powerful tools given to them in Article III—including jurisdiction-stripping and court packing) powerfully suggests that judicial review is both more normatively legitimate and more consistent with the general preferences of elected legislators than Waldron's assumptions imply.[42] While the possibility that judicial review allows legislators to diffuse responsibility for difficult policy choices presents problems for democratic legitimacy, these problems are indistinguishable from the problems created by other veto points (such as bicameralism and legislative committees) that Waldron accepts as part of a healthy legislative democratic system.

To conclude, Waldron fails to properly evaluate judicial review as one of many veto points in a democratic system. This error is a common one, dating back at least to Alexander Bickel's influential formulation of judicial review as a "deviant" institution in American politics over fifty years ago.[43] But legislative majorities may be thwarted at various points in the process, ranging from formal to informal.[44] Waldron, when arguing against judicial review on behalf of "majority decision," implies that veto points are never justifiable.[45] However, when arguing on behalf of the "ordinary legislative procedure," the various veto points embedded in both that procedure (as well as the enactment of legislative outcomes) are not directly discussed but seem to be assumed.[46]

Waldron's core error—his failure to evaluate judicial review in an institutional comparative context—is replicated by many other recent democratic critics of judicial review. Richard Bellamy's republican case for political rather than legal constitutionalism contains an even stronger version of Waldron's critique of judicial review, relying on a similar argument from the fact of disagreement as a central feature of the circumstances of politics.[47] Throughout, he distinguishes between two kinds of decision-making procedures: democratic and legal. The former is associated with majoritarianism; the latter, with countermajoritarianism. As the latter procedures elevate the views of some voters to a higher status than others, they are not consistent with the value of political equality, and open the door for potential domination. The potential for veto points associated with legislative processes are not entirely ignored by Bellamy, but are downplayed relative to judicial veto points in large part because they are closer to the act of voting, which contains the requirements for a non-dominating procedure: "Giving each and every citizen one (and only one) vote in a general election offers a rough and ready and easy to verify form of ensuring all citizens views *carry the same weight* in collective decision-making."[48]

This approach makes the same fundamental error as Waldron's: a number of veto points, particularly those found in the organization of the legislature, suggest the democratic side of political decision-making fails to live up to the standard suggested here. Beyond that, even at the moment of a democratic election, the standard of equality suggested here is rarely met. Bellamy correctly takes some of judicial review's defenders to task for contrasting idealized exercises of judicial review with the messy reality of everyday politics. Here he is guilty of a parallel

**138** Part II

problem, as he idealizes elections. Virtually all contemporary democracies feature some degree of malapportionment in one or more legislative bodies, which is persistent and generally favors some categories of voters (often rural voters) over others.[49] So even at the procedural level, democratic elections as practiced don't live up the standard Bellamy holds out for them, even before we consider the legislative veto points that will frustrate strong political equality after the election. There is no configuration of democratic politics that fully meets the procedural demands of political equality.

Another important critique of judicial review has been developed by constitutional populists such as Larry Kramer[50] and Mark Tushnet.[51] Kramer's popular constitutionalism can be placed in the context of progressive scholars using the tools of originalism to challenge the conclusions of conservative originalists.[52] Kramer attempts to demonstrate with voluminous historical data that as generally understood at the time of the framing, constitutional limits on the government were enforced through popular will, not by the courts. Certain limited forms of judicial review can be consistent with this understanding, but contemporary judicial supremacy is not. Ultimately, we think that cases both for and against judicial review must rest on pragmatic and consequentialist grounds rather than historical ones, and like Waldron, Kramer does not explain why judicial review (as opposed to other countermajoritarian veto points intended to impose limits on the state) is uniquely problematic. However, his point that "the people themselves" cannot be presumed to be incompetent to interpret the Constitution is an important one that should inform any evaluation of judicial review.

Tushnet's populist case against judicial review—even the relatively modest forms Kramer finds acceptable—is of significant potential interest in the context of comparing judicial review to other veto points. Tushnet advocates a populist constitutionalism that privileges the "thin Constitution" (most notably, the broad abstractions of the preamble and the Declaration of Independence) over the "thick Constitution" (the detailed distribution of power and establishment of procedures that dominates the first three Articles of the Constitution).[53] For example, hypothetically considering Bill Clinton's potential appointment of the Senate Majority Leader to the Supreme Court, Tushnet argues that the thin Constitution (whose principle popular sovereignty includes the right of the popularly elected president and Senate to fill Supreme Court vacancies) should trump the thick Constitution's Emoluments Clause (under which a Mitchell appointment would probably have been illegal).[54] Tushnet's version of populist constitutionalism would seem to imply serious democratic problems with *any* veto points that interfere with popular sovereignty, as veto points are quintessentially "thick constitutional" devices. Given his focus on judicial review, however, Tushnet does not pursue a comparative analysis of thick constitutional veto points.

One recent critic of judicial review, importantly, does not treat it as a uniquely problematic or deviant institution. In an important recent book, Melissa

Schwartzberg considers (with particular attention to the process of constitutional amendment but general democratic decision-making as well) the status of different veto points and procedural hurdles in both historical and analytic terms.[55] She argues that veto points and procedural hurdles can be grouped into two categories: those that straightforwardly and clearly lead to supermajority rules, and create the opportunity for minority veto power, and those that don't appear to be in conflict with legislative majoritarianism. The latter, she argues, don't violate majoritarian rule but create "complex majoritarianism."[56] Examples of rules that might comprise complex majoritarianism include popular referendums, requiring a second affirmative vote following the next election, and deliberative citizen assemblies of the sort used in British Columbia's electoral reforms.[57] Schwartzberg argues that a democratic system could plausibly be designed in such a way that the veto points of complex majoritarianism could replace most or perhaps even all supermajoritarian veto points, including judicial review, accomplishing whatever legitimate aims such rules might have with significantly fewer democratic costs. We have few quarrels with this argument, and indeed find the constitutional vision she offers potentially attractive under the right conditions. Our differences with Schwartzberg primarily revolve around the level of analysis: we wish to consider the democratic value of different veto points in the context of currently existing democratic institutions, which, without exception, contain countermajoritarian veto points, whereas Schwartzberg's approach is more broadly systemic. In embracing the assumption that countermajoritarian veto points appear to be inevitable under the current conditions for democratic governance, we are not making a claim that they are conceptually or normatively necessary for democracy in a greater sense. Insofar as countermajoritarian veto points remain common, an analysis of their comparative value is useful even if there exists a strong independent case for complex majoritarianism.

While we have focused on judicial review's critics here, we wish to briefly comment on a common strategy for defending judicial review that we do not pursue, and explain why. The most common form of democratic defense of judicial review takes the form of what Peter Railton calls a "bulwark theory" of judicial review.[58] Precisely what judicial review is promoted to provide a bulwark against varies considerably, but the structure of such theories remains the same: majoritarian democracy is associated with a threat, and judicial review empowers judges to protect against that danger. The harm prevented by avoiding this danger outweighs whatever harm (if any) is done to democratic procedure by the exercise of a judicial veto point. Perhaps the most common form of bulwark theory concerns the possibility of democratically authorized rights violations against unpopular minorities or individuals.[59] Other bulwark theories focus on the protection of one's rights in the democratic process,[60] the proper boundaries of public reason for political discourse,[61] and the proper balance between honoring democratic procedures and ensuring democratic outcomes.[62]

**140** Part II

The differences between bulwark theories are less important to us than their similar structure. As a justification for granting a specific institutionalized form of political power, they fall short. In our assessment of bulwark defenses of judicial review, we find ourselves in agreement with judicial review's critics on one narrow point: insofar as judicial review functions as a defense of minorities against majorities, it will often be the case that the minorities whose interests are defended will be those whose interests are already well-represented.[63] This isn't, however, in itself a reason to reject judicial review, but rather a reason to appreciate the dangers and flaws we must recognize in any institutional arrangement. Institutions cannot be justified solely by an account of how the persons who occupy them ought to ideally wield power. Any non-ideal defense of judicial review must start with the likely effects of that institutionalization of power, recognizing that it will be occupied by flawed and untrustworthy characters. Judicial review, like all veto points, and indeed all institutional democratic arrangements, is likely to be exploited for undemocratic and/or illiberal purposes. No veto point or institutional arrangement can avoid this possibility, yet all of them could avoid such outcomes if we could stipulate ideal behavior on the part of the relevant actors. Bulwark theories are better understood as a form of judicial ethics than a justification of judicial review as a power, and so we must look elsewhere for an institutional, non-ideal normative defense of judicial review.

## 5.4 Veto Points and Democratic Theory

What would a consideration of judicial review's democratic status look like if we treated it as one possible veto point among many, rather than a uniquely deviant institution? This is the question to which we now turn. The literature on veto points in political systems has largely emerged from social and public choice theory and not normative democratic or legal theory.[64] Before we can begin to consider judicial review's democratic status, we must first consider what a democratic approach to veto points in general might look like. For reasons elaborated in the previous section, we will not consider the question of whether veto points are ever democratically legitimate. We assume that some veto points are inevitable, even in the most majoritarian of democratic political systems, due largely to the size, scope, and complexity of modern politics, but that the quality and quantity of veto points in such systems varies considerably. The position that no veto points are ever justifiable could be entertained only by an abstract ideal theory. It simply is not useful in sorting out the relative democratic legitimacy of various veto points in modern democratic governance, or making sense of the relative democratic virtues of institutional arrangements in contemporary democratic systems. We skip the step of justifying veto points in general, and move on to a crucial yet neglected task in contemporary democratic theory: comparative veto point assessment.

Judicial Review as Just Another Veto Point **141**

So what might render a veto point more or less democratic? How one answers this question will turn on the question of what one holds to be the normative point of democracy. We align our analysis here with the conception of democracy-against-domination articulated and defended in the previous chapter. This position holds that preventing domination by government officials through the threat of removal via election is a normatively valuable feature of democracy. But democracy-against-domination must also consider other sources of potential domination. Domination is not solely the purview of the state, as private domination in various forms remains a routine feature of modern life even in liberal societies. Democracy-against-domination provides a distinctively valuable way of evaluating state action and institutions. Domination captures the fundamental danger of state power (that it can easily come to dominate the citizenry) and the importance of a powerful state, with the capacity to construct and enact laws sufficient to prevent citizenry from dominating each other. A democracy-against-domination theory of the state thus becomes a balancing act—the state must be powerful enough to effectively thwart *dominium* when possible, but not so powerful that it evades the control of its citizens and risks slipping into *imperium*.

In applying this democracy-against-domination theory to veto points generally as a way of analyzing judicial review specifically, we are following Michael Saward's timely suggestion to move democratic theory away from an all-consuming focus on identifying and defending democratic principles and their precise application, and toward a greater focus on identifying democratic devices that have the potential to activate and advance democratic principles.[65] A veto point becomes a potential democratic device when it makes a contribution to either *dominium* prevention or *imperium* prevention, without heightening the danger of the other to an equal or greater degree. This democratic theory presents a clear picture of what we should want from democratic institutional arrangements above and beyond merely being representative or majoritarian.

How can democracy-against-domination generate heuristics for comparative veto point evaluation? Pettit argues that democracy requires two dimensions: authorial and editorial. The overall goal of both is to match policy with the common good, which should guide non-dominating governance.[66] The authorial dimension of democratic politics is idea generation, which runs the risk of what Pettit calls "false positives"—ill-advised ideas that do not serve the public good or reduce domination.[67] The editorial dimension of democracy, when functioning properly, eliminates these false positives through "scrutinize-and-disallow" mechanisms. Pettit's conception of democracy is appealing, although it exaggerates the separation between these two parts of the democratic process. To the extent that veto points serve this editorial democratic function, they occur at many different stages of the process, sometimes early in the authorial stage. To the extent that democratic politics can be understood in terms of these two dimensions, they cannot be sorted out as cleanly and clearly as he suggests.[68]

**142**   Part II

Nevertheless, Pettit's image of the editorial function is a good way to think of what we can hope veto points in democratic systems might, in the best case, provide. At their worst, veto points thwart democratic majorities through the capricious whims or craven self-interest of powerful veto players (and no veto point is immune from potentially being used for this purpose). If we assume that veto points are inevitable, we should focus not on how to prevent them but on how to evaluate, shape, and reform them to serve democratic goals as well as possible. What kind of veto points might accomplish this goal? In considering this, we must construct a framework for evaluating veto points consistent with our conception of democratic values. What criteria might be implied by a democracy-against-domination approach? This section will suggest five criteria for evaluating democratic veto points. This list is, needless to say, not exhaustive, and does not deny the existence of additional important criteria unrelated to the normative ends of democracy. (The complexity of the modern state, for example, makes committee systems where legislators can acquire and deploy at least some expertise over some areas of policy inevitable, whether or not committee systems tend to reduce domination.) Nonetheless, these categories can provide a useful guide to considering the democratic impact of various veto points.

## Criteria for Evaluating the Democratic Value of Veto Points

First, *requirements that veto players and their vetoes are public and justified to a public audience increase their legitimacy.* Two closely related and central features of functional democratic systems are accountability and transparency. These are important values in both democracy's majoritarian and non-majoritarian procedures. This is why, for example, most legislative bodies have rules that permit a minority of members to force a public, recorded vote count (in the case of the United States, this is one of the few procedural rules written into the U.S. Constitution: the "journal clause" of Article 1, sec. 5 empowers a one-fifth minority to demand a publicly recorded vote).[69] If the exercise of vetoes is effectively hidden from the public, some of the goals of democracy are less likely to be well-served.[70] The use of veto points to promote domination, rather than prevent it, are less likely to be effectively hidden from the citizenry, increasing their capacity to respond negatively to such efforts. If we are to authorize and allow a veto power, we should also demand justification and accountability from that exercise. This is consistent with the notion that majoritarianism is the default guiding principle of democratic decision-making, and deviations from it should be done in a way that recognizes that status. The exercisers of veto point power will inevitably have wide discretion over their use, but that discretion should not be a cover to avoid the demand for public justification. A veto player should not be able to avoid criticism and public responsibility for an unpopular or controversial exercise of veto power. This is especially important given the recurrent, repetitious nature of many political conflicts and debates. If the justification for the exercise of a veto is poor, there are numerous ways in which that veto player might conceivably be removed, or engaged to behave differently in a future situation. Under this criterion, the modern "stealth filibuster" (in which single senators can privately put "holds" on legislation or supermajority requirements are simply assumed) in the United States Senate would be more problematic than filibusters that at least require identifiable legislators or groups of legislators to delay the passage of legislation with majority support.[71]

Second, *veto points should, to the extent it is reasonably possible to do so, be separated from the direct, personal private interests of veto players.*[72] The goal of avoiding domination is not well-served when public institutions are easily subverted to private ends. This criterion should not be construed too broadly; we are not suggesting that veto players (or any democratic actors) should be prohibited from legitimate political action on behalf of any cause where there might be an overlapping interest or goal—indeed, to do so might be consistent with a particularly high-minded version of deliberative democracy, but would not at all be consistent with democracy-against-domination. This criterion is meant narrowly and regards direct private gain accruing to the individual veto player or her associates and family, and not to a political or social movement or demographic group to which she might belong (the limitations on the latter cases are better covered by the previous criteria as well as criteria five, following). When such a separation is not possible, those private interests should be disclosed and justified. This is a particularly difficult goal when considering the veto points that exist on legislative committees, as legislators are likely to gain and maintain access to veto points through committee membership on issues of particular interest to them. Nevertheless, limiting and exposing this connection is crucial to the separation of public and private interest. Limiting the extent to which narrow, private interests can hijack public processes is necessary for preventing democratic processes from becoming complicit in private domination. Whatever democratic benefits veto points might provide, they are also opportunities for private interests to assert themselves in the democratic process. To the extent that this can be lessened or prevented, it should.

Third, *veto points should function not only to disallow "false positives" but provide a forum for weighing priorities in a context of limited resources.* Here the most important veto points in question are the committees in legislative bodies that control the budget, and the federal agencies that inevitably wield considerable power of which laws to commit resources to enforcing. The key fact we wish to emphasize with this point is that priority-setting is a form of veto politics. A good deal of legislation is irrelevant without authorized funding (authorized by budget legislation) and a will to enforce (by federal agencies and local governments). On the one hand, this is a banal fact of political life. Nevertheless, the organization of authority to exercise these powers can be done in more or less democratic

**144** Part II

ways. Domination exists to various degrees throughout the political, economic, and social realm and democracy-against-domination is not a perfectionist political theory. Weighting the importance of political attention based on degree and scope of domination is central to this approach to democracy, and to the extent that veto points can be directed toward this fundamental challenge of politics, they should.

Fourth, *veto points should facilitate public contestation of government decision and government action.* Too often, the goal of public participation and influence is understood as valuable only at the level of idea generation. But, as Scheppele has argued, democracy takes place not merely during elections but between them as well.[73] Veto points can be an avenue for public participation and input, especially in cases where ordinary legislative action has failed to reflect the priorities, needs, and will of the public for various reasons. More veto points can, among other things, mean more agenda-setting loci that lessen the chances of particular groups being shut out of the process.[74] This is particularly necessary from a democracy-against-domination standpoint because the democracy-against-domination theory recognizes the extent to which domination can arise in unintentional and unexpected ways: in Shapiro's terms, just hierarchies have an unfortunate tendency to atrophy into relationships of domination.[75] To the extent that democratic veto points can create avenues for effective contestation for minority populations subject to domination, whether that domination is due to malicious disregard in a part of the political process, indifference, or unintended consequence, they should.[76]

And fifth, *veto points are most valuable when they empower underrepresented minorities as opposed to minorities already well- or overrepresented within the political system.* While any democratic system will contain some countermajoritarian aspects, both majority rule and the desirability of responsibility and accountability mean that redundancy among multiple veto points is, all things being equal, problematic. If veto points reliably overrepresent interests who already enjoy strong representation, their potential and actual democratic value is lessened considerably, as they become more likely to serve as a tool of domination than provide protection against it. If an increase in the diffusion of power within state institutions does not represent a more diffuse array of social forces, such veto points are likely to reinforce patterns of social domination rather than alleviating them. Evidently, this is a difficult standard: virtually any repository of institutional power in a democratic political system will be in danger of overrepresenting powerful interests; power, after all, is useful for infiltrating, influencing, and capturing institutions. The comparative effects of veto points in this respect are especially important in determining their democratic value. If a particular veto point fails to substantially broaden representation and involvement in political decision-making, Waldron's normative vision becomes much more attractive.

Two final notes before we turn to evaluation of judicial review on the prior criteria. First, we do not give much consideration to different models of judicial review: strong vs. weak, review of legislative vs. executive action, standing rules for bringing a case to the court, and so on. In the real world, there is a great deal of variation in the organization of judicial review in different democratic systems, and this very likely matters when evaluating its democratic value.[77] This issue is further complicated by context: judicial review might also vary considerably in its democratic value depending on the institutional context in which it is embedded, as well as the political, legal, and cultural environment in which it is found. The best tools against domination are likely to vary considerably, depending on the nature of the most prominent local threats to non-domination. Strong conclusions about judicial review's democratic value in a particular democratic system are likely to be contingent both on the organization of the court and its powers and the larger institutional context in which it is embedded. The criteria here are the beginning, not the end, of the evaluation of judicial review as embedded in different political systems.

Second, we focus on the comparative evaluation of veto points largely in isolation. However, it is important to consider the cumulative effect of veto points in political systems. How might considering veto points together rather than in isolation matter? On the one hand, whatever the merits of judicial review or any other veto point, they may diminish should a political system become overloaded with excessive veto points. This issue has been a point of disagreement among democracy-against-domination theorists. Ian Shapiro has taken Pettit to task for embracing an "exceedingly long list" of veto points, making him appear "entirely innocent of the literature on veto points . . . which has made it clear that, as veto players become stronger and veto points multiply, so does protection of the status quo and those who have the resources to wait out opponents"[78] and argued that excessive institutional complexity "works to the disproportionate advantage of powerful interests by fostering opacity."[79] On the other hand, veto points may operate together to produce an effect that is more than the sum of their parts. An optimistic take on the democratic effects of the veto point-laden American political system can be found in the recent work of Adrian Vermuele, in which he urges readers to consider that its various countermajoritarian features produce "emergent democracy" via "offsetting failures of democracy" and the democratic distribution of undemocratic powers.[80]

Both Shapiro's and Vermuele's warnings about interactive effects are worth keeping in mind as we evaluate veto points in isolation. The political science literature on veto points, however, suggests that Shapiro's pessimism is perhaps more plausible than Vermuele's optimism. While the various veto points in the American political system are distributed across different actors and interests, they are not distributed via a particularly democratic pattern. The sheer volume of veto points has empowered economic elites to effectively resist changes to the laws that would threaten their interests or curb their power, leading to what Hacker and Pierson call legislative "drift."[81] Such a phenomenon describes elites accommodating themselves more and more to the status quo, while thwarting

**146** Part II

efforts to change the regulatory environment in ways that better check their power. In addition to this substantive worry, recent research suggests political systems with excessive veto points erode democratic cultural values as well, as public opinion research shows that countries with veto point-laden systems tend to have a much higher degree of authoritarian attitudes about politics.[82] So even if certain veto points have relative democratic value, their cumulative effect may well erode that value if they are too numerous.

## 5.5  Evaluating Judicial Review

While an effort to identify and rank all veto points and their democratic valence is well beyond the scope of this chapter, we can at least offer a preliminary assessment of judicial review by these standards, in comparison to some other important veto points. On the first criteria, judicial review would seem to stand up reasonably well. Unlike a legislator quietly killing a bill in committee, or placing a "hold" on legislation, or a bureaucrat quietly issuing a directive to "de-prioritize" the enforcement of a particular law, Supreme Court decisions are overtly and formally public, and subject to at least a modicum of popular scrutiny and debate. Even in comparison to other particularly public veto points, such as the presidential veto, the need to offer justification is formalized through legal decisions. This is not to suggest that judicial review perfectly meets these criteria, however. For one thing, there is nothing to prevent disingenuous or dishonest justifications.[83] Jeremy Waldron has argued that defenders of judicial review often, and incorrectly, hold up judicial reasoning as fundamentally superior in quality compared to the low standards of public political debate.[84] We agree with Waldron that the quality of judicial reasoning is often overstated; however, the relevant comparison here is not to public reasoning and debate, but to other veto points, many of which contain no public justification requirement at all. The justificatory requirements built into judicial review are still a net positive compared to other veto points on this criterion.[85]

On the second criteria, judicial review as a veto point would seem to have one distinct advantage over veto points invested in legislators. Specifically, the constant need of funding for re-election campaigns, as well as ties to interest groups representing private industries, provide the possibility of private interests influencing the exercise of veto power. Consider, for example, the case of Congressman Billy Tauzin. Upon his retirement from Congress in 2005, he immediately began a new job as a lobbyist for the Pharmaceutical Research and Manufacturers of America. PhRMA outbid another major lobby, The Motion Picture Association of America, paying him an annual salary of approximately 2.5 million dollars. While in Congress, Tauzin had occupied key positions on committees with a direct relevance to the interests of both these lobbies.[86] The relative isolation from the potential private interest contamination is much greater for judges than for legislators. Billy Tauzin may be an extreme (although hardly unique) case of the potential for private interests playing a substantial role in legislative veto points, but he is representative of a common and widespread concern about private and powerful interests and the legislative process. Because judges need not run for re-election and generally do not have significant post-Supreme Court careers, the pathways through which their control of a key veto point could be used to advance private interests are limited compared to members of Congress. This requires two caveats, however. First, there is no necessary link between direct financial gain and private interest. Judges, as Waldron reminds us, are people too. They have group ties, irrational biases, and allegiances to groups both political and personal that could reasonably provide pathways to private influence over their exercise of veto points. Furthermore, with politicians, the threat of private influence is widely understood, and has resulted in a panoply of measures (such as ethics rules and campaign finance laws) to track and limit it. The success of such measures has been decidedly limited, but they are at least attempted. The exercisers of the judicial review veto point are subject to considerably less scrutiny on this front.

The third criteria would seem, at first blush, to have little bearing on the democratic quality of judicial review as a veto point. Constitutional courts are generally not tasked with prioritizing various laws, but with sorting them into three broad categories: constitutionally mandatory, constitutionally optional, and unconstitutional. Moreover, the opportunity costs that might be associated with abandoning a particular path on constitutional grounds are, at least formally, often outside of the purview of courts. But courts may exercise a great deal of discretion in the cases they decide to consider. The array of cases in which they may agree to hear is vast and wide enough that they can be said to have a great deal of discretion in whether to intervene in any particular constitutional controversy. Unlike the decisions they do make, they are under no need to justify the non-use of their veto point. Finally, it is possible that judicial review as a veto point has the potential to provide a forum for considering whether a particular "costly" form of rights protection is in fact fundamental and constitutional. For example, *Brown v. Prata* recently forced the state of California to make choices about the costs of rights protection with respect to rights violations associated with overcrowding of California's prison system.[87] Courts can potentially elevate and identify a claim that a particular constitutional priority has been de-prioritized to the point that a rights violation can be identified, even if they are not in a position to offer a precise remedy to this problem. Previous scholars who emphasize judicial review's deliberative value have demonstrated its potential on this criterion.[88]

The fourth criterion invites contrasts between different systems of organizing and empowering courts to engage in judicial review. An important democratic function of veto points is to provide avenues for contestation beyond and between elections. Judicial review can provide this possibility in a limited set of cases—it is by no means likely to be sufficient to meet the demand for contestatory

**148** Part II

institutional arrangements, but it can play an important part. Some regimes of judicial review (for example, in Hungary and India) allow for direct petition of the constitutional court on behalf of citizens, without first proceeding through a series of lower courts. In the Hungarian case in particular, this has enhanced democratic participation.[89] Nevertheless, despite the high barriers, this remains an avenue for contestation of some forms of domination. So, at a general level, judicial review appears to have the potential to serve as a relatively democratic veto point on this criterion. A number of previous scholars have emphasized judicial review's positive democratic valence on participatory grounds.[90]

The fifth democratic criteria for veto points require they must be comparatively likely to empower generally disempowered minorities. Obviously, judicial review's likelihood to empower underrepresented and disempowered minorities will vary considerably, and it is difficult to reach general conclusions at a high level of abstraction. For Ran Hirschl, the case against judicial review hinges on the fact that it tends to further empower economic elites, who are overrepresented among both judges and those who create and design systems of judicial review.[91] However, in reply to some of his critics,[92] Hirschl concedes that despite the further empowerment of economic elites, "Women, ethnic minorities, gays and lesbians, and indigenous populations are likely to be far better off in the constitutionalization era."[93] Furthermore, Kim Scheppele's research on constitutional courts in Hungary demonstrates that courts can and do intervene on behalf of the economically vulnerable in some cases.[94] It would obviously be a mistake to view judicial review as a tool that reliably empowers disempowered minorities, of course, but there seems to be evidence that it may, at times, serve as a veto point for those who are unlikely to have access to other veto points—particularly those groups who fall into a category comparable to Justice Stone's "discrete and insular minorities." Still, as a contestatory rather than legislative veto point, judicial review appears to have advantages on this point compared to veto points such as the filibuster.

## 5.6 Contingency, Substance, and Procedure: Judicial Review and Democracy-Against-Domination in Practice

In the abstract, there are plausible reasons for believing that judicial review has certain comparative advantages in terms of broadening representation and attenuating domination, at least within the context of contemporary constitutional norms.[95] It is also crucial to remember that these advantages are, at best, comparative; the structure of judicial appointments in most liberal democracies ensures that courts will be far from immune from the domination-reinforcing self-dealing that can affect other political institutions. In addition, although this is a preferred strategy of some sophisticated defenders of the democratic value of judicial review,[96] it is extremely difficult to separate "procedural" and "substantive" judicial review. Even if representation-reinforcement is understood as the primary goal of judicial review, such reinforcement inevitably involves making contestable judgments about what groups have been unfairly unrepresented or excluded.

## 5.7 Abortion: Procedure, Substance, and Domination

Even among scholars sympathetic to the effects of the judicial nullification of abortion statutes, cases such as *Roe v. Wade* are often seen as courts operating (at best) at the farthest reaches of their justifiable authority. John Hart Ely, who developed the "representation-reinforcement" constitutional theory as a defense of substantively controversial Warren Court decisions, pointedly argued that *Roe* could not be defended in a similar fashion.[97] Cass Sunstein, whose theory of minimalism has some important commonalities with Ely's in terms of goals if not doctrinal methodology, has also critiqued the broad scope of the opinion (albeit without arguing that the Texas statute in question should have been upheld).[98] According to this line of critique, while important Warren Court decisions had corrected glaring defects in the democratic processes, most notably but not exclusively related to the oppression and disenfranchisement of African-Americans under Jim Crow, *Roe* simply represented the substitution of the substantive preferences of legislators with the substantive preferences of judges. While such an outcome is not impossible to defend from a democracy-against-domination perspective, it makes it more difficult. However, as we noted in section 2.3, the outcome of *Roe* fits reasonably well with the cases of the Warren era, and can be squared with the need for courts to remedy democratic defects, even as it can be plausibly argued that the court's particular holding did not. An interesting contrast with *Roe* is its Canadian counterpart *R. v. Morgentaler*, which struck down a federal law similar to the Georgia law struck down in *Roe*'s companion case *Doe v. Bolton*. While one member of the *Morgentaler* majority urged a broad substantive due process holding similar to *Roe* (but more rooted in the rights of women than the rights of physicians), the other four members of the majority struck down the legislation on more narrow, procedural grounds. Rather than attempting to resolve the conflict between the statute's deleterious impact on a woman's security of the person and the state's potentially legitimate interest in protecting fetal life, the Court held that the regulations in question were not sufficiently related to the state's legitimate interests in the abstract and too arbitrary and inequitable in their application. While the holding in *Roe* seemed to foreclose future attempts at balancing these interests, *Morgentaler* returned the ball to the legislature's court.

From a democracy-against-domination perspective, then, the Canadian Supreme Court's resolution of the issue was arguably superior, as the Canadian government would be free to react to a genuine social consensus that fetal life merited greater protection while American legislatures would not. As a practical

**150** Part II

matter, however, it is likely that this is a distinction without much of a difference. Not surprisingly, given a requirement that abortion regulations be fairly applied, the Canadian Parliament has not passed new abortion regulation (and indeed, currently, Canada has a substantially more liberal abortion regime that the United States). If the political climate in the United States changed such that draconian abortion restrictions would be fairly enforceable, it is vanishingly unlikely that courts would obstruct legislatures for a significant period of time.

## 5.8 Restrictions on the Franchise and the Courts

If *Roe* represents a case where the Court's resolution was more consistent with a democracy-against-domination approach than might be initially evident, the Court's 2008 decision *Crawford v. Marion County* sends a much more cautionary note. This would seem to be a promising issue for democracy-against-domination theorists; indeed, one legal theorist has argued that it is precisely in the area of election law that judicial review can play an important role in democracy-against-domination theory.[99] The case facts have broad similarities with the one-person-one-vote Warren Court cases that Ely saw as being the *sine qua non* of representation-reinforcement, and for this reason were particularly ripe for judicial intervention. Expanding access to the franchise represents perhaps the most successful intervention of the Warren Court, being enforced much more smoothly than its desegregation, school prayer, or criminal justice landmarks. The Indiana legislature—on a strict party-line vote—passed a draconian voter identification law that, while not affecting a large number of voters, almost exclusively disenfranchised Indiana's most disadvantaged citizens. Whatever the desirability of judicial intervention, however, the Supreme Court declined the invitation, upholding the Indiana law 6–3 (although the plurality opinion did hold out some faint hope that a future challenge after the statute had been applied might be successful).

In suggesting the Court's decision is difficult to defend from a democracy-against-domination perspective, we certainly do not mean to suggest that any voter identification requirement should be found unconstitutional under democracy-against-domination principles; as with abortion, context matters. The state's interest in maintaining fair elections is unquestionably compelling, and to rectify a severe vote fraud problem, some potential disenfranchisement might be defensible. The problem with the specific Indiana statute, however, is that the "vote fraud" problem the statute purported to address was entirely illusory. As the *majority* opinion in the case conceded, "[t]he only kind of voter fraud that SEA 483 addresses is in-person voter impersonation at polling places. The record contains no evidence of any such fraud actually occurring in Indiana at any time in its history." Even more problematically, the state did not place any further ID requirements on absentee balloting, although problems with fraud among these ballots have been a real problem. Particularly given that absentee voters are more likely Republican, concerns that the legislation might have involved self-dealing by the legislative majority rather than a genuine concern with voter fraud must be particularly acute. In addition, in a system in which the state took a more active role in voter registration, voter ID restrictions might have almost no disenfranchisement effect, which would also make the statute more defensible.

The lesson of *Crawford*, however, is that it cannot be assumed that courts will reliably be protectors of dominated social groups even when the rationale for defending their interests is compelling. The courts, being appointed by the governing coalition of the day, are also likely to reflect their interests and priorities. It is probably not a coincidence that the Supreme Court was much more aggressive about protecting access to the ballot when such actions were also in the political interests of the dominant ruling coalition of the time. Even if courts have some comparative advantages in attenuating domination, then, it is also important to remember the ability and willingness of courts to fulfill such a role is likely to be erratic and limited.

## 5.9 Conclusion

We have argued that any democratic theory needs a general comparative theory of democratic veto points before we can meaningfully assess the democratic content of particular veto points like judicial review, and we have attempted a preliminary effort in this regard from the perspective of democracy-against-domination. The line of argument we pursue here makes a neat and simple theoretical resolution to the question of judicial review's democratic status highly unlikely. While this frustrates any effort to bring our analysis to a tidy conclusion, we can safely deduce that it is theoretically and empirically unsound to dismiss judicial review as anti-democratic on anti-majoritarian grounds. Beyond that, we will conclude with a review of what we take to be the most important lessons for democratic theorists in light of this analysis.

First, democratic theorists cannot assess the democratic value of different veto points and institutional arrangements generally as a purely formal matter. We must rely to no small degree on the important work of scholars of institutions and regime politics. While it has begun to unravel, the longstanding consensus view among legal and democratic theorists that judicial review presented a uniquely countermajoritarian difficulty stood for far too long, even as our empirical colleagues painted a very different and far more complicated picture, in which legislatures and judges are as likely to work together as to be at odds, and judicial review rarely strayed much further from majoritarian preferences than legislatures. The real-life consequences of institutional political arrangements are as important as their formal structure, and the former cannot be simply derived from the latter. Perhaps the greatest democratic threat associated with judicial review comes not from unelected judges thwarting legislative majorities,

**152** Part II

but from the diffusion of power and responsibility through legislative deferrals, as Lovell among others have shown.[100] But without attention to historical and institutional empirical scholarship on courts, the nature of the democratic challenge judicial review presents would not have been noticed.

Relatedly, attention to such scholarship gives some reason to doubt the strategy of sorting institutional arrangements and decision-making strategies into two discrete categories: majoritarian and non-majoritarian. Once we recognize that any scheme of representation removes us from straightforward majoritarian decision-making as applied to citizens, two things become clear. First, the majoritarian nature of any particular decision-making strategy must be measured substantively as well as procedurally, as the latter does not directly determine the former. This makes determinative assessments of comparative majoritarianism a bit difficult to make. Second, because democracy has other associated values and demands beyond majoritarianism, it becomes one axis on which the democratic valence of the institutional arrangement can be measured, alongside the others identified here.

Finally, attention to empirical scholarship in a comparative context reveals the difficulty of saying anything too definitive about judicial review's (or other veto points') democratic value in the abstract. In addition to the potentially different values of various forms of review, the way it interacts with the rest of the democratic system may shape its democratic value. For example, the circumstances that surround judicial review's creation may matter: if it is created, as Ran Hirschl argues it was in Israel, New Zealand, and elsewhere, to extend the political influence of the current ruling coalition well into the future after they would have otherwise lost power, its democratic value may not be as great, at least initially.[101] Of course, once an institutional power such as judicial review is established, it can take on a life of its own beyond what its creators intended. The democratic value of judicial review may function differently across political systems and cultures. Scheppele's research on the democratic value of judicial review in Hungary in the 1990's hinges on the contestatory role it played in the absence of a robust contestatory civil society, alongside the weaknesses of elections in holding officials accountable, suggesting the weaknesses and fragility of Hungary's democratic culture made judicial review all the more valuable.[102] The experience of judicial review in different institutional and cultural contexts will be crucial to understanding the circumstances and forms of review most (and least) likely to effectively promote democracy-against-domination.

In the end, despite judicial review's evident limitations and drawbacks, we conclude that it appears to have some modest advantages over other veto points commonly found in contemporary political systems. We are less committed to this conclusion than we are to the approach to applied democratic theory by which we have arrived at it. If further analysis of the effects of judicial review relative to other democratic veto points suggests a net negative democratic value, or if judicial review fails on additional democratic criteria we have not identified

Judicial Review as Just Another Veto Point **153**

here, a re-evaluation of our conclusion would be appropriate. The democracy-against-domination approach focuses our attention on the problem of the dominated, vulnerable, and generally underrepresented members of society. Judicial review will almost certainly fail to provide a consistent and reliable path to successful contestation of dominating practices and structures and full democratic representation. While this is unfortunate, it is not dispositive. A democratic theory that takes power and institutions seriously cannot place its hope in a simple, single institutional fix to the problem of inequitable power relations, as no such "bulwark" can reliably exist. It is only through comparison with other veto points that we can hope to answer the question of judicial review's democratic value.

## Notes

1 Freidman, "The Birth of an Academic Obsession," 158.
2 Schumpeter's minimalist articulation of democracy's value can be found in *Capitalism, Socialism and Democracy* (New York: Harper Perennial Classics, 2008 [1942]), 269–283.
3 We take the term "democratic irrationalists" from Gerry Mackie's outstanding critique of Riker's theory of democracy; see his *Democracy Defended* (Oxford: Oxford University Press, 2003).
4 Riker, *Liberalism versus Populism.*
5 Kenneth Arrow, *Social Choice and Justice: The Collected Papers of Kenneth J. Arrow* (Oxford: Basil Blackwell, 1984). The key relevant argument made by Arrow, which itself followed from Condrocet's "impossibility theorem," is the theoretical possibility of "vote cycling." That is, when more than two voters have preferences that are clearly ranked, independent, and non-transferable, there are always multiple possible outcomes, and hence majority votes cannot be assumed to represent majority preferences.
6 Curiously, as Mackie notes, Riker holds the position that such legislative action is both undesirable and substantively indeterminate and incoherent. See *Democracy Defended.*
7 William Riker and Barry Weingast, "Constitutional Regulation of Legislative Choice: The Political Consequences of Judicial Defense to Legislatures," (Stanford, CA: Hoover Institution Working Paper Series, 1986), argue that judicial review should have a significantly broader scope than in current practice in the United States. According to their theory, not only should the judiciary aggressively enforce civil liberties such as free speech and the right against unreasonable searches and seizures, but should revert to the *Lochner* era's aggressive protection of property rights as well.
8 Cunningham, *Democracy: A Critical Introduction,* 153.
9 Adam Przeworski, "Minimalist Conception of Democracy: A Defense," in Ian Shapiro and Casiano Hacker-Cordon (eds) *Democracy's Value* (New York: Cambridge University Press, 1999), 45. Przeworski's paper is discussed here as an exemplar of the minimalist case for democracy. His all-things-considered view of democracy's value and the role of judicial review in democracy are considerably more nuanced than this chapter in isolation would suggest. See, for example, Adam Przeworski, *Democracy and the Limits of Self-Government* (Cambridge: Cambridge University Press, 2010), esp. at 158–160.

**154** Part II

10 Przeworski, "Minimalist Conception of Democracy," 45.
11 See especially Riker and Weingast, "Constitutional Regulation." On Riker's libertarian tendencies, see Mackie, *Democracy Defended*, 29–30, and Ian Shapiro, *Democracy's Place* (Ithaca, NY: Cornell University Press, 1996), 16–52.
12 Shapiro argues that "Riker and Weingast's position seems to require a return to *Lochner.*" *Democracy's Place*, 39–40.
13 On both counts, see Mackie, *Democracy Defended*, 17–18. For example, a lynchpin of Riker's irrationality thesis is the alleged prevalence of "cycling." Mackie reviews every empirical example that Riker gives of cycling and finds that *every one* fails to hold up under empirical scrutiny.
14 Ibid., 411–417. One possible line of defense for Riker here, offered by Keith Dowding, is to draw a distinction between arbitrary outcomes and random outcomes, such that "arbitrary" simply means there is some correlation, however slight, between bad behavior by politicians and the likelihood of their electoral removal. While this rather unusual understanding of arbitrariness would make Riker's theoretical point less incoherent, the correlation would need to be recognizably strong enough to affect politicians' behavioral calculus; so without empirical support, this modification does little to make Riker's theory more persuasive. See his "Can Populism Be Defended? William Riker, Gerry Mackie, and the Interpretation of Democracy," *Government and Opposition* 41:3 (2006): 327–346, at 33. As Bruce Gilley ("Is Democracy Possible?" *Journal of Democracy* 20:1 (2009): 113–127, at 117) observes, "Logical possibilities conjured by the academic mind are not in the same as empirical probabilities in real-world democracies."
15 Mackie, *Democracy Defended*.
16 Riker, *Liberalism against Populism*, 9. Emphasis retained from original.
17 The core argument of Hirschl, *Towards Juristocracy*, is that the new wave of judicial review creation in the world (with particular attention to Canada, Israel, New Zealand, and South Africa) today has had the effect of protecting neoliberal visions of property rights at the expense of social and economic rights. Hirschl is suspicious of judicial review on precisely the same grounds Riker embraces it. See also Ran Hirschl, "The Judicialization of Mega-Politics and the Rise of Political Courts," *Annual Review of Political Science* 11 (2008): 93–118.
18 Randy Barnett, *Restoring the Lost Constitution: The Presumption of Liberty* (Princeton, NJ: Princeton University Press, 2005).
19 David Bernstein, *Rehabilitating Lochner: Defending Individual Rights against Progressive Reform* (Chicago, IL: University of Chicago Press, 2011).
20 Richard Epstein, *How Progressives Rewrote the Constitution* (Washington, DC: Cato Institute, 2006).
21 Bernstein, *Rehabilitating Lochner*, 127.
22 Waldron, *Law and Disagreement*, 114–115.
23 Ibid., 118. Emphasis retained from original.
24 Ibid., 23.
25 An important critique of Waldron's assumptions here is made by Alon Harel. He argues that "the judicial process itself—the process of determining the scope of our rights and their content is not oblivious to social values and hence that courts are more 'democratic' than the opponents of judicial review believe." Harel argues that the structure and focus of legislative and judicial decision-making are both fundamentally important in the process of the political approximation of the will of the people. See Alon Harel, "Rights Based Judicial Review: A Democratic Justification,"

*Law and Philosophy* 22:3–4 (2003): 276. See also Annabelle Lever, "Democracy and Judicial Review: Are They Really Incompatible," *Perspectives on Politics* 7:4 (2009): 805–823.

26 For the sake of argument, we are granting Waldron's assumption that judicial review functionally means that constitutional court judges do, in fact, have the "last word." However, this is far too simplistic. First, it ignores the issue of complexities of court-legislature relations suggested by recent scholarly literature on legislative deferrals. See Lovell, *Legislative Deferrals*. Second, it ignores an important part of political reality—that legislatures (not to mention executives) have multiple means of continuing to pursue desired ends that have been rejected as unconstitutional. See Hiebert, *Charter Politics*; Peretti, "An Empirical Analysis," 133–136.

27 Waldron, *Law and Disagreement*, 299.

28 Ibid., 285–289.

29 To make the case that judicial review is in fact necessary for liberal democracy, one would be forced to explain cases such as the United Kingdom, which by contemporary global standards certainly appears to be a functioning parliamentary liberal democracy without a court with the power of constitutional judicial review.

30 On this point, see Tushnet, *Red, White, and Blue*.

31 Christopher Eisgruber, "Democracy and Disagreement: A Comment on Jeremy Waldron's Law and Disagreement," *Journal of Legislation and Public Policy* 6:1 (2002): 35–49.

32 Kathleen Doherty and Ryan Pevnick, "Are There Good Procedural Objections to Judicial Review?," *Journal of Politics* 76:1 (2014): 86–97. Waldron discusses May's theorem at Waldron, "The Core of the Case," 1388. May's theorem was originally presented in Kenneth May, "A Set of Independent Necessary and Sufficient Conditions for Simple Majority Decision," *Econometrica* 20:4 (1952): 680–684.

33 Jeremy Waldron, *The Dignity of Legislation* (Cambridge: Cambridge University Press, 1999).

34 Waldron, *Law and Disagreement*, 264.

35 Ibid., 232.

36 Ibid., 299–300; Eisgruber, "Democracy and Disagreement," 38.

37 Waldron, "The Core of the Case," 1361.

38 Klarman, *From Jim Crow to Civil Rights*.

39 Section 33 of the Canadian Charter of Rights and Freedoms reads: "Parliament or the legislature of a province may expressly declare in an Act of Parliament or of the legislature, as the case may be, that the Act or a provision thereof shall operate notwithstanding a provision included in section 2 or sections 7 to 15 of this Charter." See, generally, Christopher Manfredi, *Judicial Power and the Charter: Canada and the Paradox of Liberal Constitutionalism* (New York: Oxford University Press, 2000).

40 Waldron, "The Core of the Case," 1356.

41 Ibid., 1357n34. In contrast to Waldron's position, the case that legislative override provisions change the democratic questions surrounding judicial review relative to strong-form judicial review is made by Mark Tushnet and Janet Hiebert. See Tushnet, *The New Constitutional Order; Weak Courts*; Janet Hiebert, "Parliamentary Bills of Rights: An Alternative Model," *The Modern Law Review* 69:1 (2006): 7–28.

42 Lovell and Lemieux, "Assessing Juristocracy."

43 Bickel, *Least Dangerous Branch*, 17.

**156** Part II

44 For an extensive assessment of the democratic value of various legislative procedures and rules that empower minorities, see Adrian Vermuele, *Mechanisms of Democracy: Institutional Designs Writ Small* (New York: Oxford University Press, 2007), 85–114.

45 We take this lesson from Waldron's defense of legislative supremacy, in which his defense of legislative supremacy and his defense of the principle of "majority decision" blend together. See Waldron, *The Dignity of Legislation*, 124–166.

46 Doherty and Pevnick, "Are There Good Procedural Objections?"

47 Bellamy, *Political Constitutionalism*.

48 Ibid., 223.

49 David Samuels and Richard Snyder, "The Value of a Vote: Malapportionment in Comparative Perspective," *British Journal of Political Science* 31:4 (2001): 651–671. For an argument that greater degrees of malapportionment are linked to higher levels of inequality, see Yasoko Horiuchi, "Malapportionment and Income Inequality: A Cross-Sectional Analysis," *British Journal of Political Science* 34:1 (2004): 179–183. For a similar argument regarding rural overrepresentation and environmental policy, see J. Lawrence Broz and Daniel Maliniak, "Malapportionment, Gasoline Taxes, and the United Nations Framework Convention on Climate Change," paper presented at the Third Annual Conference on the Political Economy of International Organizations, Georgetown University, Washington, D.C., January 2010.

50 Kramer, *The People Themselves*.

51 Tushnet, *Taking the Constitution away from the Courts*.

52 See esp. Jack Balkin, *Living Originalism* (Cambridge, MA: Belknap Press, 2011).

53 Tushnet, *Taking the Constitution away from the Courts*, 9–14.

54 Ibid., 33–53.

55 Melissa Schwartzberg, *Counting the Many: The Origins and Limits of Supermajority Rule* (Cambridge: Cambridge University Press, 2014).

56 Ibid., 184.

57 For further discussion of the latter, see Amy Lang, "But Is It for Real? The British Columbia Citizen's Assembly as a Model of State-Sponsored Citizen Empowerment," *Politics and Society* 35:1 (2007): 35–69; Mark Warren and Hilary Pearce, *Designing Deliberative Democracy: The British Columbia Citizen's Assembly* (Cambridge: Cambridge University Press, 2008); Mark Warren and Amy Lang, "Supplementary Democracy? Democratic Deficits and Citizens Assemblies," in Patti Tamara Lenard and Richard Simeon (eds) *Imperfect Democracies? The Democratic Deficit in Canada and the United States* (Vancouver, BC: University of British Columbia Press, 2012), 291–314; and Carole Pateman, "Participatory Democracy Revisited," *Perspectives on Politics* 10:1 (2012): 7–19, at 8–9.

58 Peter Railton, "Judicial Review, Elites, and Liberal Democracy," in James Roland Pennock and John W. Chapman (eds) *NOMOS XXV: Liberal Democracy* (New York: New York University Press, 1983), 153–180, at 156–158.

59 See, for example, George Kateb, "Comments on Robert B. McKay, 'Judicial Review in a Liberal Democracy'," in James Roland Pennock and John W. Chapman (eds) *NOMOS XXV: Liberal Democracy* (New York: New York University Press, 1983), 145–152; Harel, "Rights Based Judicial Review"; Robert Dworkin, *Freedom's Law: A Moral Reading of the American Constitution* (Cambridge, MA: Harvard University Press, 1996).

60 Ely, *Democracy and Distrust*.

61 Den Otter, *Judicial Review in an Age of Moral Pluralism*.

62 Brettschneider, *Democratic Rights*, 136–159.

Judicial Review as Just Another Veto Point  **157**

63 See, for example, Bellamy, *Political Constitutionalism*, 42.
64 George Tsebelis, *Veto Players: How Political Institutions Work* (Princeton, NJ: Princeton University Press, 2002). Veto points come not just from legislative procedure, but from other political institutions as well. Under some arrangements, bureaucracies can function as a veto point. See also Thomas Hammond, "Veto Points, Policy Preferences and Bureaucratic Autonomy in Democratic Systems," in George Krause and Kenneth Meier (eds) *Politics, Policy and Organizations: Frontiers in the Scientific Study of Bureaucracy* (Ann Arbor, MI: University of Michigan Press, 2003), 73–103.
65 Michael Saward, "Enacting Democracy," *Political Studies* 51:1 (2003): 161–179.
66 Pettit articulates this through a different language: government must track "common avowable interests," a less demanding goal than a full-fledged account of the common good. See Pettit, "Republican Freedom," and Pettit, "Democracy, Electoral and Contestatory."
67 Pettit, "Democracy, Electoral and Contestatory," 115.
68 There is some controversy about the status of judicial review among democracy-against-domination theorists. Pettit is clearly in favor of it, as evidenced by his two-dimensional democratic theory. He also characterizes the empowerment of courts and bureaucracies as a way of "depoliticizing" democracy. See Pettit, "Depoliticizing Democracy." Richard Bellamy, on the other hand, argues that such empowerments cannot escape the realm of power and abandon democracy-against-domination's grounding in political equality; see *Political Constitutionalism*, "The Democratic Constitution"; "The Republic of Reasons"; "Republicanism, Rights, and Democracy." While we ultimately side with Pettit on the substance of the debate, we agree with Bellamy that Pettit's dream of technocratic and apolitical judges and bureaucrats who are somehow outside of politics isn't plausible, and is not a promising foundation for a defense of judicial review. For critical assessments of Pettit's "depoliticization" argument, see also Patchen Markell, "The Insufficiency of Non-Domination," *Political Theory* 36:1 (2008): 3–36; Nadia Urbinati, "Unpolitical Democracy," *Political Theory* 38:1 (2010): 65–92; John McCormick, *Machiavellian Democracy* (Princeton, NJ: Princeton University Press, 2011), ch. 6; "Republicanism and Democracy"; and Ian Shapiro, "On Non-Domination," *University of Toronto Law Journal* 62:2 (2012): 329–332. Iseult Honohan argues judicial review is consistent with republican governance when understood not as depoliticizing, but as an opportunity for a different form of political participation. See "Republicans, Rights and Constitutions: Is Judicial Review Compatible with Republican Self Government?," in Samantha Basson and Jose Luis Marti (eds) *Legal Republicanism: National and International Perspectives* (Oxford: Oxford University Press, 2009), 83–101.
69 See Vermeule, *Mechanisms of Democracy*, 97–98.
70 This issue is central to Ronald Den Otter's defense of judicial review in Den Otter, *Judicial Review in an Age of Moral Pluralism*, discussed in chapter two.
71 See Catharine Fisk and Edwin Chemerinsky, "The Filibuster," *Stanford Law Review* 49:2 (1997): 181–254; Sarah Binder and Steven Smith, *Politics or Principle? Filibustering in the United States Senate* (Washington, DC: Brookings Institution Press, 1997). It is worth noting that even analysts who see the filibuster as more consistent with democratic values than we do are generally unwilling to defend secret holds and similar forms of obstruction; see, e.g., Richard Arenberg and Robert Dove, *Defending the Filibuster* (Bloomington, IN: Indiana University Press, 2012), 173–175.

**158** Part II

72 For an argument that this is the primary criteria for evaluating and justifying collective decision-making procedures, see Jon Elster, *Securities against Misrule: Juries, Assemblies, Elections* (Cambridge: Cambridge University Press, 2013).

73 Scheppele, "Democracy by Judiciary" and "Parliamentary Supplements (Or, Why Democracies Need More than Parliaments)," *Boston University Law Review* 89:2 (2009): 795–826.

74 See, e.g., Frank Baumgartner and Brian Jones, *Agendas and Instability in American Politics* (Chicago, IL: University of Chicago Press, 1993) and John Kingdon, *Agendas, Alternatives and Public Policies*, 2nd ed. (New York: Pearson, 1995).

75 Shapiro, *The State of Democratic Theory*, 3.

76 This function for democracy is central for Pettit's democratic theory, but Pettit is not alone here: in his revisionist history of democracy, John Keane argues that the age of representative democracy is being replaced by monitory democracy in the post-WWII world. See Keane's *The Life and Death of Democracy* (New York: Norton, 2009); "Monitory Democracy?," in Sonia Alonso, John Keane and Wolfgang Merkel (eds) *The Future of Representative Democracy* (Cambridge: Cambridge University Press, 2011), 212–235.

77 Tushnet's *Weak Courts* makes the case for the democratic superiority of weak review powers, as found in Canada, while Scheppele's "Democracy by Judiciary" makes the case for the democratic superiority of the far more powerful Hungarian court.

78 Shapiro, "On Non-Domination," 293–335, at 328.

79 Shapiro, *Politics against Domination*, 91.

80 Adrian Vermuele, *The System of the Constitution* (New York: Oxford University Press, 2011), 51–52.

81 Jacob Hacker, "Privatizing Risks without Privatizing Benefits: The Hidden Politics of Social Policy Retrenchment in the United States," *American Political Science Review* 98:2 (2004): 243–260; Hacker and Pierson, *Winner-Take-All Politics*.

82 Shane Singh and Kris Dunn, "Veto Players, the Policy-Making Environment, and the Expression of Authoritarian Attitude," *Political Studies* 61:1 (2013): 119–141.

83 And even where legal reasoning is disingenuous or in bad faith, the need to give reasons can sometimes mean that dubious case outcomes can, by the necessity of needing to use attractive principles, have more positive future consequences. See Mark Tushnet, "Renormalizing *Bush v Gore*: An Anticipatory Intellectual History," *Georgetown Law Review* 90:6 (2001): 113–125. Even though this is not likely to occur in most cases of bad faith reasoning, there is democratic value in exposing bad faith political action.

84 Waldron, *Law and Disagreement*, 289–291.

85 Of course, especially at lower levels, courts do not always justify case outcomes with public reasoning, and other aspects of the process (such as decisions to accept or deny appeals) are often secret. Still, it is clear that courts have a clear comparative advantage in this respect.

86 John Fund, "Republican Rot: Is Congress's GOP Majority Becoming as Corrupt as the Democrats Were?," *The Wall Street Journal* (February 9, 2005).

87 Alicia Bower, "Unconstitutionally Crowded? *Brown v. Plata* and How the Supreme Court Pushed Back to Keep Prison Litigation Reform Alive," *Loyola of Los Angeles Law Review* 45:2 (2012): 555–567. This decision is noteworthy for another reason: it demonstrates a case in which the victims of rights violations who are denied participation in democracy's ordinary "democratic procedure" through felon disenfranchisement can still utilize this veto point to contest their own domination.

88 Eisgruber, *Constitutional Self-Government*.
89 Scheppele, "Democracy by Judiciary." On India see Epp, *The Rights Revolution*, 86.
90 Peretti, *In Defense of a Political Court*; Aileen Kavanaugh, "Participation and Judicial Review: A Reply to Jeremy Waldron," *Law and Philosophy* 22:5 (2003): 451–586; Dmitrios Kyritsis, "Representation and Waldron's Objection to Judicial Review," *Oxford Journal of Legal Studies* 26:4 (2006): 733–751.
91 Hirschl, *Toward Juristocracy*. Hirschl's analysis is limited to recently created systems of constitutional judicial review in South Africa, Canada, Israel, and New Zealand, although he identifies this as a broader global trend.
92 McCain and Fleming, "Constitutions, Judicial Review and Progressive Change."
93 Hirschl, "Constitutions, Judicial Review and Progressive Change," 895.
94 Scheppele, "Democracy by Judiciary." In the so-called "Bokros package" cases, the Hungarian Constitutional Court required the legislature to not cut certain social welfare benefits on constitutional grounds. The Russian Constitutional Court also issued a series of rulings enhancing and protecting employment and housing rights in the early 1990's, during the Court's relatively brief period of political power.
95 This is not to say, of course, that a *complete* break between the property rights-focused constitutionalism of the *Lochner* era is possible; see, e.g., Jennifer Nedelsky, *Private Property and the Limits of American Constitutionalism: The Madisonian Framework and Its Legacy* (Chicago, IL: University of Chicago Press, 1994).
96 Ely, *Democracy and Distrust* and Shapiro, *The State of Democratic Theory*.
97 Ely, *Democracy and Distrust*.
98 Sunstein, "Concurring."
99 Yasmin Dawood, "The Antidomination Model and the Judicial Oversight of Democracy," *Georgetown Law Review* 96:5 (2008): 1411–1485.
100 Lovell, *Legislative Deferrals*.
101 Hirschl, *Toward Juristocracy*.
102 Scheppele, "Democracy by Judiciary."

# 6

# JUDICIAL REVIEW IN A COMPARATIVE CONTEXT

## 6.1 Introduction: Democracy and Veto Points

In the previous chapter, we argued veto points aren't antithetical to democracy but an inevitable part of it, or at least part of it in the context of modern democratic political systems. The central question for democratic theory, then, shouldn't be which, if any, of these anti-democratic checks can be justified in an absolute sense, but rather which veto points are more and which are less democratic. This book is primarily about the democratic status of judicial review, and it is beyond the scope of our analysis to fully assess the democratic value of every common veto point within democratic institutions. But it is nonetheless useful to briefly consider how judicial review might compare to some of the other veto points democratic theorists who assess judicial review sometimes take for granted. This chapter serves two purposes: first, to further build the case that judicial review is a relatively democratic veto point, and second, to further refine and develop our tools for evaluating the democratic valence of veto points. We will not try the reader's patience by comparing all of these veto points based on every one of the five criteria established in the previous chapter. Rather, we will use the points that seem most pertinent to the specific veto point. If we omit discussion of how a particular veto point fares against a particular criterion, it implies a judgment that the veto point has no particular strength or weakness based on that particular factor.

The use of the kind of test developed in the previous chapter is necessary for not just democracy-against-domination, but any institutional approach to democratic theory. To simply suggest that a particular veto point encapsulates or reflects a democratic value is insufficient. Such an approach doesn't take into account the process by which values enter institutional life. Take, for example, the so-called *liberum veto*, a central institutional feature of the "gentry democracy" of the Polish-Lithuanian commonwealth in the 16th and 17th centuries. This parliamentary veto allowed any member of the commonwealth's parliamentary body, the *sejm*, to suspend deliberation and effectively end consideration of any measure presently under consideration. Defenders of this procedural rule understood it as an instantiation of the value of political and deliberative equality of all members of the *sejm*, and by extension all members of the Polish nobility.[1] Obviously, this isn't the only way to translate the value of political equality into an institutional rule, and Waldron, among many others, has made the case that majority procedure offers a better institutionalization of the value of political equality.[2] It is, however, a plausible way to institutionalize political *equality*, when distributed equally, as political equality speaks to both an equal share of decision-making power and equal access to defensive or contestatory mechanisms. We need additional criteria beyond merely the apparent fit of democratic values and institutional rules, and that is what we have sought to develop.

It is not difficult to see why the *liberum veto* is unlikely to score as particularly democratic on our account here. Rousseau identified an important reason in his *Constitution of Poland*. Even though the defenders of Polish consensual democracy took great pride in the separation of parliament's lawmaking powers and political independence from the monarch, "your kings, because of the *liberum veto*, must always have been sure that they could arrest any legislative proceeding that might displease them, and dissolve the Diet at their pleasure," as a king would only need to win over one member of the *sejm* to do so.[3] Rousseau's fear was a shrewd and accurate one, but it turned out to be not the most damaging one to the commonwealth, as the king turned out to be not the only already over-empowered actor who used the *liberum veto* to undermine the proceedings of the *sejm* and indeed the commonwealth itself. It is generally understood to be the case that various foreign powers hostile to the commonwealth bribed and compromised *sejm* members to serve their interests throughout the 18th century, eventually undermining the commonwealth itself, whose demise is generally laid at least partially at the feet of the stubborn attachment to this particular veto point.[4] A new constitution, attempting to arrest the slide into anarchy, was adopted in May 1791, but it was too late, as the following year the government fell to Russian military forces, and the dismantling and partition of the commonwealth was well under way.[5]

On this account, then, the *liberum veto* fails dramatically as a *democratic* veto point. It fails on the first criterion: even as a rule designed to force deliberation to reach a consensus, it does not include a requirement for public justification.[6] All that was required to invoke it was the utterance of a particular phrase, which changed over time but generally translated as "I will not allow it" or "I put a stop to these proceedings."[7] It fails perhaps more dramatically, though, on the second and fifth criteria: it authorizes veto for private reasons, and empowers already over-empowered minorities, including

**162** Part II

those outside the deliberative body whose empowerment is not democratically authorized. While the focus of historical critiques of the *liberum veto* has tended to focus on their role in the demise of the commonwealth, its use had paralyzing effects on the *sejm* that should give pause to anyone concerned with the state's capacity to prevent *dominium*. For example, the veto was used in a manner that led to the commonwealth being prevented from collecting any taxes at all in 1580.[8] The *liberum veto* is instructive because it serves as a clear example of what constitutes an undemocratic veto point, even one nominally connected to a democratic principle or value (in this case, a particular interpretation of democratic equality). While recognizing the potential of veto points requires decoupling democracy and majoritarian procedure, this cannot go too far. The empowerment of majorities to act must remain central to any democratic theory; democratic veto points can challenge, complicate, delay, edit, and occasionally prevent exercises of majority power, but they must not be able to undermine it as fundamentally as the *liberum veto* did. The rest of this chapter will explore the democratic potential and democratic dangers of contemporary veto points in light of the analysis provided here, beginning with the filibuster, with an eye toward comparisons with judicial review. It has been observed that the privileges of the states bears a family resemblance to the *liberum veto*,[9] and the growth of the filibuster as a central procedural rule of the operation of the U.S. Senate has only made this connection more clear, so it should be no surprise that the filibuster scores as a profoundly undemocratic veto point.

## 6.2 Veto Points and Concentrated Power: Filibuster

The filibuster rule in the United States Senate is an institutional feature that is very difficult to defend from a democracy-against-domination perspective. In practice, the filibuster has tended to exacerbate *dominium*, and played a particularly dismal role in reinforcing white supremacy in the post–Civil War South: "Beginning during Reconstruction and continuing for nearly a century, anti-civil rights filibusters played a major role in blocking measures to prohibit lynching, poll taxes, and race discrimination in employment, housing, public accommodations, and voting."[10] The rule has never been used in a similarly systematic way to protect the interests of underrepresented groups, and even in theory, there is no particular reason to expect it to do so. The representational rules of the Senate suggest that one minority the filibuster can be expected to potentially offer protection is small states—a potentially legitimate goal, common in large, diverse democracies.[11] Because such groups are already greatly overrepresented in the composition of the Senate (which exercises a veto over executive and federal judicial appointments) and somewhat overrepresented in the House of Representatives and the Electoral College, it is difficult to argue that the filibuster is democratically legitimate. "The filibuster," Binder and Smith conclude, "is used

Judicial Review in a Comparative Context  **163**

in ways that are hardly relevant to the nation's welfare, in ways that undermine Senate effectiveness on legislative matters unrelated to the targeted measures."[12]

The filibuster's great flaw is that it fails in spectacular fashion on the fifth criterion—the minority it effectively grants a veto is not in much danger of domination, in no small part due to the small state-empowering representational scheme of the Senate. But how does the filibuster look on our other criteria? On the first criterion, public justification, it is possible to argue that a classic talking filibuster does not necessarily do so poorly. While, as Huey Long's famous Shakespeare recitations and recipes demonstrate, the filibuster contains no requirement to actually justify blocking the legislation in question, it does require the veto players to say something—potentially very many things—to continue the delay. While this arguably could be interpreted as closer to meeting this criteria than the modern procedural veto, any democratic value gained on public justification grounds should be understood as fairly limited; the kind of speech used in filibusters generally don't appear to be particularly useful in this respect. The modern procedural filibuster both lowers the stakes of invoking it (one need not grind Senate business to a halt) while also diminishing whatever meager public justification value the filibuster may have once had.

## 6.3  Bicameralism

The filibuster, while it retains some defenders,[13] is one of the most derided and least defended contemporary veto points from a democratic perspective. To consider a less obvious case, bicameralism also functions as a veto point. Can it be democratically justified? While disavowing some examples of bicameralism, such as the profoundly unrepresentative U.S. Senate, Waldron thinks so. The democratic value of bicameralism, for Waldron, comes from the potential value of difference, as long as the two legislative bodies are both generally majoritarian. Arguing against Bentham's critique of bicameralism, Waldron suggests it may have added democratic value compared to a unicameral system if properly designed.[14] For Waldron, bicameralism is potentially valuable because no system of representation—no single legislature—can capture every virtue and value we might want from a legislative body, and this is inevitable because legislatures are not perfectible:

> No matter how good we make the scheme of representation in a given chamber, no matter how many of our good thoughts about election, representation, and deliberation we have already taken on board . . . it is always possible to improve things by complementing that scheme of representation with another.[15]

Different schemes of representation, on Waldron's logic here, can capture different shades of majoritarian representation, which might complement each other in

**164** Part II

important ways. It is easy to imagine how this might work: if a particular minority is spread out across districts evenly in a first-past-the-post single member district legislative body, they might have little to no voice or power. If the second chamber adopted a different scheme of representation, such as proportional representation, it could enhance their political power and give them an important tool to resist domination. We certainly agree with Waldron that a bicameral system could plausibly be designed to accomplish such an end, but the democratic benefits of such a proliferation of veto points must be weighed against the democratic costs. A second co-equal chamber doubles the intra-legislative veto points associated with committee hierarchies and procedural rules, doubling the opportunities for status quo bias. It doubles the chances of an electoral majority finding itself unable to pass legislation due to the configuration of districts or the particulars of a scheme of representation. Bicameralism also potentially dilutes political accountability by allowing for blame-shifting between branches that can both claim to be democratically legitimate.

Whatever advantages bicameralism might have must be weighed against the costs that come with it. The most prominent democratic flaw inherent in bicameralism is a significant enhancement of status-quo bias, inhibiting government's potential to enact policies that respond to private domination.[16] While Waldron does identify some potential democratic benefits from bicameralism as a veto point, its status as a legislative veto point does not eradicate their democratic dangers. While making a case for bicameralism as a democratic veto point is easier to do than for the filibuster, it is far from clear that its status as legislative and majoritarian is sufficient to declare it more democratic than judicial review on our criteria, particularly because giving a veto to each of two majoritarian legislatures produces a countermajoritarian effect, which is generally exacerbated by countermajoritarian representative features in at least the upper house.

One the first criterion outlined in the previous chapter—requiring public justification—bicameralism provides no discernible democratic value that a unicameral legislature does not. With respect to the remaining criteria, whether a bicameral legislature provides additional democratic value is a more complex question. There is a potential clash between the second and third criterion. It is theoretically possible that a second legislative body could result in a more careful assessment of legislative priorities, but this comes at the cost of potentially empowering particular veto players over broader public or institutional interests—a legislative body that overrepresents rural areas (such as the United States Senate) is likely to provide relatively more agricultural than urban housing subsidies, not because of a considered deliberative judgment but because institutional design puts its thumb on the scale for a particular interest. Given that bicameralism that does not represent constituencies differently in the two houses is redundant, in most bicameral systems, the value potentially added under the third criterion and subtracted under the second is likely to be a wash at best.

The value of bicameral systems on the fourth and fifth criteria is highly contingent on specific institutional designs and norms. A bicameral system might facilitate more opportunities for public contestation, and indeed in the abstract this is probably the strongest democratic argument to be made on behalf of the system—constituents who cannot get a hearing from one legislative chamber might be able to get one from another. Whether this increased contestation actually occurs is evidently an empirical question that should be evaluated on a case-by-case basis, but its potential value cannot be dismissed out of hand. Similarly, the case for bicameralism is much stronger when a second chamber provides greater representation to a historically underrepresented group (fifth criterion). A second chamber that overrepresents a group already overrepresented within a country's political institutions is nearly impossible to defend from a democratic perspective. But a second chamber that provides representation to groups that are historically underrepresented might be valuable, although whether this is sufficient to justify the costs of a major additional veto point is a question of judgment that will depend in part on how many other major veto points exist in the political system.

## 6.4 Federalism

Federalism's status as a veto point is complex. Delegating authority to sovereigns with a nation-state or to subdivisions within governments does not always effectively act as a veto point, and indeed, in some cases, it might be easier for state or local governments to achieve consensus and act. Federalism can make it more difficult to achieve national policy but make it easier for states to experiment. In other cases, federalism can function in tandem with judicial review to act as a veto point—for example, the United States Supreme Court's holding that the expansion of Medicaid in the Affordable Care Act was unconstitutionally coercive frustrated the goal of Congress to create a more robust level of health care coverage for the poor, as many states opted out of the offered federal money after the statute was effectively rewritten by the Court.[17] Such cases, however, cannot be easily disentangled from the democratic virtues and vices of judicial review itself, so we do not consider them here. Instead, we consider the extent to which delegating power to subnational governments is likely to affect democratic legitimacy when compared to a relatively unitary state.

Jacob Levy argues that federalism as it actually exists in most contexts is a poor candidate for what is often asked of it—goods generally associated with competitive or assortative federalism.[18] In the former, federalism improves policies via competition for residents within a polity. In the latter, federalism sorts people and their preferences into the local government best suited for them.[19] Both of these theories exaggerate the extent to which personal mobility is likely to be politically motivated at the margins, but more importantly, they appear to be based on a misunderstanding of not just citizens but actually existing federal systems, which are too large and unwieldy to deliver these values, and likely to be tied to ethnocultural or regional identities that raise the costs associated with the kind of citizen mobility he's promoting.

Instead, Levy argues, federalism's potential value is largely defensive, and in some senses accidental. The general tendency toward centralization has dangers associated with the creation of a homogenizing and totalizing center; one that might threaten liberty and stability because of its size and strength.[20] Insofar as ethnoculturally sorted federalist systems might produce a set of divided loyalties among the citizenry, they might lead to a check—a bulwark, in Levy's terms—against some of the worst excesses of a totalizing central state power. Levy doesn't frame this argument in the context of democracy-against-domination, but it fits well—federalism's potential virtue, on his analysis, is its capacity to reduce the likelihood of *imperium* on the part of the central state. While federalism prevents domination by neutralizing national solidarity for Levy, Weinstock offers a more balanced account of federalism's value along these lines. By allowing regional diversity in local governance, federalism has the capacity to defuse the threat local identities might pose to a state, partly by limiting secessionist energy, but also by limiting some conflicts about how to govern and live together.[21]

Kyle Scott's defense of federalism goes quite a bit farther than Levy's, and offers a defense not just of federalism as it is, but a far more robust federalism as it could be. Scott offers a strong defense for a heavily decentralized state, in which federal units retain a number of privileges they rarely have today, including veto, nullification, and secession powers.[22] For Scott, such powers are essential for federalism to retain its primary democratic value: resistance of the majoritarian tyranny of major brokerage parties. If federal minorities retain such strong veto powers, federalism will prevent domination by thwarting majority tyranny. Scott sees his theoretical antecedents in 17th-century defenders of federalism such as Athusius,[23] but his position bears a strong resemblance to that of consensualists such as Calhoun.[24] His hope is that the threat of the use of significant federal power will bring the dominating tendencies of the central state to heel, thereby preventing it from becoming a dominating power.

From a democracy-against-domination perspective, what both of these approaches fail to account for is the second form of domination: *dominium*, or private domination. The concern for these defenses of federalism focuses on how to prevent the state from slipping into domination, but often at the expense of the state's capacity to prevent private domination. Our fifth criterion for democratic veto points demands we look at which minorities are likely to be empowered. Federalism empowers minorities organized geographically as majorities in certain regions, but perhaps at the expense of other minorities either residing in that region in lesser numbers or distributed in more spread-out geographic patterns. Under such circumstances, some federal arrangements might serve an important democratic purpose: if a particularly vulnerable minority is predominantly located in a particular geographic territory—perhaps a traditional territorial homeland—it could potentially protect them from domination by the majority population through the state, and allow them to make laws to protect their members from the majority community or culture.

In many other cases, though, federalism can exacerbate the power of one minority to dominate another. The case of federalism in the U.S. is a clear and obvious example here: federalism allowed a minority (southern whites) to dominate another minority by vetoing federal action restricting the very forms of domination they were engaged in—not through Scott's formal veto power but through a number of informal ones. It is striking that Scott never gives any significant consideration to this glaring counterexample. Federalism's value, on the fifth criteria, is highly contingent on geographic distribution. While Levy is right to argue that federalism often has an ethnocultural or identity-based component to its distribution, such distributions are likely to be insufficient to put federalism in the domination-reducing category. Similarly, federalism is sometimes provoked as a protector of smaller federal units—giving them discrete forms of power that might otherwise be overwhelmed by sheer numbers in a unitary arrangement. Again, true enough, but how many federal arrangements take that form? Is small state domination at the hands of larger states a significant problem as a general matter? It is not clear that this is so.

What of the other four criteria? The fourth criterion demands participatory and contestatory benefits. Federalism can certainly add some value here: when a particular policy is effectively frozen at the federal level, perhaps because of the exercise of certain veto points there, federalism can offer a venue for experimenting with strategies to reduce domination that would otherwise be foreclosed. Efforts to legalize or decriminalize medicinal and recreational marijuana, in an attempt to reduce the abusive *imperium* associated with the war on drugs, stands as a current and prominent example. But federalism also provides venues for politicians already in power to exercise prerogative with little democratic input. Many of the states currently governed by Republicans' refusal of the Medicaid expansion attached to the PPACA, for example, are doing so in the service of a national political strategy to undermine the PPACA in any way possible, keeping it unpopular and undermining its effectiveness in the hopes of someday overturning it. This kind of political strategy as a general matter isn't inherently objectionable; our democratic theory doesn't preclude hard-nosed partisan politics. Still, the politics of federalism are being deployed in a way that seems distinctly at odds with the purported democratic value of federalism—the concrete, urgent needs of vulnerable populations in those states aren't being well-served by a government closer to them and more sensitive to their needs. Instead, federalism creates the opportunity for the politicians closest to them to treat them as pawns in a national political struggle. The shared agenda of local and national Republican politicians demonstrates federalism's failure to live up to this mandate: it is merely a tool for a highly homogeneous national movement to use to resist another, fairly homogenized national political movement. It is not

**168** Part II

empowering any minority with a new perspective or complaint. Another way in which a possible case can be made for this veto point might be through federalism offering an avenue to become a more active and contestatory citizen through political activism and engagement that would be unlikely to occur at the national level. While we do not wish to dismiss this possibility, it is not clear to us how much work federalism, rather than just the general existence of local government in some form, is doing here. Perhaps more people are attracted to the higher stakes of local governments under a federal system, and as such, more people are socialized into becoming politically savvy contestatory citizens. However, it is not clear this hope is supported by the available evidence; the mere existence of opportunities to get involved in local government may provide a similar level of democratic benefit in this area.

On the third criterion, federalism could be understood as a form of democratic competition for resources. Federal units assert their claims to a share of resources based on their challenges, needs, and plans, and through an ongoing political struggle, goods are eventually allocated in light of these claims and requests. Indeed, some would argue that the fight for resources for one's constituency, often defined in geographic terms, is a central preoccupation and purpose of modern legislatures. However, does this represent a weighing of different substantive state priorities, or merely different groups of people? In *Brown v. Plata*,[25] the Supreme Court upheld an earlier ruling ordering the state of California to release prisoners to prevent overcrowding, following through on a decade-old threat to do so if the state didn't reduce its unconstitutional overcrowding problem. In this case, the court weighed two legitimate state mandates (protect citizens from criminals; not violate the 8th Amendment's prohibition of "cruel and unusual punishment" with substandard prison conditions) and decided in this case the latter should take precedence. This wasn't merely a case of interest groups duking it out for resources, as is often associated with politics at any level of government. Certainly, federalism's enhancement of local governments might lead to micro-level evaluations of tradeoffs, but it's not clear this is a major point for federalism from a democracy-against-domination standpoint.

Finally, we consider federalism in light of the second criterion: avoiding direct conflicts of self-interest and public interest for veto players. Judicial review has an occasional case of corruption and slip-ups here, but in general, for reasons of socio-economic standing and professional ethics, these kinds of conflicts of interest are relatively rare among the judiciary in many countries. This is, however, a real worry when it comes to federalism. In general, the smaller the local government, the easier it is for the wealthy and powerful to gain political access and potentially obtain political favors. The circumstances of federalism will generally produce some very corrupt local governments (although not uniformly so), due in part to their discretionary control over resources. Evidently, however, how problematic federalism is with respect to the second criterion will depend

Judicial Review in a Comparative Context  **169**

on contingent factors such as the size of the constituencies governmental subdivisions represent and the strength of anti-corruption norms within a given polity.

Last but not least, we consider the first criterion: providing requirements for public justification. Here judicial review has an advantage in the phenomenon of "the opinion." These opinions are not always the platonic ideal of moral/legal reasoning, but judicial opinions constitute an exercise in self-justification that can come to bolster good decisions and perhaps even undermine bad ones, and is generally understood to be a wise and powerful choice.[26] That said, federal acts of non-implementation often produce little to no call for greater public scrutiny, and there is no official requirement they offer such a justification. It is perhaps better on this issue than the worst veto exercises—a lobbyist getting a bill killed in committee quietly, when there is no knowledge and no opportunity to demand a public justification, for example. But this is not a criterion on which federalism fares particularly well or particularly badly in most cases.

In summary, the case for federalism as a democratic veto point rests on two assumptions, both of which are problematic. First, that the minority groups who are most vulnerable and most otherwise underrepresented will in many cases be geographically organized in such a manner as to stand to benefit from federalism's basic structure. And second, some justifications of federalism assume that the central government presents a greater domination threat than both private actors, individual and corporate, and local governments. In some circumstances, both of these assumptions may hold. Our contention is that in most contemporary democratic states, they are unlikely to do so. At the very least, we cannot assume that these conditions will apply. With respect to the second assumption, for example, it is worth noting that James Madison—despite generally being a proponent of decentralized government—assumed in *Federalist #10* that state and local governments provided a greater threat to domination by a faction opposed to the public interest than the central government. Particularly because Madison wrote the essay in the context of defending a Constitution with a more centralized system,[27] his analysis is hardly dispositive, but it does indicate that it is not *obviously* true that central governments constitute a greater threat of domination. Federalism's democratic virtues appear to be, if not overshadowed, at least matched by her vices. The case for federalism's democratic value remains, at best, incomplete.

## 6.5  Conclusion

As we discussed at the outset of the chapter, it is beyond our scope here to fully evaluate other countermajoritarian or non-majoritarian mechanisms in comparison to judicial review. Our comparisons here are meant to be suggestive and tentative. But comparing judicial review to other common features of

**170** Part II

constitutional democracies does not show obvious comparative deficiencies for the institution of judicial review. While we did not intend to cherry-pick institutional features that would make judicial review look good by comparison, and only the filibuster isn't a fairly common feature of constitutional democracies, it is certainly possible that a different set of comparisons would yield different results. The limited comparisons here are meant as a guide for future research and reflection, as opposed to being a definitive statement about the comparative value of judicial review.

We do wish to reemphasize the critical importance of contingency and specificity. As with judicial review, it is impossible to determine the value of a broad principle of institutional construction like "federalism" or "bicameralism" in the abstract. How any particular institutional feature fares according to the criteria established in the previous chapter will depend on precisely how such features are designed and how they operate within a political system. In addition, veto points have interactive effects. A high-veto-point system places a greater burden of proof on additional veto points than a low-veto-point system. This does not mean that consideration of these features in the abstract is without value—general rules don't have to apply in every case to be useful, and we can in many cases establish tendencies for institutional features to have more or less democratic value. But no institutional feature has a fixed democratic value that applies equally in every context, and this is as true of bicameralism as it is for judicial review.

## Notes

1 Jakob Filonik, "The Polish Nobility's 'Golden Freedom': On the Ancient Roots of a Political Idea," *The European Legacy* 20:7 (2015): 731–744.

2 Waldron, *Political Political Theory*.

3 Jean-Jacques Rousseau, *The Constitution of Poland*, (ed). Willmoore Kendall (Indianapolis, IN: Hackett, 1985); for astute commentary on Rousseau's discussion of the *liberum veto*, see Melissa Schwartzberg, "Rousseau on Fundamental Law," *Political Studies* 51:2 (2003): 387–403.

4 Jerzy Lukoski, "The Political Ideals of the Polish Nobility in the 18th Century (to 1788)," *The Slavonic and East European Review* 82:1 (2004): 1–26; Robert Frost, "'Liberty without License?' The Failure of Polish Democratic Thought in the 18th Century," in Mieczysław B. Biskupski and James S. Pula (eds) *Polish Democratic Thought from the Renaissance to the Great Emigration: Essays and Documents* (New York: Columbia University Press, 1990), 29–54; Jon Elster, "Constitution-Making in Eastern Europe: Rebuilding the Boat at Open Sea," *Public Administration* 71:1–2 (1993): 169–217, at 199–201.

5 Elster, "Constitution-Making," 201.

6 Rousseau also flagged this issue in the Constitution of Poland. For discussion, see Schwartzberg, *Counting the Many*, 84.

7 Jerzy Ludowski, *Disorderly Liberty: The Political Culture of the Polish-Lithuanian Commonwealth in the Eighteenth Century* (New York: Continuum, 2010), 21.

8 Norman Davies, *God's Playground: A History of Poland, Volume One: Origins to 1795* (New York: Columbia University Press, 1984), 346. For some libertarians, who are a great deal more concerned with *imperium* prevention than *dominium* prevention, this weakening of state capacity is a reason to celebrate the *liberum veto*. See, for example, Dalibar Rohac, "'It Is By Unrule That Poland Stands': Institutions and Political Thought in the Polish-Lithuanian Commonwealth," *The Independent Review* 13:2 (2008): 209–224.

9 Wenceslas Wagner, "Some Comments on the 'Old Privileges' and the *Liberum Veto*," in Samuel Fiszman (ed) *Constitution and Reform in Eighteenth Century Poland: The Constitution of 3 May 1791* (Bloomington, IN: Indiana University Press, 1998), 51–67, at 62. Wagner makes this comparison in the service of an argument that the standard historical judgment of *liberum veto* has unfairly maligned it.

10 Fisk and Chemerinsky, "The Filibuster," 200.

11 However, this veto point is built into the very structure of the Senate in the first place. The filibuster merely allows an even smaller minority to exercise it.

12 Binder and Smith, *Politics or Principle?*, 159.

13 Arenberg and Dove, *Defending the Filibuster*.

14 Waldron, "Bicameralism," *Political Political Theory*, 72–92.

15 Waldron, *Political Political Theory*, 77.

16 Adrian Vatter, "Bicameralism and Policy Performance: The Effects of Cameral Structure in Comparative Perspective," *Journal of Legislative Studies* 11:2 (2005): 194–215.

17 Leah M. Litman, "Inventing Equal Sovereignty," *Michigan Law Review* 114 (2016): 1208–1273.

18 Jacob Levy, "Federalism, Liberalism and the Separation of Loyalties," *American Political Science Review* 101:3 (2007): 459–477.

19 For a defense, see Ilya Somin, "Foot Voting, Political Ignorance, and Constitutional Design," *Social Philosophy and Policy* 28:1 (2011), 202–227; "Foot Voting, Federalism, and Political Freedom," in James Fleming and Jacob Levy (eds) *NOMOS LV: Federalism and Subsidiarity* (New York: New York University Press, 2014), 83–119. A similar argument can be found, from an expicitly anti-domination perspective, in Taylor, *Exit Left*, ch. 4.

20 The theme suggested here—that centralization in itself tends to be a threat to liberty, which must be countered by pluralism and local control, although there are real trade-offs to each—is developed in much greater historical and philosophical detail in Levy's *Rationalism, Pluralism and Freedom* (Oxford: Oxford University Press, 2015).

21 Daniel Weinstock, "Toward a Normative Theory of Federalism," *International Social Science Journal* 53 (2001): 75–83.

22 Kyle Scott, *Federalism: A Normative Theory and Its Practical Relevance* (New York: Continuum, 2011).

23 On Althusius' contribution to a political theory of federalism, see Patrick Riley, "Three 17th Century German Theorists of Federalism: Althusius, Hugo, and Liebnitz," *Publius* 6:3 (1976): 7–41, and Alain de Benoist, "Johannes Althusius: The First Federalist," *Télos* 118 (2000): 25–58.

24 For a thorough, sympathetic reconstruction of Calhoun's federalist, consensual, and minoritarian political theory, see James Read, *Consensus versus Majority Rule: The Political Thought of John C. Calhoun* (Lawrence, KS: Kansas University Press, 2009).

25 563 U.S. 493 (2011).

26 To reiterate, in citing the value of judicial opinions, we are not endorsing a naïve or formalist view of the law that sees "law" as somehow easily distinguishable from

**172** Part II

"politics." However, even if one assumes that judges in politically salient cases use their policy preferences as a baseline, the need to justify decisions in legal language itself can have an effect. And even if "politics" determines the appellate judge's final vote on the merits, "legal" factors will influence what issues a judge considers justiciable and structure how the court approaches an issue. For discussion of these points, see, e.g., Michael McCann, "How the Supreme Court Matters in American Politics: New Institutionalist Perspectives," in Howard Gillman and Cornell Clayton (eds) *The Supreme Court in American Politics: New Institutionalist Interpretations* (Lawrence, KS: University Press of Kansas, 1999), 63–97, and Howard Gillman, "What's Law Got to Do with It? Judicial Behavioralists Test the 'Legal Model' of Judicial Decision Making," *Law and Social Inquiry* 26:2 (2001): 465–504.

27 See Michael J. Klarman, *The Framers' Coup: The Making of the United States Constitution* (New York: Oxford University Press, 2016).

# 7

# CONCLUSION

## Toward a Realist, Institutional Democratic Theory

This conclusion offers a reflection on this project in light of some recent realist interventions into democratic theory. From the outset, we declared our intention to offer an institutionally and empirically grounded account of democracy (and judicial review's value within it) that would meet most widely acknowledged desiderata for a "realist" theory of democracy. An important recent work, Christopher Achen and Larry Bartels' *Democracy For Realists* (hereafter, *DFR*), has offered a challenge and alternative to contemporary democratic theory.[1] In addition, the field of democratic theory has recently seen the emergence of an approach to democracy that can be read as taking into account and responding to the realist lessons of *DFR*, although almost certainly not in the way Achen and Bartels would probably expect. We'll term them "shadow of unfairness" theorists, in the evocative phrase of Jeffrey Green, who has given this approach its fullest and most sophisticated statement of defense.[2] We treat our comparative institutional approach and the "shadow of unfairness" approach as offering two distinct responses to the problems posed by the *DFR* challenge (complementary, but occasionally in tension with each other), and give an account of why we take the route we do in responding. We close with a consideration of how the challenge effectively posed by *DFR* holds up in light of these responses. In particular, we consider the resistance offered by both our approach and the "shadow of unfairness" approach to one particular critique leveled by *DFR* against the slogan that the solution to democracy's problems is more democracy. We resist it for different reasons than "shadow of unfairness" theorists, but agree it should probably be resisted (even if we accept some of the specific institutional arguments made by Achen and Bartels).

**174** Part II

## 7.1 The Realist Challenge of Achen and Bartels

In this important new book, Achen and Bartels, drawing on their previously published work and related research, seek to demonstrate the accuracy of the book's subtitle: that elections do not produce responsive government. There are two specific democratic theories of "responsive government" they seek to refute. The stronger of the two is what they call the "folk theory" of democracy, which is described in a variety of ways. It is a "set of accessible, appealing ideals assuring people that they live under an ethically defensible form of government" (*DFR*, 1) that "celebrates the wisdom of popular judgments by informed and engaged citizens" (9) in a polity where voters are "represented, not just governed" (297). According to the folk theory of democracy, the notion that sovereignty lies with the people is in some sense a substantive, not procedural, observation. Achen and Bartels see the folk theory as dominant in both popular and theoretical discourses, although not consistently so. On some level, we surely know something is very wrong with it, but return to it anyway—a habit characterized by a kind of theoretical schizophrenia (12). The second, less demanding theory of democracy they seek to refute is relatively weak compared with the folk theory, but also too demanding for the reality of democratic politics: the retrospective theory of voting that suggests voters punish misdeeds, failures, and bad behavior after the fact.

There is a wealth of scholarly research that suggests that both of these theories of democratic politics are overly optimistic about democracy, and Achen and Bartels present it systematically and persuasively. The most recurrent theme is the shortcomings of the voters: they are simply not up to the task of democratic citizenship as laid out by the folk theory or even the relatively modest tasks required of them by retrospective voting. (There is evidence that the latter does occur, but in such a haphazard, myopic, inconsistent way that it simply can't be where we place our democratic hopes; see chapter five of *DFR* for a good discussion of these shortcomings.) The shortcomings of the voters are not just criticized but explained; the authors draw on psychology as well as political science research to make sense of voter behavior. This is important because it raises the stakes for a common dodge of so-called[3] "ideal theory": that the specific shortcomings of this or that society shouldn't get in the way of understanding how things should be. If democracy is failing not just because there's some contingent failure or breakdown, but because of persistent core features of political behavior, underpinned by psychological and sociological facts, ideal theory's dodge becomes particularly unsatisfying, particularly from the perspective of *political* political theory in Waldron's sense.

It should probably be noted that Achen and Bartels' attribution of the folk theory of democracy to academic democratic theorists isn't entirely persuasive. As Andrew Sabl has noted, democratic theorists "have rarely imagined that democracy normally translates public preferences into policy, or judged that democracy's health depends on whether it does."[4] Sabl is surely correct that most democratic theorists offer an account of democracy's value that isn't reliant on the folk or retrospective theories. On the other hand, we do think Achen and Bartels have something of a point here, if underdeveloped: even if democratic theorists don't explicitly endorse this position, it retains a place and a role in many of their theories, just as empirical political scientists, not to say citizens, who understand the shortcomings of these approaches but still find themselves clinging to them.[5] Beyond this characterization, Achen and Bartels engage normative democratic theorists in two relatively direct ways. The first comes in chapter three. A common response to the shortcomings of democracy, for activists and theorists alike, has often been "more democracy." Achen and Bartels argue here that this is a dodge—that more democracy compounds, rather than resolves, democracy's shortcomings. To make that case, they examine the historical record regarding two ways in which politics has been allegedly "further democratized"—first, the introduction of greater democracy into political parties themselves (in particular, the democratization of the candidate selection process), and second, the introduction and continued use of initiatives and referenda in American politics.[6] Their assessments here are somewhat mixed but largely poor; the general ignorance and irrationality of voters takes on a more specific form as it manifests itself in a costly optimism bias—the public wants to believe it can get something for nothing, and votes accordingly. The second point of engagement with democratic theory comes from Achen and Bartels' fascinating and important effort to build an alternative justification for democratic politics. It is all too common for academic commenters on democracy's shortcomings to simply abandon a normative commitment to democracy,[7] something Achen and Bartels are (for somewhat underexplained reasons) loath to do. Instead, they develop what they call the "group theory" of democracy. The group theory recognizes that social identity, not ideology, drives our political behavior, and indeed largely shapes our political preferences. But it is as groups—and sometimes through interest groups representing those groups—that policy preferences make their way into political outcomes. Achen and Bartels are well aware that the previous incursion of group theory into political science—1950's pluralism—presented too rosy a picture of American democracy (223), noting Schattschnieder's famous line about the "upper class accent" in the song of the pluralist chorus (321). This leads them to close the book with a reassessment of what "more democracy" would actually mean in our current context. Rather than more elections, they suggest a more democratic society would in fact be one of greater social and economic equality (325), which would translate not into the blooming of folk democracy at long last but more even influence among the social groups that make up our society.

**176** Part II

## 7.2 Realist Democracy and "The Shadow of Unfairness"

In the next section, we will discuss directly how democracy-against-domination might respond to the two arguments presented in the previous section, and what those responses might suggest about the status of democracy-against-domination as a realist democratic theory. Prior to that discussion, however, we want to briefly discuss another path—one that mostly complements, but might occasionally conflict with, our own. I call this school of democratic thought "shadow of unfairness" theory, after the evocative phrase coined by Jeffrey Green in a book that was published at roughly the same time as *DFR*. Green sets out to write a "Plebian" democratic theory; that is to say, a democratic theory for those of us who are, self-consciously, Plebians. For Green, a basic fact about liberal democratic societies—one that should orient our theorizing and that we should not hold out meaningful hope of eradicating—is our (that is, non-elites) second-class status. The modern condition of the Plebian is the product of three features of our political condition. The first two, taken together here, are "remove" and "manyness." Remove speaks to the fact that we cannot be democratic citizens in the Athenian sense; we simply lack the standing, access, and power to be a political actor in any significant sense. We are not powerless altogether, though—through "manyness," ordinary people can hope to act in politics; it is only in the aggregate as part of a large group that invariably strips out much of what is generally regarded as edifying, virtuous, and valuable about political activity. The third feature of Plebianism stems from the fact that the conditions of remove and manyness are neither randomly nor universally distributed. Some avoid those conditions, and do so reliably and predictably, and are able to protect and reproduce that privilege through inherited wealth and other avenues of power. He calls this third feature "plutocracy."[8]

Once we acknowledge that while remove, manyness, and plutocracy cannot, ultimately, be eliminated and ought to be understood as constitutive features of liberal democracy, we can get down to the business of developing a Plebian theory of democracy. Green's efforts on this front can be divided into two broad categories. First, we need to rethink our assumptions about political ethics and virtues in light of Plebianism. Green argues, convincingly, that much of our thinking about political ethics assumes something along the lines of the folk theory of democracy, which Plebians should actively unlearn. In this spirit, he urges Plebians to relax some norms of decorum and debate and goodness, and devotes considerable energy to the project of rehabilitating envy (specifically, "reasonable" envy) as a useful political value. In the same spirit, but distinct from his account of Plebian virtue, lies his account of what he thinks and hopes a Plebian politics might look like. This discussion contains a number of proposals for policies that violate some feature of the universal values generally associated with democracy. His advocacy of singling out the super-rich for greater scrutiny might violate liberal norms of equal treatment, and the designation of a threshold for such scrutiny risks violating the republican norm against arbitrariness. But

Conclusion **177**

these norms are, in their strong form, a product of the misplaced faith in the folk theory of democracy; too much fidelity to them interferes with the Plebian's entry into politics as a self-conscious Plebian.

It is this kind of proposal—veto points against the plutocrats—that unites the current work we call "shadow of unfairness" theory. Once the basic unfairness and second-class citizenship is understood as inevitable, they argue, a number of new ideas that go beyond the standard democratic approach need to be considered, including tribunals with an upper socio-economic bound, and other similar restrictions on the rich. The "shadow of unfairness" theorists look to fix the problems created (in part) by the failure of the folk theory with a new array of institutional arrangements meant to lessen the shadow.

## 7.3 Bringing It Together: DFR, the Shadow of Unfairness, and Democracy-Against-Domination

Democracy-against-domination and shadow of unfairness theories are trying to accomplish something similar. They're trying to develop a democratic theory that can help us identify and think about how to address an inevitable and ultimately ineliminable problem. For democracy-against-domination theorists, the problem is the ubiquity of the threat of domination, whether by more powerful citizens over less powerful ones, or the government over its citizens, or various combinations and permutations of the two. For shadow of unfairness theorists, it's a bit more specific of a problem—the problem of the failure of the folk theory of democracy and the resultant second-class status. They differ, too, in their ambition. Throughout this book, we haven't spend much time contemplating new mechanisms and policy structures for preventing or reducing domination—we've been content to take the existing slate of options and evaluate their value and disvalue for the project of resisting domination. It might appear as though we're driven by a more rigorous anti-utopianism than the self-consciously realist shadow of unfairness theorists exhibit. But it's more simply a question of division of labor; we certainly don't disavow such a search, but we don't prioritize it either. Our conception of what democracy must work against overlaps with the shadow of unfairness theory—certainly, the problems of plutocracy and second-class citizenship exacerbate the risk of domination a great deal, and ought to be of central concern. However, we take a view that the threat of domination is more distributed than the image of society the shadow of unfairness invokes. Men and women and white people and black people can all be Plebians, but that doesn't remove the thread of the domination of women by men and black people by white people. In the remainder of this final section, we'll consider how our approach as well as the shadow of unfairness theory might respond to the two challenges *DFR* poses for democratic theorists.

The first challenge *DFR* poses for democratic theory is the critique of "the solution to democracy's problems is more democracy" thinking. Here, we think

**178** Part II

democracy-against-domination theorists, "shadow of unfairness" theorists, and many other schools of democratic thought would reject the conclusion a good deal more strongly and uniformly than they'd reject the underlying analysis. Democratic theorists regularly advocate for more and deeper democracy. Deliberative democrats, for instance, have taken a keen interest in various institutional innovations that they hope would lead to greater deliberation, producing better democratic decisions. But they don't define more democracy, necessarily, as more elections generally, or direct elections in particular. Rather, they advocate for deliberative forums and mini-publics and other small-scale political innovations that only a tiny fraction of people might participate in.[9] The anti-elite innovations of the shadow of unfairness theorists follow a similar innovative path. In fact, one shadow of unfairness theorist, Gorden Arlen, suggests a new understanding of the mixed regime as one with institutions that promote and embody mass democracy, deliberative/epistemic democracy, and Plebian democracy.[10] It has been suggested that a related, earlier social choice critique of the efficacy of voting and elections (which has some real similarities to the one offered by Achen and Bartels) motivated democratic theory to look beyond majoritarian election, perhaps contributing to the explosive growth of deliberative democratic theory.[11]

The premises of democracy-against-domination help us make sense of this. The implied premise of the argument against more democracy to solve democracy's problems is that more democracy would look more or less like the electoral democracy we've already got—more mass voting, or something that looks a lot like it. But if we take such elections as one possible manifestation of the value of democracy—a way to reduce the likelihood of one kind of domination while seeking solutions to others—then it's less obvious it should be simply replicated to expand and deepen democracy. In their own way, "shadow of unfairness" theorists, deliberative democrats, radical democrats, and others are exploring new ways to do just that.

A democracy-against-domination approach will generally see a lot more common ground with *DFR*'s second contribution to democratic theory,—the advocacy of the "group theory of democracy." While individuals can be dominated, both *imperium* and *dominium* often target groups, in part or in whole. Membership in the wrong social group is how people get marked for domination, and why their domination is tolerated.[12] So emphasis on the democratic value of being a part of a group with some social power makes good sense; democracy-against-domination might find some value in non-ideological group-block voting. Of course, the way we tend to talk about demographics and voting tends to be a bit overdetermined, and that flaw can be found in *DFR* as well. Virtually all social identity groups have a sizable minority—usually well into the double digits in percentages—who vote "the wrong way," so to speak. This might be because of an overlapping and overriding social identity taking hold (say, an African-American who is a police officer, or extremely wealthy, voting Republican), but it also might be because of idiosyncratic individual

Conclusion  **179**

decision-making. This means, though, that we can retain the anti-domination value without needing group voting to be particularly strict.

It might seem as though "shadow of unfairness" theorists might also see much to like in the group theory of democracy as well. Their diagnosis is almost a mirror image of the closing pages of DFR. While DFR suggests the group theory of democracy might work better if we could find a way to get to more social and economic equality, "shadow of unfairness" theorists might think we could target the plutocrats more effectively if we could mobilize and empower "the poor" or "Plebians" or "the 99%" or something along those lines. But this kind of scope for "groups" doesn't really track how social identity works in practice. This group is too large, too general, and too varied in interests and goals. This is perhaps why "shadow of unfairness" theorists seek new institutional bodies and structures to empower this kind of group.

While we think democratic theory has much to learn from the defense of group democracy here, it is unlikely that democratic theorists will be content to treat this as the only value of democracy. Democratic theorists are likely to continue to look for ways to further advance democratization, even if they accept the specific critiques of party-level democracy and initiative and referenda. Democratic theory can appreciate the value and importance of the group theory of democracy without being content to stop there. Does that mean we're just unwilling to be the kind of "realists" DFR is encouraging us to be? Are we idealists after all? We don't think so, at least not necessarily. It is incumbent on democratic theorists who take the demand for realism seriously to take the realist limits of particular forms and practices of democracy seriously—and DFR helps us do that. But democracy-against-domination theorists see the need for a broader range. Domination is adaptive; democracy must be as well. One tricky thing about realism in political theory is different invocations of realism can come to very different conclusions depending on what, exactly, we ought to be realists about. DFR implores us to be realists about electoral democracy, in the U.S. and elsewhere. Democracy-against-domination implores us to be realists about the distributed, adaptive, unpredictable threat of domination, broadly conceived; "shadow of unfairness" theorists implore us to be realistic about the problem of plutocracy. All these realisms are necessary, even if they ultimately point us in different directions.

Still, we recognize that scholars will evaluate judicial review from a variety of perspectives about what makes democracy normatively valuable. Our overriding purpose with this book is not to establish democracy-against-domination as the sole legitimate conception of democracy. Instead, our core purpose is to argue that when evaluating judicial review, democratic theory needs to be taken *seriously*. Simplistic comparisons based on crude majoritarianism are neither empirically accurate nor consistent with how the vast majority of people in general and scholars in particular conceive of democracy. Scholars who understand democracy's core values differently than we do are likely to reach different conclusions in

**180** Part II

some cases about the value of judicial review, but if these conclusions are based on a rich, empirically attentive vision of democracy, they will contribute more to the discussion about judicial review than evaluations of judicial review based on the "countermajoritarian difficulty." We hope our analysis in this book has helped to move the discussion forward to more promising avenues.

## Notes

1 Christopher Achens and Larry Bartels, *Democracy for Realists: Why Elections Do Not Produce Representative Government* (Princeton, NJ: Princeton University Press, 2016).
2 Jeffrey Green, *The Shadow of Unfairness: A Plebian Theory of Liberal Democracy* (Oxford: Oxford University Press, 2016). Other examples of work in this vein include John McCormick, "Contain the Wealthy and Patrol the Magistrates: Restoring Elite Accountability to Popular Government," *American Political Science Review* 100:2 (2006): 147–163; *Machiavellian Democracy* (Cambridge: Cambridge University Press, 2011); and Gorden Arlen, "Aristotle and the Problem of Oligarchic Harm: Insights for Democracy," *European Journal of Political Theory* (forthcoming).
3 We say "so-called" because we're skeptical the notion of ideal theory can be defended; all political theory makes stipulations about what can and can't be assumed away. For a persuasive presentation of a skeptical take on the idea of ideal theory congenial to our own, see Jacob Levy, "There's No Such Thing as Ideal Theory," *Social Philosophy and Policy* 33:1–2 (2016): 312–333.
4 See his review of *Democracy for Realists* in *Perspectives on Politics* 15:2 (2017): 158–159. He develops this argument in greater detail in "Two Cultures of Democratic Theory: Responsiveness Democratic Quality and the Normative-Empirical Divide," *Perspectives on Politics* 13:2 (2015): 345–365. (This paper was published prior to *DFR* but anticipates several of that book's moves, in part from a reading of an earlier paper by Achen and Bartels.)
5 We acknowledge this claim demands evidence beyond stipulation, which we hope to add at some later time.
6 This chapter is one where the effort to look beyond the U.S. becomes less prominent; on political parties, a couple of studies suggesting the American story can be found elsewhere are cited, but not discussed in any detail (67–68). Unless we missed something, the direct democracy discussion is entirely American.
7 For a recent example, see Jason Brennan, *Against Democracy* (Princeton, NJ: Princeton University Press, 2016). The *locus classicus* here is Riker's *Liberalism against Populism*.
8 These concepts are introduced in Green, *The Shadow of Unfairness*, ch. 2.
9 For an overview of such innovations, see Robert Goodin, *Innovating Democracy: Democratic Theory and Practice after the Deliberative Turn* (Oxford: Oxford University Press, 2008), esp. part 1.
10 Arlen, "Aristotle and the Problem of Oligarchic Harm," 18–19.
11 Gerry Mackie, "The Reception of Social Choice by Democratic Theory," in Stephanie Novak and Jon Elster (eds) *Majority Decision: Principles and Practices* (Cambridge: Cambridge University Press, 2014), 77–102.
12 One important democracy-against-domination theorist, Iris Marion Young, distinguishes between domination and oppression, and puts what we're calling group domination in the latter category. See *Justice and the Politics of Difference*, ch. 1–2. We have no quarrel with her nomenclature, but use domination in a broader sense that encompasses both her meanings.

# INDEX

abortion law 15, 46, 52–58, 68–70, 74, 76, 79–80, 83–84, 85, 149–150
Achen, Christopher *see Democracy for Realists*
agonistic democracy 11, 46, 59, 105, 110–118, 123
*Akron v. Akron Center for Reproductive Rights* 57
Alito, Samuel 65, 81, 82, 84, 85, 87–92
Arlen, Gorden 178
*Ayotte v. Planned Parenthood* 83

Bales, Kevin 116–117
Balkin, Jack 4
Barnett, Randy 133–134
Bartels, Larry *see Democracy for Realists*
Bellamy, Richard 137–138, 157n68
Bernstein, David 133–134
bicameralism 136–137, 163–165, 170
Bickel, Alexander *see* countermajoritarian difficulty
Blackmun, Harry 55, 58, 61n49, 69, 94n32, 97n116
Brettschneider, Corey 47–48, 51
Breyer, Stephen 77, 78, 87
*Brown v. Board of Education* 13, 36n12, 74, 75, 77
*Brown v. Prata* 147, 158n87, 168
Buccola, Nicholas 46–47
bulwark theories 103, 139–140, 153, 166

campaign finance law 66, 85–87, 147
Carey, Brian 3
*City of Boerne v. Flores* 78
committees (in legislatures) 10, 14, 136–137, 142, 143, 146, 164, 169
Conant, Lisa 13
countermajoritarian difficulty 2, 9–44, 47, 60n7, 63, 103, 106, 130–132, 134, 151
*Crawford v. Marion County* 150–151

Dahl, Robert 14
deliberative democracy 3, 11, 12, 17–19, 20, 27, 35, 71, 89, 105, 110–123, 143, 147, 178
democracy-against-domination 3, 11, 12, 18–19, 21–32, 34, 52–59, 105–115, 123, 130–131, 133, 141–145, 148–152, 160, 162, 166, 176–179
*Democracy for Realists* 173–179
Den Otter, Ronald 47–51
Devins, Neal 67
Dowding, Keith 154n14
drift (legislative) 145–146

economic inequality 24, 30–31, 115, 129n77, 156n49
Ely, John Hart 20, 53, 149
Epstein, Richard 135
essentially contested concepts 39n36
executive power and judicial review 26–28, 145

**182** Index

*F.E.C. v. Wisconsin Right to Life* 85, 91
federalism 3, 77, 81, 165–169, 170
filibuster 143, 148, 157m71, 162–163, 170
*Flast v. Cohen* 84–85
folk theory of democracy 174–177
Frankfurter, Felix 66
Friedman, Barry 2, 43n101, 130–131
Fung, Archon 119–122

Ginsburg, Ruth Bader 54–55, 61n44, 78,
  95n65
Ginsburg, Tom 13, 75
*Gonzales v. Carhart* 83–84
Goodhart, Michael 107–108
Graber, Mark 2, 13, 15, 58
Green, Jeffrey *see Shadow of Unfairness, The*
*Griswold v. Connecticut* 13, 36n12, 53,
  94n32
Gutmann, Amy 112, 119

Habermas, Jurgen 17–18, 39–40n45, 49,
  112–114, 119
Hand, Learned 17–18
Harel, Alon 154n25
*Harris v. McRae* 55
Heibert, Janet 15
*Hein v. Freedom From Religion Foundation*
  84, 91
Hirschl, Ran 24–26, 29–31, 148, 152,
  154n17
Honig, Bonnie 51, 52, 113–114
Hungarian Constitutional Court 25–26,
  29–32, 148, 152, 159n94
Hyde Amendment 55, 61n49

Indian Supreme Court 30, 148
interbranch relations 11, 14–16, 26,
  32–33

Jackson, Robert 56

Keck, Thomas 14
Kennedy, Anthony 68, 78, 84–87
Kramer, Larry 138
Kreimer, Seth 28

*Lawrence v. Texas* 68
Levinson, Sandy 4
Levy, Jacob 165–166, 167, 171n20, 180n3
*liberum veto* 161–162
*Lochner v. New York* 31, 134
Lovell, George 15–16, 152
*Loving v. Virginia* 48

Mackie, Gerry 133
*McConnell v. FEC* 85–86
*Miranda v. Arizona* 72, 76, 78, 81
Mouffe, Chantal 114

Nozick, Robert 122

O'Connor, Sandra Day 77–81, 83, 87, 88, 92

Pettit, Philip 19, 22–23, 106–109, 120,
  123–124, 129n73, 138, 141–142, 145
*Phillip Morris v. Williams* 87
Pierson, Paul 14, 145
*Planned Parenthood v. Casey* 52–58, 69, 72,
  75, 81, 83
popular constitutionalism 54, 58, 138–139
Powe, Lucas 54
process theory 19–22
Przeworski, Adam 132
public opinion 36n10, 36n12, 54, 61n43, 146
public reason 48–51, 112, 139, 146

Railton, Peter 139
realism in political theory 1, 3, 4, 133,
  173–179
Rehnquist, William 76, 78–82, 90
Rehnquist Court 65, 76–82, 88
retrospective voting 174–175
*Reynolds v. Sims* 36n12, 48
Riker, William 16, 38n34, 132–134
Roberts, John 64–65, 81–82, 84, 85, 87,
  88, 90, 92
Roberts Court 65–68, 76, 81–92
*Roe v. Wade* 13, 34, 52–58, 68–70, 74,
  79–81, 149–150
Rosen, Jeffrey 73
*Rumsfeld v. Padilla* 80
*R v. Morgentaler* 53, 149

Sabl, Andrew 174–175
Saward, Michael 141
Scalia, Antonin 65, 71, 73, 78, 80–82, 84,
  85–90
Scheppele, Kim Lane 25–26, 29–31, 144,
  148, 152
Schwartzberg, Melissa 139
Scott, Kyle 166
*sejm* (Polish-Lithuanian Parliament)
  161–162
*Shadow of Unfairness, The* 173, 176–179
Shapiro, Ian 11, 19–21, 23, 32, 33, 51–59,
  105, 108, 122–124, 138, 144, 145
Shue, Henry 31, 42–43n88

Index **183**

slavery 4, 15, 72, 104, 116–118
Souter, David 78, 83, 84
*Stenberg v. Carhart* 83–84, 91
Stevens, John Paul 78, 87, 88
Sunstein, Cass 3, 46, 53, 64, 65, 67–78, 80, 82, 84, 149

Thirteenth Amendment 3–4
Thomas, Clarence 65, 78, 82, 84, 85, 87–91
Thompson, Dennis 112, 119
Tilly, Charles 124n1, 128n77
Tushnet, Mark 27, 32, 42n81, 43n96, 64, 77, 81, 138

*U.S. v. Lopez* 81

Vermeule, Adrian 145
veto points 3, 48, 58–59, 107, 130–172, 177

Waldron, Jeremy 1–3, 21, 27, 45, 47, 50, 116, 134–138, 144, 146–147, 161, 163–164, 174
Walzer, Michael 108–109
*Webster v. Reproductive Health Services* 58, 79, 81, 82
Weinstock, Daniel 166
Wolin, Sheldon 113–114

Young, Iris Marion 109, 180n12

Zurn, Christopher 18

 Taylor & Francis eBooks

## Helping you to choose the right eBooks for your Library

Add Routledge titles to your library's digital collection today. Taylor and Francis ebooks contains over 50,000 titles in the Humanities, Social Sciences, Behavioural Sciences, Built Environment and Law.

**Choose from a range of subject packages or create your own!**

**Benefits for you**
- Free MARC records
- COUNTER-compliant usage statistics
- Flexible purchase and pricing options
- All titles DRM-free.

**Benefits for your user**
- Off-site, anytime access via Athens or referring URL
- Print or copy pages or chapters
- Full content search
- Bookmark, highlight and annotate text
- Access to thousands of pages of quality research at the click of a button.

 **REQUEST YOUR FREE INSTITUTIONAL TRIAL TODAY** — **Free Trials Available** We offer free trials to qualifying academic, corporate and government customers.

## eCollections – Choose from over 30 subject eCollections, including:

| | |
|---|---|
| Archaeology | Language Learning |
| Architecture | Law |
| Asian Studies | Literature |
| Business & Management | Media & Communication |
| Classical Studies | Middle East Studies |
| Construction | Music |
| Creative & Media Arts | Philosophy |
| Criminology & Criminal Justice | Planning |
| Economics | Politics |
| Education | Psychology & Mental Health |
| Energy | Religion |
| Engineering | Security |
| English Language & Linguistics | Social Work |
| Environment & Sustainability | Sociology |
| Geography | Sport |
| Health Studies | Theatre & Performance |
| History | Tourism, Hospitality & Events |

For more information, pricing enquiries or to order a free trial, please contact your local sales team:
**www.tandfebooks.com/page/sales**

 **Routledge** Taylor & Francis Group | The home of Routledge books

**www.tandfebooks.com**